C000008510

The Sex Tsar's guide
to Electile Dysfunction

By

Geoff Hackett

Copyright © 2023 by – Geoff Hackett – All Rights Reserved.

It is not legal to reproduce, duplicate, or transmit any part of this document in either electronic means or printed format. Recording of this publication is strictly prohibited.

Table of Contents

Dedication

- The late Dr Graham Jackson, "the man who knew too much" – my greatest inspiration and one of the finest physicians of his time.

- Professor Mike Kirby, "font of all knowledge" – a great friend, collaborator, and fitness fanatic.

- Dr Bollinger for being "larger than life", inspirational, and a generous friend and provider of many memorable moments.

- Mr Mike Heal, a Urologist from Crewe, who first showed me how to induce an artificial erection.

- Mr Amged El-Hawrani, Consultant ENT surgeon and my appraiser in 2019 and 2020, and tragic victim of COVID-19 on 28th March 2020.

- Julie Spinks, my long-suffering NHS hospital secretary.

- Bob Stokes (bob@bobstokes.co.uk) for the excellent cartoons.

- And not least,

- My wife Sally, for over 40 years of support of the "Sex Tsar"…and counting.

- I have attempted to respect the privacy of colleagues and patients who might not wish to be identified. Dates and times have been altered to prevent identification, along with certain details that might have allowed recognition of the various scenarios.

The rise, fall, and rise of the "Sex Tsar".

- The title "Sex Tsar" was awarded to me by a Men's Health journalist in 2005 during an article on the health benefits of sex. Throughout my career, I have always struggled to find a title that describes precisely my unique interests, insights, and skills that I have acquired over the last 30 years. I felt the term "Sex Tsar" captured this rather nicely, if somewhat humorously grandiose. I wore the badge with pride until the Russian invasion of Ukraine. Then in January 2021, I had a narrow escape from death after severe COVID-19 with several weeks in intensive care with two blood clots on the brain and meningitis. I was determined to get back to work and managed this in June 2022. I felt I had further stories to tell.

About the Author

The Author of 180 original papers, 5 textbooks, and 18 book chapters on sexual medicine, Professor Geoff Hackett received the Zorgniotti-Newman Prize in 2012 at the International Society for Sexual Medicine's World Meeting on Sexual Medicine in Chicago for his work on testosterone deficiency in Type 2 diabetes. He is a past winner of the Duke of Edinburgh Prize for Sports Medicine in 1992 and the Charles Oliver Hawthorne Clinical Prize from the British Medical Association for original research in 1986.

Professor Geoff Hackett was a consultant in Urology at University Hospitals Birmingham Foundation trust from 1994 – 2020 and Professor of Sexual Medicine at Aston University Birmingham since 2017. He works as a Consultant in Urology and Sexual Medicine at Spire Hospital, Little Aston, Birmingham. He was also as a primary care physician for 34 years, from 1978-2012.

Why this book is important

Whilst menopause has been quite rightly prioritised in recent years with the help of high-profile celebrities, testosterone deficiency in men has lagged behind, despite the increasing recognition that low testosterone levels are associated with increased rates of type 2 diabetes, kidney failure, sexual dysfunction, depression, and premature death. As 78% of men maintain adequate levels of testosterone, the is no such thing as "male menopause".

Symptoms in men are often dealt with by advice such as "man-up" or "buy some Viagra". Men are more often drawn to the "dark side" for "supplements from the internet or the guy at the gym" rather than seeking support from their GP. The message from this book is that we need to stop the "battle of the sexes" or "them and us" approach and realise that our relationships and the well-being of our partners are at least as important as our own health.

I often say that the treatments that I give treat two people (at least), whereas I have never seen a man or woman say how much better they have been feeling their partner was prescribed cholesterol tablets!

The important message is that we all need to look after our own health and relationships and take control of our own lives. With all the pressures on health care services, we can no longer depend solely on our GP to care for all our needs.

I hope that this book will be read by both men and women who are seriously interested in improving their health and relationships.

Introduction

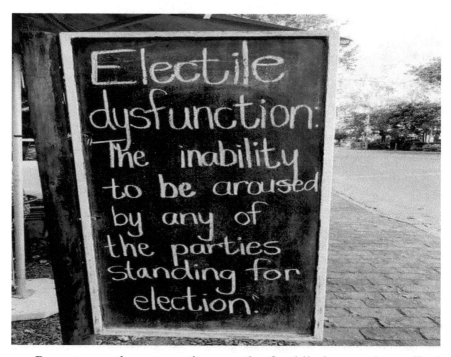

Electile
dysfunction:
The inability
to be aroused
by any of
the parties
standing for
election.

Recent years have seen the growth of public interest in medical autobiographies, and the COVID-19 lockdown certainly led to record numbers. These often reveal behind-the-scenes activities, which are a mixture of fascination, information, amusement, and at times, sadness. It is also a way of providing insights into particular areas of medicine. There can be no more interesting subject than sex, and I feel honoured that so many patients have trusted me with their secrets and fantasies. Had I not found the subject so fascinating, I would have retired years ago, like so many of my colleagues.

The hardest job of all was to find a title for such a book. My first edition in 2020 was entitled "Just a tiny prick" a title that my wife, Sally, still hates to this day, calling it cheap and tacky, yet she has never had another suggestion. I chose it because I used to say to patients, "just a tiny prick with a needle" as I approached their penis with a needle. The odd one would reply, "yes, I can see that". I always felt that they were unwise to upset this particular tiny prick at that moment. I then shortened it to "just a tiny prick", which drew replies like "speak for yourself" or "yes, I think it must be the cold weather". We British always use humour for these darker moments.

For my second book, I settled for "another tiny prick". The subtitle "the sex tsar's guide to Electile Dysfunction" was chosen to reflect the intense politics surrounding men's (and women's) sexuality. To put it bluntly, patients have suffered over the last couple of decades because of ill-informed political meddling. I will touch on some of the most absurd government regulations that have made my job virtually impossible over this time. In the final chapter, I will tell you the real reasons why you cannot get to see any GP, never mind answering the question, "who is your regular doctor?"

None of this is helped by a change in Prime Minister every few months, or in the case of Liz Truss, every 42 days, with her entire economic strategy dismantled overnight by her second chancellor, Jeremy Hunt, who in the past was one of the least popular Ministers of Health, after her first chancellor had been "thrown to the wolves" after a couple of weeks We now celebrate the appointment of Rishi Sunak as her replacement, only 7 weeks after his heavy defeat in a head-to-head contest. We then have a series of ministerial failures, resignations and re-instatements within a matter of weeks.

If we ever needed an example of Electile Dysfunction, then surely this fits the bill.

As the Sex Tsar, I have often wondered whether a manifesto based on "firmer erections" and "enhanced libido" might have been more enticing for the electorate.

I might just have left it at that until COVID-19 struck me down in January 2021, narrowly surviving several months in ITU on a ventilator and eventually returning to work through the sheer determination not to let this "mugger" beat me. Whilst lying in bed and learning to walk again, I had plenty of time to reflect on the impact of this illness, especially as it relates to my speciality, as the UK has completely overlooked these significant issues. I hope that these chapters are interesting as I don't believe that many senior doctors have described their "COVID-19 journey".

Although the feedback on the first edition seemed pretty positive, I noted that a few (or some) women reviewing the book stopped short of using the term misogyny. I wondered why we never seem to hear the word "misandry" or, indeed, what percentage of the population would be able to define the word. In this book, I try my best to get readers not to think in these terms. I remember my favourite sex therapist Trudy Hannington, during the course of a single lecture stating that "men could not possibly understand how women are feeling", followed fifteen minutes later by "women are best placed to understand how men are feeling". I realised at that stage that thirty years of work had been ineffective as I was in the wrong body! I have tried to redress these stereotypes and tried to see things as a "couple problem" rather than taking sides. In this edition, as well as a mixture of "tumescent tales", old and new, I have included a chapter "Women, what's in it for me", as I believe that women's sexual problems are neglected, with the assumption that all problems can be dealt with by "intensive counselling", which is, in reality, rarely available. Of course, counselling is important, even in patients with clear medical conditions, but too often, it is not the first-choice intervention. In their medical training, doctors learn to always exclude potentially serious medical conditions before focusing on psychological solutions, but seemingly we think differently when a sexual problem is mentioned. In reality, what therapists term "bio-psycho-social" approaches are ideal if the necessary expertise is readily available. In reality, prescribing a pill is seen as the quickest, cheapest, and most convenient solution for the patient.

Whereas most doctors like to pretend that they planned every stage of their medical career, in all honesty, mine was a series of chance events. Despite that, there is little that I would change, apart from passing the exams that I failed. Although this book focuses on the junior hospital life of the 70s, where the 95-hour weeks described by Adam Kay in "this is going to hurt" would have seemed like utopia, it also describes a golden age of general practice, when there was time to talk with patients, and the GP was a trusted friend. Whereas Adam Kay gave up medicine in his thirties, I have seen it through the bitter end, perhaps because I would have starved had I pursued a career as a stand-up comic.

At times progress has been frustrated by hospital administrators who fail the realise the importance of sexual medicine and the impact that sexual problems have on our patients. In these pages, I am at times critical of the system, especially NICE. After publication, I expect any remote chance of appearing on any honours list will be extinguished, despite 45 years of service to the NHS.

I feel very lucky to have been in at the very beginning and travelled the world to International conferences and on speaker tours. I have also been involved in some of the most bizarre clinical trials, as will become evident to the reader. I have met many wonderful patients and colleagues along the way. Hopefully, most of them will remain friends, after they read these chapters.

CHAPTER 1 – This book might change your life.

Sex is fundamental to good health, and relationships are crucial to human happiness. No relationship has ever broken up because of a raised cholesterol, but countless marriages have failed because of a lack of penile tumescence. Most couples spend more time talking about what colour to paint the bedroom than why nothing has happened there for several months. Every erection, orgasm (men and women) and ejaculation should be a cause for celebration. Sexual activity should be enjoyed at least 3 times per week for a healthy heart and youthful looks, fully endorsed by a medical certificate from the Tsar.

CHAPTER 2 - The Rise of the Sex Tsar

This chapter charts the development of the Erectile Dysfunction Clinic at Good Hope Hospital in Sutton Coldfield and the case histories of couples attending. It highlights the importance of sex, especially in older men seeking new relationships in later life, demonstrating that there is more to look forward to than countdown, cocoa, and an early night. I have been privileged to share life experiences with a number of wonderful couples over the years. I make no apologies for getting straight into some top tumescent tales.

CHAPTER 3 – COVID-19 Strikes…as bad as it gets.

Just as I was looking to wind down gently to retirement, I was struck down by acute COVID-19 in January 2021, just a few weeks before the vaccinations were introduced. Six weeks in ITU on a ventilator and 3 months of rehabilitation later, I decided that I was not going to be beaten by this, even though several medical colleagues were not so lucky.

CHAPTER 4 – COVID-19 – the hidden impact.

My personal experience of this dreadful illness made me more determined not to be beaten. COVID-19 has become a particular interest, especially in the way that it attacks male hormones with long-term effects on sexual function and relationships. These are important issues for victims and their families that are being completely overlooked by government policies. The clear message is that we need to take control of our own lives.

CHAPTER 5 – Junior hospital doctor years.

Tyrannical consultants insisting on 24/7 on-call rotas, falling asleep through exhaustion during operations, rats in the on-call quarters, these were really tough times. Tell that to junior doctors today, and they do not believe you. The Tsar describes a number of surgical disasters and close shaves that would never happen today, or would they? Could a porter really administer anaesthetics for years without being noticed? Could a man really wedge a TV aerial up his rectum simply by seeking better reception? The answers are in this chapter.

CHAPTER 6. The Sex Tsar in general practice.

Nothing in hospital medicine can prepare a doctor for what awaits them as a country general practitioner. Whether it is dealing with cardiac arrests or surgical emergencies in remote areas, trouble down below, dealing with a highly strung violin instructor, or simply knowing where to store your thermometer when visiting nudist colonies, this chapter has helpful tips for all occasions.

CHAPTER 7. General practice – pastures new.

The time had come to move on room country practice to a midlands partnership in Lichfield with the chance to work as a hospital consultant with plenty of emergency scares along the way.

Here you will get some advice on dealing with psychopaths flailing an Arabic sword and the severe psychological consequences of being labelled as a "high-prescribing outlier".

CHAPTER 8. Testosterone, the true story.

This chapter comes with a serious health warning and is packed with science. For those of you who thought that testosterone was all about bodybuilding and weight lifters, think again. Learn why testosterone should be considered the "heptathlon therapy" for men's health. After reading this chapter, you will learn why any men out there who have noticed something embarrassing hanging out over their trousers, increasing need for a bra, or lack of activity in the trouser department, especially in the mornings, need to get their testosterone checked. Most importantly, make sure that you know your numbers and not just accept that everything is "normal".

CHAPTER 9 - Viagra Years and Beyond

The Sex Tsar explains the incredible story of the development of the most famous drug in the world and how it changed medical practice. You will learn the details of the sexual practices of a precision grinder and the risks of running a 4 x 100m relay after taking a dose of Viagra. There are key messages for those of you with body image concerns or those contemplating genital piercing.

CHAPTER 10 – A drug of limited clinical value!!!

Time moves on, and tadalafil is now the most important medication for men's health. Learn why it is the "decathlon therapy" with potential benefits for most of the major systems of the body. This chapter could save you a fortune on vitamins and supplements. For years, doctors have been searching for the "polypill" and now the Sex Tsar explains that it is already available and how to get it.

CHAPTER 11 – Media triumphs and disasters.

The media constantly seek the Sex Tsar for media work. This chapter explains the benefits of sex in recharging lust levels. Media training courses will not be required if you follow the Tsar's five top tips for dealing with the press and TV. This chapter also contains helpful advice on the sex benefits of antique furniture, how to hide in a celebrity bush, and training tips for aspiring world masturbation champions.

CHAPTER 12 – The Sex Tsar's medical research secrets.

The Tsar has conducted multiple original research projects for both men and women, and the findings are revealed here. The reader will learn how to master the controls of the ejaculometer, the preferred positions for sex in an MRI scanner, or the medical benefits of fellatio. The more bizarre the project, the more likely that the reader should be able to get a grant. Next year one of my readers might be presenting at the Scandinavian Society for the Study of Sexual Statistics.

CHAPTER 13 – Travels with Dr Bollinger.

With the future of international travel uncertain, what could be better than travelling to exotic locations with one of sexology's greatest bon viveurs? There is never a dull moment travelling with Dr

Bollinger. You might never have contemplated international flights with a large set of buttocks or considered the best batter for Korean tempura dog's testicles. The Sex Tsar provides top tips. You will learn the best way to handle the common embarrassing situation of being locked out of your hotel room stark naked, the correct way of tipping your female golf caddy in Indonesia, and how to deal with common mid-air medical emergencies. This chapter is the complete almanac for international jet setters.

CHAPTER 14 – Women – what's in it for me?

This is the most important chapter in the book. Women, quite rightly, feel pleased as they might feel that their man has "perked-up" thanks to the discovery of Viagra. I can reassure them that medical science has been working hard on their behalf. The problem is that a woman's sexuality is more "complicated", especially in relation to the impact of pregnancy and especially menopause. The reality is that there are two major issues in women's sexuality, desire, and arousal. Desire problems are more common and highly impacted by menopause, whereas most men maintain adequate levels of male hormones throughout life, despite the gradual decline. The traditional sexual response was that desire, in appropriate circumstances, leads to arousal and often, but not always, orgasm. Loss of arousal in women is related to deficient blood flow, often associated with medical conditions and potentially corrected by drugs such as sildenafil (Viagra) or tadalafil (Cialis). In reality, these drugs improve blood flow to the genital areas in women, potentially increasing arousal, but "desire" needs to be addressed, and this may require both HRT (oestrogen)and testosterone (currently unlicensed). We are now getting into a more complex situation than simply "popping a pill" before the match of the day on Saturday night. Having been involved in the development of an important drug, "flibanserin" to improve desire in women, I witnessed the vitriolic attacks that the manufacturers endured in Europe before they settled for a licence and clinical use in the USA. Get ready for some controversy in chapter fourteen.

CHAPTER 15 – Your doctor won't see you now.

Surely everything you have learned in the previous chapters will be common knowledge to your general practitioner...unfortunately, not. Here you will learn how to get the most out of your GP and how you need to take control of your own health. We all know that the NHS is in crisis and cannot provide all things to all people. Specialities such as vision, hearing, and dental treatment have largely been passed out of NHS care to those who can afford to pay. We readily accept that elegant spectacles, discrete digital hearing aids, and dental implants frequently need to be funded as the NHS only covers a basic level of care. HRT and treatments for ED have been discretely passed to over-the-counter prescribing, as we have had to address the issues as to whether bedroom romping or "wellness" can realistically be considered a core duty of care issue for the overwhelmed GP.

The Tsar has condensed thirty years of experience into this single chapter. If you read this and follow the take-home messages, no other books or magazines on health will be required. The Tsar explains why, post COVID-19, you cannot expect your GP to look after all aspects of your health, as, contractually, they are working toward a different agenda. In reality, general practice will never be the same again. We need to accept this and become masters of our own health. This chapter contains "the Serious Stuff" telling you precisely what needs to be done. It also includes important information relevant to the COVID-19 crisis and possible future pandemics.

APPENDIX – The Boring stuff...health and lifestyle advice from the Sex Tsar and some useful self-help questionnaires to check out your own health.

CHAPTER 1

This book might change your life.

Authors usually start by asking the question, "why did I write this book?"

Thirty years specialising in sexual problems and general practice has taught me many lessons and earned me the unfortunate title of the "Sex Tsar" from the Daily Mail. With recent events in Ukraine, I realised that the time has probably come to shed that particular title. I will also make it clear that this is not just for men, as I feel that the most important chapter of all is chapter 14, "Women, what's in it for me."

I will attempt to reach out (how I hate this term) to my readers with a few key messages in these chapters, supported by several medical *vignettes*!

My first book, *Just a tiny prick,* in 2020 was moderately successful for a first attempt, especially with a release in the middle of the pandemic when just about everybody published their memoirs. *Just a tiny prick* was effectively my "*journey*" (how I hate this term, even more, I promise not to use it again!) from a mere country GP to international recognition, at least in my own household. The book comprised a series of bizarre and embarrassing stories that patients had shared with me over the years. In the last chapter, entitled *the serious stuff,* I tried to lay out some important health issues, mainly for men. I still live in the hope that an innovative TV producer might see the potential for a series based on the *Sex Tsar* and I often fantasise as to who would play myself; I thought perhaps, Russell Crowe or

Gerard Butler, as they reflect my Australian roots and now both past their prime. With my luck, it will probably be Barry Humphries, alias Sir Les Patterson. When it comes to playing Dr Bollinger, who will become a cult figure in your life after reading this book, Michael Gambon, alias Dumbledore, is the obvious choice.

The feedback was that, although the readers enjoyed the funny *ditties,* many felt that *the serious stuff* really packed some important messages, so this is precisely what I have set out to do in the following chapters.

The first idea for this book came in 2006, so it has been many years in evolution. I was at a meeting in Sydney when I was rung by a journalist from "Men's Health" magazine, which I had only previously read in order to develop my buff, chiselled, waxed physique. They had heard me speak on the health benefits of sex, and this is how it was published in Australia.

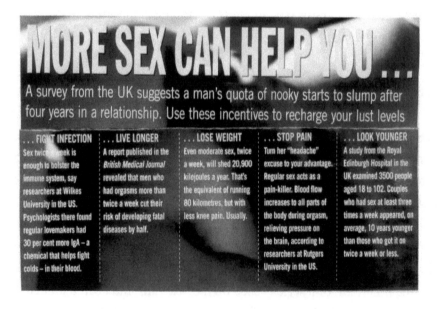

MORE SEX CAN HELP YOU . . .

A survey from the UK suggests a man's quota of nooky starts to slump after four years in a relationship. Use these incentives to recharge your lust levels

. . . FIGHT INFECTION	. . . LIVE LONGER	. . . LOSE WEIGHT	. . . STOP PAIN	. . . LOOK YOUNGER
Sex twice a week is enough to bolster the immune system, say researchers at Wilkes University in the US. Psychologists there found regular lovemakers had 30 per cent more IgA – a chemical that helps fight colds – in their blood.	A report published in the *British Medical Journal* revealed that men who had orgasms more than twice a week cut their risk of developing fatal diseases by half.	Even moderate sex, twice a week, will shed 20,900 kilojoules a year. That's the equivalent of running 80 kilometres, but with less knee pain. Usually.	Turn her "headache" excuse to your advantage. Regular sex acts as a pain-killer. Blood flow increases to all parts of the body during orgasm, relieving pressure on the brain, according to researchers at Rutgers University in the US.	A study from the Royal Edinburgh Hospital in the UK examined 3500 people aged 18 to 102. Couples who had sex at least three times a week appeared, on average, 10 years younger than those who got it on twice a week or less.

Clearly, "nooky" twice per week is an excellent way to boost the immune system to fight infections, especially COVID-19, but more of that in a later chapter. Cutting the risk of dying from a fatal disease with three orgasms per week seems like a complete no-brainer, although this study in the Lancet, the Caerphilly Cohort study, was unclear whether this was as a duet or whether occasional solo performances were in order. I remember first hearing of this research on the Terry Wogan show, with his conclusion, "my God, she's trying to kill me". The case gets even stronger with research showing that sex is an excellent way for two people to lose weight as, assuming that they are both awake, they will each consume around 20,900 kilojoules per year, more than some couch potatoes would shed in a lifetime, with less risk of sports and repetitive strain injuries. The resolution of headache by relieving pressure on the brain through orgasm, as shown by US scientists, could reduce the horrendous impact of pain-killer addiction. The most persuasive evidence of all comes from the Royal Edinburgh hospital, where the researchers reported on the sex lives of 3500 *couples* aged 18-102, and those having sex three times per week or more looked, on average, ten years younger. I am sure that this was excellent news for the couple of 102, but not the 18-year-old who kept getting arrested for underage sex. Consider the sheer magnitude of this study and the fortune that can be saved on Botox injections and plastic surgery when a couple of additional morning romps will do the trick.

"You know, darling, since we've been having sex twice a day, I think I'm looking 10 years younger."

By now, the reader should be convinced that more sex is beneficial for both men and women, so the title of my book is fully justified. The next question is, "what about those of us who cannot have sex through lack of a partner or medical illness?" I will develop the argument in future chapters that not only will medication provide benefits by enabling you to have sex three times per week, saving your life and your partner's, but the medication itself can prolong life by preventing several serious diseases, even if you do not have a partner.

I am often asked by doctors, "if there was one question you could ask a man that would accurately tell you if his life was at risk, what would that question be?" For me, that question has been obvious for years and has nothing to do with chest pain or shortness of breath. The answer is, "do you wake with regular morning erections?" This simple question tells you more about the condition of a man's arteries and the likelihood of a cardiac event than any other. Importantly, it is just as relevant for widowed, divorced, or celibate men of any sexual orientation and is unrelated to relationship stress or any performance pressure. This conclusion was fully supported by the 2022 publication of the European Male aging Study, involving over 3000 men followed up for over twenty years. The authors concluded that the absence of morning erections and low levels of testosterone predict premature death. Despite this, an older or widowed man is unlikely to be asked this question for fear of it seeming to be in "bad taste". After a heart attack, a man is far more likely to be assessed for "fitness to hoover", which is probably the last thing on his mind.

Unfortunately, there is no equivalent question for women, although the more complex questionnaires about sexual function do predict cardiac risk but are unlikely to be used in day-to-day practice.

The final decision on this book was made in the winter of 2022 after three months in hospital with five weeks in the intensive care unit in the Queen Elizabeth Hospital, Birmingham, in a deep coma facing near-certain death from COVID-19, followed by several months of rehabilitation. At that point, the COVID-19 "mugger", as Boris called it, became very personal, and I have devoted much of my time since to COVID-19 research, publishing three papers in prominent medical journals. Since then, my career has taken more of an upward trend than Boris's. Be assured that everything in the ongoing pages is the absolute truth; no lies here. More of this is in chapters 2 and 3.

A 2018 US research study on "happiness" found that relationships were rated as the most important issue, followed by health. I would hope that after reviewing these chapters, the reader will agree that solving sexual problems ticks both boxes. Preventing relationship breakdown has a huge social and budgetary impact on society. In fact, a major problem in health care is that we often fail to deal with relationships and "couple issues," choosing only to consider problems on an individual basis. I had been trying to treat these issues as "couples' problems" for years until I learned that the clinic clerk at my hospital was sending the female partners off for a nice "Costa" rather than waiting around for me.

Women with sexual problems are likely to be referred to a gynaecologist, who not only rarely, if ever, sees male patients but whose contract prevents them from even accepting male referrals. In contrast, for intimate problems in men, a urologist can see the man along with a partner, but they can only comment in correspondence about the problems of the referred male patient, even if the major issue involves their partner, male or female. This is because of the funding pathway, where two fees might be charged for the consultation. Likewise, a request for payment would be declined if the specialist detected a problem in the partner that needed to be addressed and attempted to charge a fee to the NHS provider.

I remember vividly a case of a man, George, who had been back to my clinic on four occasions. I had prescribed several medications for his erection problem, but nothing seemed to be helping, so I went back to basics and asked him precisely what went on with his wife, Doris, in the bedroom. It soon became obvious that he had been barred from the bedroom for a long time. I tried to explain to him that no tablets that I prescribed would solve that problem. I thought that the message had got home to him, but as he rose from his chair, he quietly mumbled, "So, won't I be getting a prescription today?" I confirmed that, in my opinion, giving him further tablets would not help. The next I hear is that the following week, a letter of complaint *has arrived from Doris, addressed to the hospital manager. It appears that Doris had asked George, on his arrival home, "What did Professor Clever Dick have to say today?" George answered, "He said that it is all your fault!" If only I had had the chance to meet Doris personally to discuss the issues, I might have avoided not only the above title but her alternative "nom de plume" of "Professor high and b****y mighty." On his next visit, I laid out a programme of "medication-assisted masturbatory training" to address his future needs.*

Another problem of UK healthcare is the obsession with "lifestyle" and the unerring belief that lifestyle changes cure most, if not all, medical problems. What is worse is that the advice is often delivered by a doctor or nurse who looks as though they were usually first in the queue for the buffet. Billions of pounds are wasted by re-inventing the lifestyle message and transferring blame, whenever possible, back onto the individual.

Studies of lifestyle issues are often poorly designed with a bias towards a positive message. It is very difficult to implement a "placebo" lifestyle. For example, many studies on dietary interventions result in weight being regained within months as old habits die hard, especially the bad ones. Despite multiple expensive health programmes re-invented by the NHS, obesity rates in the country continue to rise. Surely the definition of insanity is continuing to throw money at a process that is clearly not working. Readers will be pleased to know that this is not a book about developing a firm butt or ribbed abdominal muscles, written by a "soap" celebrity with plenty of spare time during the lockdown. Neither will you need to spend a fortune on new trainers or exercise equipment. There will also be minimal risk of repetitive strain injury.

Along with the huge waste of money on gym memberships, often with defaults within a few weeks, we also spend a fortune on vitamins and supplements with little evidence to support their use in a well-nourished society. Sometimes overdosing with inappropriate vitamins proves dangerous. Just because a "natural" product comes from African tree bark does not mean that it is safe.

In contrast, evidence for licensed medications requires multiple double-blind placebo-controlled trials with peer review over several years at a massive expense, averaging around £20 million pounds, for the companies involved. Because of these rigorous requirements, we can be pretty confident that products actually work and are safe; otherwise, the companies would not have spent millions to get to that stage. The problem that we have as physicians is that we have to be slaves to "licensed indications" and "evidence-based guidelines". These are usually drawn up by experts, many of whom have stopped seeing patients; hence they have endless hours to sit on guidelines committees. The recommendations made by these committees have to be supported by evidence from clinical trials, all of which have been graded by strict criteria devised by even more experts. In the end, these guidelines usually stop short of saying anything meaningful for fear of litigation. Individual doctors risk sanctions for making statements not supported by "expert guidelines", even if based on many years of treating thousands of patients.

Drug companies risk severe fines if they make claims about their drugs that are not supported by their product licence or guidelines, whereas "snake oil salesman" can make unregulated sensational promises. On occasions, I have been asked to modify my statements at meetings to avoid making any comments that might be perceived as "outside the product licence". As these licences usually run for fifteen years, it is often a relief when the patent runs out, and any "generic" company can manufacture the product. At that stage, doctors can actually express opinions as no specific company will gain, and there can be no suspicion that the doctor concerned is being sponsored in any way. This brings me back to the point as to "why now?" for this book. The reason is those important medications discussed in this book are off-patent and, therefore, cheap. Even if not endorsed by their GP and his commissioning group, they will be affordable for the patient to fund for themselves through private prescriptions.

This raises the important question as to what the NHS should provide for every patient. With increased pressure on the NHS, certain aspects of health care, such as "wellness" (how I hate that term) and "sexual health and satisfaction", seem to be appropriate areas to be delegated as a responsibility of the patient. This is similar to hearing, visual, and dental issues now having to be self-funded by the majority of the population, apart from those on very low incomes. The benefits of this are that the physicians will be freed from the shackles of NICE or endless NHS "peer-reviewed" guidelines and might be able to give some honest, genuine advice, telling you what they would do for themselves or their families. As a good tip, ask your doctors what they would do in your position, as it frees them to be honest and allows them to deviate from the "script" imposed upon them by guidelines.

Another major driver for this book was an article in the Times, in July 2022, from the Government's newly appointed "women's health Tsar" which really annoyed me. As far as I knew, there was only one "true Tsar". I have always hated these "gender issues in medicine". I never had any preference to see a male or female doctor, just someone who knew their stuff and their limitations. I have never felt the need for a chaperone, mainly because there were not many spare ones hanging around in the surgery, just waiting to "eavesdrop" on the consultation. The perception is that women need a female chaperone when being examined by a male doctor, whereas a male patient being seen by a female doctor will usually get another woman as a chaperone. Clearly, the perception of two women examining his embarrassing deficiencies is somehow different.

I always felt that the consultation never "flowed" when someone was sitting in, and the patient must have been thinking, "Why me? Why does the doctor feel that they need protection?" I had much experience in Obstetrics, Gynaecology, and Contraceptive services, and yet, as soon as I had trained a young lady doctor, many patients immediately opted for the "seen one, do one" female doctor rather than the highly experienced male physician who taught her. I regularly hear receptionists saying to women, "you'll be wanting to see a lady doctor for that", further compounding the problem. Medicine is plagued with such stereotypes and sweeping generalisations. As a senior colleague once taught me, *"people who constantly make sweeping generalisations are, generally, all the same!"*

Getting back to the "women's health Tsar", the message was that this female senior gynaecologist was going to sort out all the health service "inequalities" working against women, and this got me thinking. A couple of hours later, I had written my first ever letter to the Times about these so-called "inequalities". I rattled off a series of facts that I believe countered her theories:

21

1. Men die four years on average earlier than women, and normally differences such as this should merit attention, even perhaps a specialist "men's health Tsar". If this difference were spotted between other groups in society, then government action would certainly follow.

2. Male mortality is 60% higher from COVID-19, and in the early stages in Italy, it was reported as double, but more about the reasons for this in another chapter. Despite this stark difference, I have never seen this reported on any of the daily news programmes as "experts" appear, usually from their living rooms, wearing their gardening clothes, in front of their laptops, with endless COVID-19 statistics. An internet search revealed that the UK country was the only major European company not to publish gender differences in COVID-19 deaths. Imagine the national outrage of a "men first" vaccination programme.

3. Each major UK city has a "women's hospital"; there are no men's hospitals. I often drive up to reception at Birmingham Woman's Hospital and ask for directions to the "Men's Hospital". The receptionist at the front desk usually just laughs at the regular appearance of this complete extrovert. I think that they actually look forward to my drop-in visits!

4. Women have their own speciality, "obstetrics and gynaecology", with their own royal college. There is no such specialism for men.

5. Doctors are not trained in men's health. I received substantial training in women's health, including four months of my medical degree course, with four weeks of residential obstetric training. In terms of textbooks, there are roughly ten women's health

textbooks for every one on men. When my colleague Mike Kirby told his wife, Sue, that he intended to write a textbook on Men's Health, her reply was, "Book? Surely a pamphlet would suffice!"

6. 60% of GPs are women, and 88% of nurses - there is no chance of an embarrassed man seeing a male nurse of his choosing. Things are set to get worse as the current ratio of female to male GPs in training is approaching 2:1, allowing for a higher career dropout in women.

7. The Royal College of General Practitioners has a women's health spokesperson, Dr Sarah Jarvis, well known on TV and radio. They have no spokesperson on Men's Health. I am sure that their staff looks forward to my regular phone calls wanting to speak to this non-existent expert.

Matt Hancock (remember him), in early 2021, prior his celebrity appearances in the jungle, stated that women GPs earned 15% less than their male counterparts for the same hours, but I always worked in practices where all income was shared equally. The reality is that women GPs with essential breaks in service for family reasons might hold "less senior" posts at lower salaries, but with these higher-paid posts often comes longer hours, more responsibility, and higher burnout rates. There is another side to this, as I have frequently seen practices seeking "preferably female partner" because of the correct perception that women patients are more frequent attenders and prefer to see female doctors. Indeed, I have actually been told at interviews that they were seeking to appoint a female doctor. It is, of course, illegal to advertise posts for a specific gender, but this still seems to be acceptable in medicine, related to the reasons above. I remember when I had a successful interview for my second GP practice in 1993, only to be told that they had been looking to appoint a female partner and that I had taken them by surprise. Nowadays, practices are lucky to get any applicants for GP posts, so these problems should not arise.

8. Women patients consult (on average) nearly twice as often up to the age of 65, and GPs get paid nearly twice as much because of payment for services for women (contraception, smears, breast checks, maternity). Men are a bad deal for GPs as there are no male-specific payments. A specialist GP with an interest in Men's Health is likely to be a "loss leader" as the extra time spent with men will not be bringing in extra payments. Luckily this is less of an issue today as GPs of either gender are becoming impossible to find. When I went into general practice in 1978, there were over a hundred applicants for many posts, whilst today, there are often none at all. This does not fit the general public perception that GPs are underworked and overpaid. I will touch on some of the reasons for this in later chapters.

9. The government has appointed a "minister for women" - there is no "men's minister". Whitehall is spared my regular phone calls as it is impossible to get through to any responsible person, although I did write to the Minister of Health, receiving a response unrelated to the question I raised.

Strangely we seem quite happy to accept these inequalities when general practice might actually be the most equal of all the professions. General practice is clearly in a bad state at the moment due to low morale. I will touch on many of the problems in future chapters.

My only wish is that we could all forget these divisive gender issues in medicine and just get on with the job and give the best possible care, irrespective of gender. By now, you must be thinking, "what an irritating chap I must have been to have as a practice partner, and you would probably be right. I was once described by a former partner as "the greatest patient advocate he had ever met". I replied "thank you very much". He replied, "that wasn't a compliment!".

CHAPTER 2

The rise of the Sex Tsar.

Well, stories have to start somewhere, and in my case, it begins at 6.30 pm on Tuesday 14th December 1994. My Erectile Dysfunction (ED) Clinic at Good Hope Hospital in Sutton Coldfield was really getting up a head of steam after a sluggish start. I wondered what had been done for all these men with sexual problems before I was appointed. The reality was nothing at all. I remember presenting a business case to Good Hope Hospital NHS trust, pointing out that erectile dysfunction was a "large potential growth area".

I had seen about twenty patients in the afternoon and was just about ready for home when the clinic clerk told me that Mr John Thomas (not his real name, of course) had returned after his treatment four hours earlier. This was some four years before the availability of Viagra, but more about that later. At that time, treatment usually consisted of an injection into the penis with a drug called papaverine, although we had recently started using alprostadil as a special mixture made up in the pharmacy at Leighton Hospital, Crewe, under a government licence.

My "Road to Damascus" moment occurred in 1988, when, as a GP, I carried out a couple of vasectomies with Mr Mike Heal, a Urologist at Leighton Hospital, Crewe. I was looking for ways to boost my meagre GP earnings by carrying out minor surgery, but I rapidly realised that vasectomy was a very hard (or difficult) way to make money. Throughout the procedures, I was constantly reminded why I decided against a career in surgery. By chance, Mr Heal was called back to out-patients to review a man who had been injected in the penis earlier that day. The sight of that large bender was like a flash of light. I had discovered my calling. A random event changed my life.

This method of injection treatment gained popularity in the mid-80s when a famous British Urologist, Giles Brindley, famously injected himself on stage at an International Urology meeting in Las Vegas. Nobody had informed him that his prestigious lecture was being attended by the wives of several eminent American Urologists when he chose to expose his impressive erection on stage. Several ladies fainted, and others were treated for shock.

John Thomas was in his late 60s. He suffered from high blood pressure and raised cholesterol and had been alone for several years after a traumatic divorce. He had just met Doris, 62, and recently widowed, at a local tea dance. In his own words, they both had a "lot of catching up to do". It was clear that neither had been looking for long evenings by the fireside, watching Countdown and Deal or no Deal. He wanted action, and quickly. Initially, the suggestion of an injection into his penis prior to sex was not something that he had contemplated, but he was prepared to "give it a go".

The problem in 1994 was that none of us were certain what dose to use for this first test. If we used too little and with no sexual stimulation, then most men might lose heart. I was unsure of the starting dose for Mr Thomas, but luckily, I had been to a seminal lecture a few weeks earlier from Mr Clive Gingell, an eminent Bristol Urologist, and I had posed this very question to him. I remember his answer to this day:

"Well, Dr Hackett, that is a very good question, and this is the way I approach it. I normally start with 10 micrograms (mcg), but If I have a young man with little in the way of medical problems, then I might give 5 mcgs; if, on the other hand, I have a man with severe diabetes, I might start with 20. Sometimes there is no alternative but to just "suck it and see!"

Although I never fancied taking up his last piece of advice, it seemed to leave something of a bad taste, but, in the case of JT and his search for a fast start, I went for 20 mcg. As he undressed, he made the very familiar comment, "it's a cold day; I'm afraid it's rather small". I tended to agree but made light of the diminutive size and delivered a full dose of 20 mcg. To this day, I have never heard a patient apologize for being over-endowed.

We were all aware of the need for sexual stimulation to augment the effect of any medication, so, in the early days, I provided several copies of Playboy that I had found under the bed of an ex-roommate. I even persuaded my accountant to allow my online prescription against tax. Unfortunately, few copies of Playboy were ever returned to the clinic. I had been reduced to subscribing to the Sun and leaving copies open at page three in the examination rooms. I still mourn the absence of page three girls. I blame the rise of the feminist movement for the lack of appropriate stimulatory material. Health and Efficiency, the leading naturist magazine at the time, rarely did the trick.

For John Thomas, the response to the injection was almost instantaneous, with a quite splendid erection. "My word," he gasped, "that is really the most impressive thing I have ever seen," and left the clinic cock-a-hoop.

Now four hours later, he was back in considerable discomfort. Doris was at the hairdresser's all afternoon, and despite several attempts at masturbation and watching a 1-hour Fanny Craddock cookery special, it had not gone down. He felt that his penis was "on fire" and might explode any second. He was in agony and crying with excruciating pain. He dropped his trousers to reveal a throbbing rock-hard erection termed priapism. I have realised that, in this situation, a man would willingly give all his money, his wife, his house, his Aston Villa season ticket, anything to be relieved. I inserted the largest size needles I could find into both sides of the throbbing mass, and dark blood began to run out into the dish. "Ahhhhhh..." he uttered – the relief was palpable. He was the first patient ever to offer me a tip for the services provided. Half an hour later, suitably deflated, he went home. I realised that his future follow-up might not be quite as straightforward, but that was a problem for another day. Clearly, in his case, I should probably have adopted the "suck it and see" approach.

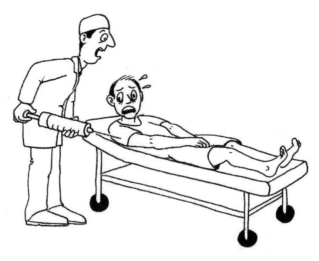

"The dose? Sometimes I just have to suck it and see."

Around this time, I was involved in a weekend conference with a famous female Urologist, Christine Evans, teaching GPs about ED. UK urologists would agree that Christine was definitely "one of a kind". She explained to the audience that she liked to give the men of North Wales a "jolly good priapism" so they knew "what it felt like". This was because of the remoteness of the area, meaning that emergency services were limited. Even in 2022, a young patient of mine travelled all the way to San Diego to see a world expert, Irwin Goldstein, who was still following this approach. Christine Evans also suggested that she only treated older men if they had an attractive younger partner. I had to hastily add that I could not endorse either of these views. Christine later became a TV celebrity on "Under the knife with Dr Christine," but for me, her finest moment was an appearance on BBC TV's "The Celebrity Weakest Link" with Anne Robinson, where she was narrowly beaten in a final question decider about a member of the cast of Emmerdale. Her victorious opponent was none other than Basil Brush. The thrilling conclusion of that particular episode is still available on YouTube.

It was December 21ˢᵗ, 1994, and my first appointment was with a 72-year-old Irishman, James O'Flaherty. He has been widowed for twelve years but has just moved into a retirement apartment where he was the only male. His first wife was staunch Catholic, and sex had always involved "pull the nighty down when you are finished" (his words, not mine). All sex had ceased when his first wife, Magdalen, developed cancer and died after a long-protracted illness. Within days of moving into his new flat, ladies were knocking on his door with invitations to tea and crumpets. A couple of ladies had made open advances. It was quite clear that nothing was stirring down below, such that he had to make a hasty retreat. He wondered if anything could be done to help Mr Tinkle (I never cease to be amused by the names men have for the old lady's best friend). I explained to him that his problem was almost certainly related to his previous heart attack and the years of depression associated with his wife's death and subsequent grieving. As there were no signs of life in Mr Tinkle (he even had me going now), the only possibility was an injection for Mr T just before the planned activity. "Begorrah – you won't be sticking that fecking thing into Mr Tinkle!". I explained how simple the process was, and he presented Mr Tinkle, who had clearly been hibernating below ground level for some time. "Just a tiny prick," I said, regretting my comment almost immediately. "I know," he said; I've needed a mirror to find him for the past ten years!" Five minutes later, Mr T showed considerable signs of life, but I had learned from my earlier "suck it and see policy" and given 10mcg instead of 20mcg. "Saints be praised," he said, "I'll take 20 of the fecking things, can I use 2 at a time?" I explained that I would recommend the higher dose to guarantee maximum performance, warning him that the erection might last an hour. "Begorrah" he shouted, "Wait until Maud sees this tonight!" I then had to be the bearer of bad news. The NHS in its infinite wisdom allows a maximum of one injection per week (more about that later). "To be sure that won't last me until lunchtime tomorrow, I've got Doris for coffee in the morning!"

In the same clinic, at around 6pm, I received a phone call from Ivor Hardy (not his real name), a 92-year-old former golf professional who was flying out to Antigua the following morning with his considerably younger wife for a 6-week break. He has realised that he was down to his last four injections. I explained that, as the pharmacy was closed, there was no way that I could get the considerable supply down to London that night. "Damn," he says, "never mind, I'll switch the flight until next Thursday!" Never in their wildest dreams would any GP in the country consider that a 92-year-old man would not even contemplate taking a Caribbean holiday without guaranteed erections.

These two cases, along with many others, have convinced me that, as doctors, we have little idea of what is important to the lives of our older patients. They could not care in the slightest about their lipids or their eGFR (a test of kidney function) if all was working in the trouser department. This was all made clear by a long-term study of "happiness" from Harvard University in 2018, which showed that "relationships" were number one, well above health and money, in terms of what made people happy. As it is sexual attraction that usually draws us into the most important relationship in our lives, it should surprise nobody of the huge impact of losing that sexual contact and intimacy. In medical school and in hospital practice, I was taught nothing about this. It was only years of really getting to know and understand people in general practice that made me realise that much medical education had little relevance to what was important in people's lives. For many couples, when that physical attraction is lost, there is often little that binds them together. The misery and financial hardships that result from relationship breakups have a profound impact, not only on the couple and their children but on society in general. If we could only ask questions about sex, especially of men, then we could detect problems, intervene, save relationships and keep families together. I often comment that I spend most of my time trying to save second and third marriages, as the first had failed long before.

Enough of the serious moralising; back to some more tumescent tales!

It was January 1995, and the clinic was beginning to pick up big time. According to Parkinson's Law, we now, of course, need more staff, so a GP clinical assistant, David Milledge, was appointed for two sessions per week to assist in a clinic that nobody knew that we needed eighteen months earlier.

On the 12th of January, Cyril Pike, a 75-year-old widower, returned. He was yet another senior gent about town. His newly discovered erectile potency was proving a huge hit with the local ladies of Erdington. He currently had four different members of the pink rinse brigade in tow, and life was getting complicated. With one 72-year-old spinster, Elsie, he was helping her to act out several of her fantasies. He visited her Mondays and Thursdays, having carefully administered an injection at least fifteen minutes before. Of course, Elsie had no idea of the "magic potion" that Cyril injected that allowed him to perform like a 20-year-old stallion. She was just along for the ride, having endured many years of sexual repression with her late husband.

Cyril's role in these fantasies was to knock on the door pretending to be a local tradesman, from window cleaner to chimney sweep and pool maintenance man, not that Elsie has an open fire, let alone a swimming pool. Cyril looked like a sorry soul in the clinic today, and Dr Milledge was sitting in on my clinic to learn the secrets of the Sex Tsar. Last Thursday, Cyril duly arrived at Elsie's house at 7.15pm and rang the doorbell, shouting, "Gas Man – come to read the meter". Sex in the Gas Man position was Elsie's favourite sexual fantasy, as she always said, "You can stay in all day, and nobody comes". This time there was no reply, so Cyril shouted again, "Gas Man here", then to his horror, he realised that in his excitement, anticipating an evening of endless passion, the old fella was lifeless – he had forgotten to inject himself. He grabbed for the syringe in his pocket and unzipped his overalls – no time to lose. At that moment, Elsie thrust open the front door and wrested Cyril to the ground, "Naughty Mr Gas Man, take me, now," she screamed, clutching at his nether regions. The syringe went flying through the air, spilling all the contents over the carpet. Dr Milledge had been totally silent throughout the consultation but suddenly interrupted, "Was it a shag pile?" "No, an Axminster, I think", replied Cyril. This was the first lesson for Dr M – all humour needs to be pitched at an appropriate level. Clever Dicks are not appreciated in the ED clinic. Alas, for Cyril, that was the end of his relationship with Elsie. Cyril's experiences were an eye-opener for Dr Milledge as to the sexual expectations of older men and the voracious demands of older women anxious to make up for lost years.

A commercial preparation of alprostadil had been licensed as Caverject by aptly named Upjohn Ltd. I was invited to present on "self- injection techniques" at a meeting In Sutton Coldfield in May 1995. I had shopped around for some sort of "aid" to demonstration and came across a product that seemed to fit the bill. It was called "Grow your own Pecker" and was essentially a small rubber penis that grew to greater than real size when placed in water. On arrival at the meeting, I found that the medic for Upjohn was called Simon Vane Percy, and the speaker before me was a Reader in Law at Reading University, called Chris Newdick, who reliably informed me that he lived at 4 Knobcock Lane. The meeting went well, and my inflated pecker stole the show, but unfortunately, I left my pecker in the wash bag in the hotel room, along with my range of expensive toiletries. Two weeks later, I summoned up the courage to ring the hotel to try to recover my bag, hoping that the staff had not opened it to reveal my pecker. I overheard the girl on the phone say to another staff member, "It's him!" When I dropped by that evening to collect the bag, it was evident that my pecker had been well handled in those two weeks.

The success of the clinic was causing me to question whether we had the appropriate name. Whilst the title "Erectile Dysfunction Clinic" might seem crisp and to the point, I was dealing with many more issues than simply supplying more lead to the pencil. I was keen to be dealing with problems of ejaculation, desire, low testosterone, and even problems affecting the female partner and the relationship. Management suggested "Sexual Health Clinic", but to the NHS, Sexual Health means contraception, unplanned pregnancy, and STIs; in fact, everything to do with having less sex, or indeed, no sex at all. Other names such as "The men's clinic"," Eros", or "Priapus" clinic were simply too pretentious. We decided to stick with the ED clinic, with all the limitations. Recently, a close colleague of mine, Dr Angela Servis, came up with the title "Eden Clinic," which does seem to have a bit more class.

My youngest son walked in that evening in tears after his teacher had asked them to write a short essay in French about "What their father did for a living". He had been selected to read his essay in class. It began "Il est un docteur du penis". He was given two weeks of detention. Clearly, this experience has not held him back, as he is now a headmaster and recently invited the Tsar to give a talk to his 9-year-olds!

The problem is that the NHS "commissioning system" had made things worse: the patients were now "units" of referral that had to be "costed". In many cases, I was seeing a man who might have little wrong with him – apart from being married to the wrong woman. The problem was that the man was the unit of referral, and, as such, I had no right to question the partner, let alone offer treatment or advice.

This was clear to me when George Dingle first consulted in May 1995. He was 52 and had let himself go, piling on the weight. He had poorly controlled blood pressure and cholesterol, largely because he did not take his tablets. He had been started on injections into the penis and, over the course of six months and three dose increases, had reached the maximum dose. This seemed strange, so I decided to go back to basics and ask him precisely what was going on in the bedroom. It became quite clear that once a week, he would go to the bathroom, inject himself and venture back into the bedroom, expecting his wife, Daphne, to succumb to the majesty of his erection, only to find that she was once again feigning deep insomnia, as she had done for the last eight years. The reality was that she was no longer remotely interested in "that sort of thing" and whatever "hardening material" I produced would make not a scrap of difference. I suggested that he have a serious "heart-to-heart" with Daphne, and the look on his face clearly showed that I had hit the nail on the head. I felt certain that he was now going to realise the futility of the last six months, only for him to reach the door, turn around and say, "so there's nothing stronger that you can give me!"

Sometimes, of course, the wife may not be the object of the man's fancy. Often, they have a "dancing partner", or they just want to indulge in solo performances just in case an opportunity arises. As Woody Allen famously said, "don't knock masturbation. It's sex with someone I love". Some of my favourite comments are "Physics is to mathematics what sex is to masturbation," or "the only shame in masturbation is the shame of not doing it well," or "if God intended us not to masturbate, He/God would have made our arms shorter". For most of my masturbatory education, I put myself into the careful hands of Angela Gregory, one of my favourite sex therapists and self-proclaimed "mistress of masturbation".

My expertise was later recognised with an invitation to act as a judge in the 2009 World Masturbation championship in San Francisco, where Asanobu Sato retained his world title with a new world record of 9 hours and 58 minutes. As many of you might know, the 10-hour barrier, one of the "holy grails" of sport, has since been shattered, but more about that, including whether masturbation should be considered a sport and, therefore, worthy of inclusion in the Olympics.

One of my favourite websites to recommend is www.masturbation.com which reliably informs us that 95% of men and 89% of women masturbate regularly and explains more than twenty different techniques. In contrast to the old guys, I saw many young men with ejaculatory problems. I was becoming increasingly aware that, to some men, ejaculation is an Olympic sport with "personal bests" for categories such as height, distance, volume, and texture. They had little concept that if you can no longer do your personal best for the 100 metres or long jump, then your best ejaculatory years might also be behind you.

Although premature ejaculation or PE (much more about that later) is the major problem, many complain about retarded ejaculation or totally impossibility to come.

Shane Lingam was 21, a quiet lad seemingly a bit of a geek. He attended with a problem of inability to ejaculate with his new partner, Phoebe, aged 18. The important question to ask is not "if" he masturbated, but "how often?" "Roughly ten times," he answered. He

37

seemed to detect a look of surprise on my face. "Is that too much?" he replied. "Well, ten times per week would be considered above average", was my considered response. "Not weekly", he retorted, "I meant daily!" I resisted the temptation to look at my watch and say, "Am I keeping you from something?" My diagnosis here was, of course, idiosyncratic masturbation, meaning that the intensity of stimulation required to reach a climax was unlikely to be replicated during vaginal intercourse with his new girlfriend unless she was a sexual contortionist. We negotiated cessation of masturbation (if possible) to reset the threshold with only once weekly relief being allowed.

I often say that the average UK couple spends more time talking about what colour bathroom suite to buy than they spend discussing their sex lives, yet I have never seen a couple divorce over the colour of their bathroom suite – yet some in avocado must come close. Many men keep their appointments secret from their wives, hoping to "surprise" them after several years devoid of action.

Such a case was Brian Everard, 75, who informed me that his wife was getting desperate, although I noted that she had not attended with him. I duly administered 20 mcg of alprostadil, and ten minutes later, we had a pretty impressive "lift-off". I tried to persuade him that he should wait around for an hour or so to check if things had settled, but he seemed very keen to exit the department, almost as though he had a "fast horse" tied up outside. I recorded Brian as another stunning success for the Tsar and thought nothing more about the case until 3 weeks later. I was greeted on arrival at the clinic by a gentleman from PALS (Patient Advice and Liaison Services). He had received a letter of a formal complaint from a Mrs Ada Everard, who wrote that 3 weeks earlier, she had been putting a freshly stuffed chicken in the Aga when her husband Brian, without warning, "approached her" from behind "like a wild animal" having just returned from an appointment with Dr Hackett. Luckily my suitably contrite response seemed to do the trick.

As a result of my experiences with Brian and Ada, I decided to rigorously question men as to their level of co-operation with partners.

Sometimes attendance with a seemingly devoted partner is not helpful, as the following case shows.

Cecil and Gladys Weiner attended with problems in the bedroom for several years, and the cause was not obvious at first. I note that Gladys seemed to be answering several of the questions that would normally require a subjective response from Cecil, such as "do you notice morning stiffness?" "Not with my new arthritis tablets," he replied. Gladys then suddenly revealed, "We were referred to you by Professor Kevan Wylie from Sheffield when we recently attended the "small penis clinic". Immediately, the elephant in the room revealed itself! During the remainder of the consultation, Cecil's experiences at the "small penis clinic" were mentioned by Gladys three more times. Cyril was a large gentleman, and an examination of his genitals duly confirmed that his attendance at the said clinic was entirely appropriate. It was clear that he would not have been able to visualise his own penis and testicles for many years. I offered them some advice, loaned him one of our designer penis scopes (as shown below), and asked them to consider some options and make a follow-up appointment. As I walked past the reception a few minutes later, I overheard Gladys saying to the clinic clerk, in front of a full waiting room, "Cecil might not be able to make that date as he has a small penis clinic appointment in Sheffield". I was prepared to go to great lengths to help this couple, but unfortunately, I never saw Cyril and Gladys for their planned follow-up.

LE PENISCOPE DU "PETIT VIEUX"

The following week I received a phone call from a scientist working for a Biopharm company called Senetek about a new drug in development called Invicorp. This was also an injection but was reported to be completely painless. They wanted to conduct clinical trials of their new drug and required a UK expert to conduct these. I was acutely conscious that the alprostadil we were using caused intense pain and that we needed something better. The other good news was that Invicorp was reported to carry zero chance of prolonged erection. The drug also came as an auto-injector, perfect for the needle-phobic man, which in terms of injecting the penis, applies to most of us. They would be providing the drug for me to use in the clinic and wanted to film the Tsar in action treating patients. I put this to my hospital managers, who were a little sceptical about ethical issues, but the offer of a £20k payment soon sorted this. I managed to negotiate that £5K should be allocated for staff attendance at educational meetings – how naïve I was to think that we would ever see this money again!

A week later, the camera crew arrived at the department just before a busy clinic. I delivered some words of wisdom to the camera, and a couple of patients agreed to have consultations filmed. I had been introduced to a small, shy gentleman who arrived with the Senetek team. His name was Jacob Rosenberg. I was unsure of his role in the proceedings. He had said nothing throughout the process, but just as we seemed to be closing, he suddenly interjected, "I am actually a major investor in the company; I wondered if I might try the injection". I looked quickly over to the product manager, who gave me a nod that clearly indicated that investment from Mr Rosenberg was critical for success. I quickly ascertained that Mr R, who was around 45, had no important medical conditions and was not sexually active. For some reason, I suspected this was probably permanently. I proceeded to inject the lowest dose of Invicorp via the "novel" auto-injector, and he verified that the process was completely painless – so far, so good. He seemed very impressed when he developed an absolute "stonker" (a term we regularly use in the ED world) within a couple of minutes. I glanced over to the product manager, who gave me the immediate thumbs up as though the full investment was now in the bag. As we were ending the session, I told Mr R that normally, I keep patients in the clinic for at least ninety minutes, but he had a train to catch and business in London that evening and Paris the next day. He reminded me of my recorded interview that listed the post-injection problems with this injection as "virtually zero". He glanced at his watch, and he and the manager promptly left to catch the train. I was now well behind the clinic and subsequently headed home at 8pm, looking forward to a nice glass of Chablis. I was just drifting off in my chair at around 10pm, when the phone rang. It was Mr R, ringing from the Grosvenor Hotel in London. His penis was rock hard and throbbing but not painful. I suggested that he might like to try some "self-relief", but he had already tried this four times, and the erection kept coming back. I advised him that the lack of pain was reassuring and that there were no recorded cases of priapism with Invicorp. He seemed relieved. I got up early the next morning for a full day of general practice and reached home at about 9pm, hoping my dinner would not be too spoilt. I had barely started when the phone rang. A lady with a strong French accent announced that this was the Ritz in Paris; she was putting me through to Mr Rosenberg in room 101. He could barely speak. "I think it's on fire," he mumbled. I asked some of my standard questions on erection hardness, and we agreed that "Yes, he could probably use it to bang in a 3-inch nail". He had called off his business meeting and sought the help of the duty manager at the Ritz. Being French, he seemed to have a novel suggestion that none of us in the UK would have considered. He rang a lady who often helped discerning clients of the Ritz in need of relief. Two hours later, she had left, apparently requesting twice her normal call-out fee. There was no alternative but to give him the emergency phone number of a top French Urologist I knew, Professor Stephane Droupy (I jest not). I heard nothing further from Mr R, but I am sure that he will always remember his European Adventure and his impulse suggestion to "give it a go". He clearly had a night in Paris that he will never forget. I bumped into Professor Droupy at a meeting a couple of months later, and he had no recollection of Mr R, so I was uncertain as to whether I should record him as the first priapism with Invicorp or simply an innocent Jewish gentleman who could tell an interesting tumescent tale of 2 cities.

My documentary for Senetek led to a couple of clinical trials and lecture trips to San Francisco and Kuala Lumpur in the summer of 1996. I was becoming an international Sex Tsar, but things were about to get even better. In early March 1996, I had a call from a Dr Ian Osterloh of Pfizer UK that an oral drug was being developed to treat ED, and I had been selected as a possible centre to carry out research. As I had witnessed the way, NHS hospital's approach to research which essentially consisted of "You do the work, and we'll take the money," along with the disappearance of the £5K allocated for doctor education, I developed a different approach. I had developed a small clinic in a barn conversion adjacent to my home, specially for clinical trials avoiding much of the red tape involved in the NHS. In early June 1996, Dr Osterloh attended with Professor Alan Riley to explain the first UK clinical trial of a drug called sildenafil. I was aware that a couple of oral drugs had been tested and failed miserably, so I was dubious to hear of a drug developed to treat blood pressure and heart disease. The interesting fact was that the patients refused to return to tablets at the end of the study. After the meeting, I remember going back to Sally and saying, "I've just met a couple of wackos who think they have a drug to give you an erection"; how wrong I was! Much more of this in later chapters.

Sally broke the news that, once again, my son, Dan, was in tears. The project at school had been to construct a poster on "How to look after your heart". Whereas the other children had cut-out pictures of men exercising, plates of healthy food, or bottles of vitamins, he had attached a box of Viagra. They had failed to appreciate that my son was years ahead of his time, condemning him to two hours in detention. Life was tough for the family of the Sex Tsar.

CHAPTER 3

COVID-19 STRIKES –

As Bad as it gets!!!

Struck down by the COVID-19 "mugger"

From the story of my early days in the previous chapter, we fast forward to the current day for my own gruesome experience that made it imperative that I write this book as soon as possible. It has been suggested that I contrived to catch COVID-19 to explore all the complications from this dreadful disease, or "mugger", as Boris termed it, merely to enhance book sales. I can definitely assure you that this was not the case.

My story begins on 6th January 2021, at the very height of the UK COVID-19 virus pandemic, the very peak of those graphs they show on the news. This was a couple of weeks before the first UK vaccinations. My wife, Sally, and I had been virtual recluses for the previous three months, following all the rules. I had even sacrificed my passion for shopping, and even my favourite pastime, golf, was banned at that stage.

Sally and I were both feeling tired for 3-4 days, but we had delayed testing as I had a negative PCR test three days earlier prior to my weekly out-patient clinic, where I saw only two patients face to face (plus three via Zoom). This was with full protection with mask, gowns, and gloves.

I had been very aware of safety as my appraiser for the last two years; Mr Amged El-Hawrani, an ENT consultant, became the second UK doctor to die from COVID-19 in March 2020, only days after my appraisal. I remember his last words vividly to me after I expressed concerns that this might be my last appraisal, "I am certain that I will be seeing you again next year". He was an excellent surgeon and a perfect gentleman.

Sally and I took a PCR test at the NEC Birmingham on the morning of Thursday, 7th January 2021, and both received positive results by text the same evening. Around 5.30 pm on that same evening of January 7th 2021, I took the dog for a walk on a misty evening and felt a bit short of breath after about 100 yards. At this stage, we were all told to avoid pressure on the NHS by self-isolating. I had actually volunteered to be available as a physician for the helpline service, but due to the predictable NHS, red tape had not yet started. The training that I had received for the emergency response team probably made me aware of not putting the emergency services under stress by "over-reacting". I decided to follow the standard advice to get an early night but woke several times, and by 4am, I was acutely short of breath. I called for Sally to ring for an ambulance, which arrived within 15 minutes. I was admitted to Good Hope Hospital on Friday, 8th January, at about 5am (?) and was immediately placed on oxygen. Lying in the A&E department, I remember catching a glimpse of my chest x-ray on the wall of the admission room and thinking, "I hope that this is not mine!" as the left side was totally opaque, as was 70% of the right side. As the two doctors looked over at me, the bad news hit home – it most definitely was mine!!

Nothing that I had heard in the media or at educational meetings prepared me for the rapid deterioration that then ensued.

Progress after Admission

I was transferred to a side room on the general ward, given dexamethasone, which at the time was considered the "life-saving injection" and treated in a prone position with high-flow oxygen. Regular blood gases were taken from the arteries in my wrist and groin and were all low at around 93% as I drifted into periods of restlessness and confusion over the next 3-4 days; I was too ill to get out of bed and remember nothing more from my third day in hospital until I woke from a coma five weeks later. I had required intubation and ventilation after multiple seizures and was transferred to the high-dependency ICU at the Queen Elizabeth Hospital Birmingham (QEHB) a few days after the original admission. This was at the very height of the maximal pandemic admissions, with over 300 patients on high dependency care. Removal of my endotracheal tube was attempted on day 11, but I was re-intubated on day 14 and subsequently had a tracheostomy, with a long-term tube inserted through the neck and put onto a mechanical ventilator over the next three weeks. Blood cultures on day 28 grew dangerous bacteria, Klebsiella, and very powerful IV antibiotics Tazocin, Vancomycin, Meropenem, and Ceftriaxone were given. These high-dose drugs subsequently caused marked deafness.

Lumbar puncture (a truly fun procedure best enjoyed at least three times in my case) also showed meningitis, and a CT scan showed encephalitis (infection of the brain) with a 1-inch blood clot in the hippocampus, a part of the brain concerned with learning and memory plus a small clot in the left temporal lobe, the part concerned with processing mood, emotions, language, and perceptions. Patients with this collection of complications would generally have a low chance of survival, and Sally had been prepared for the seemingly inevitable news. She had even been given power of attorney due to the likelihood that I might not regain mental function. It is interesting that, had I not survived at this stage, I would have been outside the 28-day classification for COVID-19-related deaths.

I remember a curious experience of a nurse being beside my bed, holding my hand, and my breath became shallower. I actually felt that "this is it," and I was peacefully drifting away. After all, I had been through, this seemed a relief, and I was prepared to go. I seemed to have stopped breathing, but I could still hear the first nurse speaking to another one. It seemed that she thought that I had gone, so I closed my eyes to drift away, but nothing was happening. I then had the strangest feeling that everybody thought I was dead, but I was still alive but unable to move. I truly believed that I had died and was waiting for the angel in white to greet me. I feared that I might not be on their list and have to turn around and head "down under", despite my Catholic school education. I even had a recollection of a recent paper that I had read from the Catholic Medical Association (see below) that suggests that, after 30 years of dedication to men's health, often facilitating extra-marital and gay sex or immoral acts, even acting as a judge for the world masturbation championships, I was destined for that bad place after death. I had clearly failed to promote chastity and facilitated a multitude of immoral acts. Had I declined to offer treatment to any patient on judgmental grounds, I would certainly have faced a complaint and probably been struck off the medical register.

I also remember in my gynaecology job; I was pressed into an increased TOPs (termination of pregnancy) load as my colleague was a conscientious objector. I recall that I used to come out of a long operating list to find him watching the test match and enjoying tea and crumpets. There was also the occasion that I was at church in Dublin, having taken an examination at the Royal College of Physicians the previous day. I had emptied my pockets of a load of shrapnel into the collection plate, only for the priest to announce in his sermon, "it has come to my notice that a large quantity of coins has been deposited in the collection. I inform you that those responsible will answer for it in hell fire. I thought "hell fire, that's a bit steep".

Things were looking worse when this extract from the Catholic press suggested that doctors prescribing Viagra to assist sex for non-procreation purposes were also designed for hell fire. Once again I seemed doomed.

Luckily, I was not destined for eternal damnation on that day and was given another opportunity for a better life!

The Linacre Quarterly
2022, Vol. 89(3) 329
© Catholic Medical Association 2022
Article reuse guidelines:
sagepub.com/journals-permissions
DOI: 10.1177/00243639221094475
journals.sagepub.com/home/ulq
$SAGE

Erectile Dysfunction (ED) Treatment: Position Paper of the Catholic Medical Association

CATHOLIC MEDICAL ASSOCIATION
Upholding the Principles of the Catholic Faith in the Science and Practice of Medicine

In recent years, Catholic and other Christian clinicians have inquired about the ethical status of prescribing erectile dysfunction (ED) medications to unmarried men.

The Catholic Medical Association does not object to the utilization of medications for ED for men in a married, monogamous, and heterosexual relationship. This is, of course, after an appropriate medical evaluation and discussion of the risks of the medication. The same recommendation can be extended to injections, implantable devices, and vacuum devices to treat erectile dysfunction. It is appropriate that the clinician encourage the patient to discuss the proposed treatment with his wife.

If a clinician is aware that a patient is requesting an ED medication for use outside of a legitimate marital relationship, a prescription should not be provided. The clinician should not cooperate in such an act, either by formal involvement by writing the prescription, or endorsing a consultation to a urologist for ED treatment. Methods of transfer for the patient may be employed to remove any form of formal cooperation with the prescription of medication. A medical work up for ED is not a form of cooperation.

It is beyond the competency of the clinician to assess the sacramental marital status of his or her patients, and only a civil declaration of marriage would be reasonable before assessing the moral status of prescribing a therapy for ED. In all circumstances, the clinician's commitment to promoting chastity and avoiding cooperation with immoral acts should be clearly visible in speech and action.

I imagined the strange scenario that Sally had been told that I was dead and then I tried to ring her at home, only for somebody else to answer and respond "you sick b*****d", as I tried to think of something I could say to tell them that it really was me. In retrospect, these bizarre experiences must have been the effect of drugs used for sedation whilst in ITU.

I have no memory of anything else during my 5-week stay in the QEHB until my return to Good Hope on 21st February 2021.

Rehabilitation

My first real recollection was on 23rd Feb (day 46) when I woke up in the general ward back at Good Hope hospital. At this stage, I was still totally confused, with no idea of the date, time, or place. I was convinced that I was in Dubai and was constantly making time adjustments. I remember being concerned that I did not have my passport and kept asking the staff how I was ever going to get back to the UK.

I quickly learned to write the date on my hand as I knew that I would be asked the question regularly, and the more confused I was, the longer I was going to remain in hospital.

I began to make a series of strange phone calls at odd times to friends and family and even believed that I had two women (one a wife and one a carer) competing for me after my discharge! Chance would be a strange thing. I remember speaking to Sally on the phone and asking her to pay some money to the other woman for being so kind. The other woman, also seemingly called Sally, was considerably younger. She seemed more patient and understanding. Of course, there was never any doubt which Sally I would choose.

I had lost 3 stone (19kg) in weight, mostly muscle, as, unfortunately, it is much easier to lose muscle than fat. I had profound muscle wasting in the legs; gone were the muscular thighs and chunky calves. I barely recognised them as my own. I was unable to stand or walk and attempts to do so resulted in intense burning in the legs, such that I had to lie down immediately. I feared that, at this stage, I might never walk again. Rehabilitation was slow and hard work, especially with the staff shortages due to COVID-19, as these were prior to vaccination.

It had been nearly three months since I had seen Sally or any of my family, and I feared that I might never see them again as the reality of the visiting ban hit home. Long-term stays on COVID-19 wards at this time were not like any prior experience; no family visitors, bunches of grapes, or chats with the nurses. There was little or no sleep to be had, especially as I was seemingly still on Dubai time and constantly telling staff that I had lost my passport! Most depressing was the daily sight of empty beds the next morning when it was clear that those poor souls were not so lucky. I was beginning to wonder when my time might come.

I had been two months with an indwelling catheter and was desperate to get rid of it. I persuaded the ward sister to let me try without. Unfortunately, on one of my first solo attempts at reaching the toilet using a frame, I slipped and fell directly onto my right hip. I was very fortunate not to break anything, and the staff checked me several times, almost in disbelief. The fall was quite a setback as I was again confined to bed. The acute shortage of physiotherapists at this time was all too clear, as some days, they did not appear at all due to more pressing demands. All too quickly, we seem to have forgotten what these wonderful dedicated people have gone through. There was no direct contact with staff as they all wore protective equipment throughout, as these were the darkest stages of the pandemic.

At this stage, I was suffering marked urinary symptoms. I was also experiencing marked postural drops in blood pressure, so the suggestion of an alpha-blocker, tamsulosin, for the urine symptoms, but commonly associated with dizziness or drop in blood pressure, was not ideal, and I declined. It must have been difficult for the nursing staff to deal with a so-called "expert", in these things, even if he had no idea of the month and thought he was in Dubai.

I asked Sally to send in my daily tadalafil, which had been stopped on my admission. I could imagine the nurses saying, "he won't be needing this in here (as it is usually prescribed for erection problems!)"

Within a couple of days of starting the tadalafil (more about that later), the urinary symptoms had settled, and, in case any readers are remotely interested, the first morning erections in two months appeared. Many might be thinking, "how can a man think about such things when he is fighting for his life". Being the Sex Tsar, I was aware that the return of morning erections is the best sign that the heart and arteries are working well, but more about that in future chapters. All I can say is that, for men of a certain age, this feeling can be very uplifting. Over the last few days, all the worst possible outcomes had been flooding through my mind, so at least one big concern could be put to rest. Strangely this was not a question that the nurses had asked at all. I had constantly been asking for my testosterone to be measured, as the link with COVID-19 had been my major area of interest before admission. It was no surprise that when they eventually checked my blood, my levels were very low, and, mostly due to my insistence, they started me on testosterone injections. I suppose it was a little strange that they accepted my judgement, given that I thought that I was stuck in Dubai without a passport and regularly wore my pyjamas back to front!

After ten weeks in hospital and four weeks back in a general ward, I was becoming desperate to get home, despite barely being able to take more than a few steps. Sensibly, I decided to go with Sally as my "preferred wife," as she is a senior physiotherapist with many years of experience! Without her, I am sure that I would have been in hospital much longer.

Undoubtedly the worst part of this experience was the inability to see any family or friends for the 3-month period. For those of you who might have had long stays in hospital, nothing is quite like this. It is only by going through this experience that you really understand how bad it feels. You realise that it is quite possible that you won't survive, but you always thought that it would be with the family around the bed or friends visiting, but there was none of this on the COVID-19 ward. There was the real possibility that you had seen them all for the last time.

Even worse than that was the appearance of at least three of my old patients suddenly popping up in the beds next to or opposite me, and there was no way to escape them by day or night. It never continues to amaze me that patients express complete surprise that doctors actually get ill, never mind end up in hospital. An update on their health in general and erectile performance, in particular, wasn't what I needed for a morale boost.

In terms of past medical history, I was pretty fit until age 59, when, in 2010, I noted a single episode of passing blood in the urine whilst at a medical conference in Veracruz in Mexico, the site of a famous Humphrey Bogart film. The clear message is that passing blood in the urine always needs assessment. As it only happened to me once, I could easily have missed it as it was in the middle of the night. Ultrasound Scan and biopsy confirmed an early transitional cell cancer of the bladder, treated with excision and Mitomycin cytotoxic infusions resulting in full recovery. Subsequent follow-up cystoscopies over 3 years were all fine, but, at random, I received an admission date for prostate surgery but politely declined. I was offered an alpha-blocker which caused a postural drop in blood pressure. I subsequently started taking tadalafil 5mg daily, which I have taken for nine years with excellent effect, but more about the effect of this medication in another chapter.

REHABILITATION

I mobilised very well at home after COVID-19 discharge for over 3-4 weeks with the use of a walking frame, and eventually, I was able to get up the stairs by six weeks. I was able to resume driving after six months as, because of seizures at the height of my illness, I surrendered my driving licence. Not being able to drive during the lockdown period was less of a problem as there were few places to go. I eventually got back to playing golf and Zoom consultations with patients by September, 7-8 months after my admission. I am left with residual deafness, worse in the right ear, presumably due to the powerful intravenous antibiotics, slight incoordination in the left hand, impaired balance, and breathlessness on exertion. I also take much longer to answer quiz questions, as my brain has to go through several extra files to find the answers. I wish the BBC would develop special quizzes with five minutes to answer each question, but I think that viewing figures would suffer.

A major worry is long-term pulmonary fibrosis, given the severity of the infection in hospital, as this is being reported in journals 12 months (a year) after severe infection. Time will tell if I have managed to avoid this complication of COVID-19.

I still have complete memory loss for the 6-week period in ITU with no sign of this returning. I am not worried about this, as nothing pleasurable happened, although my beloved Leeds United collected 15 out of 18 points when I was in a coma, their best run of that season.

I also realised how lucky I was to survive, and I am very appreciative of the excellent care I received at QEHB. During convalescence, I wrote a medical textbook and published three medical papers on the subject of COVID-19. For those small-minded people who become obsessed with a few typos and grammatical errors, I would invite them to embrace these as entirely appropriate for a victim of hippocampal thrombosis and enjoy a unique literary experience!

As cases of COVID-19 continue, despite vaccination, I fear the risk of a second infection, but I feel that it is important to continue in clinical work seeing patients, even if only one day per week.

My research on the subject of COVID-19 has convinced me that the higher hospital admission rate and mortality in men are associated with the catastrophic falls in testosterone levels in men compared with the protective effect of oestrogen in women. Testosterone levels should be measured at COVID-19 admission, and appropriate therapy should be prescribed to reduce mortality. The high-risk factors for male mortality in COVID-19 are similar to those for low testosterone, namely age, obesity, type 2 diabetes, and certain ethnicities. Explaining catastrophic falls in testosterone levels on the basis of "stress reaction" misses a potential opportunity for life-saving intervention. There is no doubt that receiving the testosterone injections helped my recovery. Clinical trials are clearly required, but we seem to ignore this issue in the UK, whilst the rest of Europe, particularly Italy, is well aware. Perhaps it is all down to Brexit.

From my own experience, I am certain that daily tadalafil, licensed to treat erectile dysfunction, lower urinary symptoms and raised pressure in the arteries of the lungs through improvement in endothelial dysfunction (or endotheliitis, inflammation of the lining of the arteries, the primary lethal process in the lungs in COVID-19) should be widely used as protection from acute and chronic complications As several European Guidelines support this, in later chapters, I will explore why the UK has lagged further behind, especially since Brexit. One of our finest cardiologists, Dr Graham Jackson, told us "PDE5 inhibitors such as tadalafil are important cardiovascular drugs hijacked by urologists!". Graham also told us that ED = ED = ED, meaning that erectile dysfunction = endothelial dysfunction = early death. He also told us that "the way to a man's heart is through his penis, not anatomically correct, but it gets the message home. How right he was on all these points.

My experience of long COVID-19 clinics is that they were hastily set up with little thought. I remember attending my appointment at a private hospital in Birmingham six months after the acute illness. I remember waiting with three ladies in the waiting room while a junior nurse read questions to one lady who spoke little English. She was clearly embarrassed, and I could see her getting distressed, so I left the room. A few minutes later, the resuscitation team arrived. I hope she survived. All the blood tests were taken before any history of symptoms was taken, and I was left to enter my history on an iPad. When I eventually saw the doctor, I was reassured. I summoned up the courage to ask why I had not been asked about ED and whether my morning erections had returned. He looked shocked, as though this was the first discussion he had ever had on the subject. His response was that he assumed that, had there been a problem, the patient would have mentioned it. In France or Italy, that might be the case, but not in the UK!

Recently I have resumed face-to-face patient contact, and I am regaining full fitness. The view of the doctors in the follow-up clinics is that my recovery has been nothing short of remarkable, even if they always forget to question me about morning erections.

I found the recent indignation about the lockdown parties and the requirement for instant resignation rather "over the top". As a front-line health care worker who nearly died from this dreadful disease and suffered probable long-term complications, I might be expected to have reason to feel angry, but I don't. These have been very difficult times for all of us, and I found all the discussions as to whether the Conservative leader was at a party and the Labour leader was not made us look petty and frivolous during a time of world crisis. My most recent long COVID-19 clinic follow-up was by telephone on the very afternoon, 8th September 2022, when the Queen passed away. Despite the immense feeling of sadness, I was able to report that my recovery had been remarkable.

As I was well aware of the high risk that I might not survive the first 12 months following my illness, I realised that I needed to crack on urgently with this book.

CHAPTER 4

The Hidden Impact of COVID-19

I was already involved in COVID-19 research, especially its greater impact on men, even before my illness struck. I must now issue a warning that this chapter contains some real science. Suggested mechanisms were that men present later to doctors, take more risks, wash their hands less often and smoke more cigarettes. Surprisingly, although smoking rates are a little lower in women, they are more likely to get COPD (Chronic Obstructive Pulmonary Disease) and respiratory failure as their lungs are smaller and more vulnerable to the effects of both active and passive smoking.

Of course, men are greater risk-takers. I remember when a new drug was being developed to treat sexual problems in women, I would go to great lengths to explain all the safety data, but invariably the woman would decide not to put "anything into her body that had not been properly tested!" In contrast, men were usually happy to take any new drug, even if it had only been tested in five rats, as long as at least two of the rats had survived.

Much has focused on the higher death rate in men of South Asian origin, but there are several possible explanations. Men from Bangladesh, India and Pakistan have three times the rate of type 2 diabetes mellitus (T2DM), largely due to genetic factors combined with poor diet and lifestyle. These conditions lead to testosterone levels being 10-15% lower. In addition, smoking rates are three times higher than in white UK men. Forty-Four per cent of Bangladeshi men smoke, 26% of Indian and 23% of Pakistan men, but only around 1%

of South Asian women are smokers. Likewise, Afro-Caribbean men suffer from more severe and aggressive blood pressure, often unresponsive to conventional therapies. This results in higher rates of heart disease and stroke with shorter life expectancy. For genetic reasons, Afro-Caribbean men have higher risks of prostate cancer and are monitored more closely for this. Likewise, certain jobs, such as taxi drivers and security guards, have been associated with increased mortality when it is well established that such jobs are associated with higher rates of obesity and diabetes. These ethnic groups also form a higher percentage of health care workers, meaning that these higher-risk groups are put on the front line to catch the infection. This is not a matter of any social prejudice, just that for cultural and educational reasons, the NHS has a highly dedicated immigrant workforce, and this is what puts them at risk. Unfortunately, none of these issues have been adequately explained by the media. An NHS policy to vaccinate men before women because they were at double the risk would, of course, have been totally unacceptable. The subsequent success of the vaccination rollout has wisely been followed up with long-term repeat doses. The likelihood is that these will be added to the flu vaccinations provided to the vulnerable on a seasonal basis.

These health issues have been known for years, but the COVID-19 crisis has polarised views, with some blaming social suppression of ethnic groups for the increased deaths. In reality, the healthcare system has been actively targeting these groups for years with variable success. In reality, they are the backbone of the NHS. Hopefully, the post-mortem after COVID-19 will see more positive interventions to improve outcomes for these higher-risk populations without issues descending into debates about social inequalities and prejudice.

At some stage, UK experts are going to realise that if all these men die more readily with these chronic conditions, such as T2DM, when they have low testosterone, then surely, we would expect a serious predator (or mugger) as COVID-19 to pick these patients with great efficiency. Studies from Germany and Italy have already shown that men with low testosterone levels on admission to hospital are significantly more likely to die. The lower the level of testosterone on admission, the greater the mortality rate, as we have shown in our studies from the West Midlands supporting earlier findings from Italy.

Without getting into too much science, the virus entry into cells is linked to the attachment to a "spike protein" on the ACE2 receptor primed by an enzyme TMPRSS2. The important thing about this process is that it is linked to the X chromosome. Women have XX and men XY chromosomes, meaning that women who have received two X chromosomes from their parents are, therefore, likely to have greater genetic protection.

Studies from China show that the COVID-19 virus attacks the testosterone-producing cells of the testis, causing further significant falls in levels and increased mortality. In many cases, scans show abscesses in the testicles, confirming the severity of the infection. These resolve with some scarring over a few weeks.

Studies from Italy have suggested that men with prostate cancer on anti-testosterone therapy had a better outcome than those not on therapy. It appears that the mechanism of COVID-19 entering the cells of the body is enabled by testosterone, explaining why men fare less well than women. This has led to suggestions that drugs that lower testosterone might be helpful in the *acute stage of the illness,* but studies have not supported this theory. In the long-term low testosterone levels are associated with increased heart disease, diabetes, osteoporosis, depression, sexual dysfunction, and reduced quality of life. The trials that we conducted in acute COVID-19 have found that men with the acute illness have very low testosterone levels (less than 3 nmol/l when normal levels are above 12 nmol/l) and the lower the testosterone, the greater the mortality. This would suggest that giving drugs to further lower testosterone would seem potentially catastrophic. In contrast, restoring testosterone levels to normal would increase physical strength and preserve muscle. Of course, if nobody in the UK is being asked about sexual function, the long-term detrimental effects will only be seen later. Unfortunately, the approach in the UK has been that if we don't measure testosterone, then it won't be a problem. In terms of funding for research, there is generally only funding for new drugs for the problem, as there is no profit in repositioning cheap generic drugs for a new indication.

Mortality Rates from COVID-19

An Italian study in November 2021 reported on 220 acute male COVID-19 admissions and found that 176 had low testosterone levels. Overall mortality was 17.6%, and of the 39 deaths, all but 1 were in the low testosterone group.

Along with my colleagues, I have reported results from 110 acute admissions to Walsall Manor hospital and found exactly the same, but our patients' testosterone levels were even lower; but we made exactly the same conclusions: the lower the testosterone level on admission, the greater the mortality. Inexplicably in the UK, there is no interest in even measuring the testosterone on admission or at any stage in the process, with the assumption being that the drop in testosterone is simply because these men are very ill. Seemingly it is also OK to accept death as long as one is very ill. Of course, if you don't do the measurements in the first place, these difficult decisions can be avoided, although this is not an argument that I have ever accepted.

Not surprisingly, being over 70 and having T2DM increases the risk of death, but we know that 40% of men with T2DM have low testosterone and that testosterone levels also fall with age. Surely studies such as these demand that these men with clearly low levels should receive testosterone therapy *now,* not when somebody gets around to designing the perfect clinical trial. Such trials are difficult to design and conduct in the middle of a pandemic. We also need to consider how addressing these issues might improve the long-term recovery of those non-fatal cases. In reality, there is no need to conduct such a study as current guidelines show a clear benefit in treating low levels of testosterone. These findings also beg the question as to whether men with T2DM should be screened for testosterone and treated in order to reduce their risk of death should they catch COVID-19. My colleagues and I had precisely done this in 857 patients in our testosterone study (BLAST) discussed in other chapters, and showed, before the COVID-19 epidemic, that there was a significant reduction in mortality when men were treated with testosterone, especially in the older patients who were at greater risk. Logically, if this benefit was clear, then the impact of COVID-19 has made it even more relevant. The problem now is that any patients asking these questions or requesting a blood test for testosterone levels from their GP would be greeted with a dismissive statement such as "really, not at your age!"

What about long-term effects or so-called "long COVID-19"?

Over the years, I have had discussions with health economists and statisticians, who confirm that medical diseases that lead to death in older and vulnerable patients can be very cost-effective, not a view that doctors would usually admit to their patients. There are no long-term care funding issues and no pension payments for deceased patients. Those who survive but with long-term disability are, of course, a completely different matter. How do we distinguish between ongoing complications of the acute illness, such as lung fibrosis after intense pneumonia and inflammation of the lungs, residual strokes, or renal failure, as compared with long COVID-19 in somebody who did not require hospitalisation? Men seem to be better at dying acutely from COVID-19, but women suffer more from long COVID-19. Women are more prone to illnesses such as depression and anxiety and the effects of menopause as possible aggravating factors. Another logical explanation is the hormonal differences between men and women, effectively testosterone versus oestrogen. Recent research has shed much light on this concept.

NICE defines post-COVID-19 syndrome as "signs and symptoms that develop during or following an infection consistent with COVID-19 which continue for more than 12 weeks and are not explained by an alternative diagnosis". Symptoms are wide-ranging and fluctuating and can include breathlessness, chronic fatigue, "brain fog", anxiety and stress.

In June 2021, the government came up with £10m for a long COVID-19 "task force", £100M to follow with £30M for general practice and a 5-point plan (sounds good) comprising:

1. NICE guidance,
2. Online "your COVID-19 guideline".
3. Public Facing information website.
4. NIHR funded research
5. NHS long COVID-19 taskforce.

This all sounds very impressive, with lots of new non-clinical jobs, lots of meetings and webinars, but what is it all about?

I already wonder about the value of long COVID-19 clinics and the way that they are set up, as the following case demonstrates.

Dr Hugh Janus (not his real name) was 53, a local GP, who contacted me soon after I returned to work after COVID-19, having heard me speak at a webinar. He has also been seriously ill, having been for a month in hospital and now, 12 months later, has not returned to work. He was suffering from "brain fog" and did not feel that he could safely do his job. Although his practice partners were highly sympathetic, as he had caught COVID-19 through his work, there was now less sympathy 12 months later, especially as two of his partners had also had COVID-19, albeit after triple vaccination, and were back at work within a couple of weeks. He was aware that sympathy was now wearing thin, and procedures were in motion to replace him. His attendances at long COVID-19 clinics had been unhelpful, really just telling him that this was "common" and that patience was required. In true "Sex Tsar" style, I quickly asked about morning erections and his ability to maintain an erection and immediately, he looked relieved. He had not been able to get any erection since being in hospital, and he felt that his marriage was at risk as his "extremely patient and understanding wife" was becoming less sympathetic. He was always tired and could not be motivated to go out. The two different antidepressants prescribed by his GP had been ineffective; in fact, he felt that they made things worse. Of course, nobody in any of the long COVID-19 clinics had asked these questions.

I checked his testosterone levels and found these to be 2 nmol/l (normal is over 12 nmol/l) and commenced him on a depot testosterone injection and daily tadalafil, but more about that later. Within a week, his erections began to return, and by 2-3 weeks, he felt much better and, by four weeks, returned to normal as his testosterone level climbed. His "brain fog" had significantly improved by four weeks, and he has remained well and intends to stay on this treatment long-term. He has lost weight and feels much fitter. I feel pretty certain that Hugh would have been squeezed out of his practice and his marriage had he not been treated. The other lesson from this case is how easily doctors reach for antidepressants as a panacea when all else fails, often to the detriment of the patient. Incidentally, when he was followed up in the long COVID-19 clinic, his endocrinologist suggested that I might have been "overzealous" and that he would have recovered eventually had he been patient! Hugh was not convinced.

This case made me reconsider my own situation. I am aware that beyond 12 months, most COVID-19 patients are probably considered "malingerers", especially as the majority of the population now have personal experience of COVID-19, albeit post-vaccination. I can assure all of them that the post-vaccination COVID-19 bears no relationship to the infection that I experienced. It is noticeable that the initial sympathy expressed at the time soon wears off.

All cases are different. In my case, with meningitis, encephalitis and two large blood clots on the brain, I found that the part of the brain involved in "usernames and passwords" was entirely wiped. One of the most frustrating issues is being treated as a simpleton when I struggle to remember a pin number. When I reset a password, I am reminded not to use any of my previous 12 passwords! How can I possibly remember the previous 11 when I cannot remember the most recent? I was also aware that patients with my complications, including intensive care and ventilation, had, at best, a 50% chance of surviving beyond 12 months. On reaching that landmark, I allowed myself a glass of champagne, reflecting on the fact that I had further delayed adverse judgement at the pearly gates for leading such an immoral life!

As a doctor, aware of some residual deafness, memory issues or "brain fog", it has been difficult to balance the need, professional or financial, to return to work against the concern that you might not function medically as well as before the illness. Realising that not all aspects of memory have returned makes it difficult to be objective as to whether I might be putting my patients at risk. This still causes me concern. I was recently reassured when I returned to work in July 2022, after 18 months, when a patient turned back as he got to the door and said, "even at 90%, I'd rather have you back than the other b*****s". This random comment went a long way to restoring my confidence.

The system also demands, quite rightly, rigorous appraisal and revalidation. The longer a doctor is out of medical practice, the less likely that he or she would regain previous career status. As a result, when asked about residual problems post-COVID-19, I immediately announced myself to be fully recovered!

CHAPTER 5

This Really Did Hurt

– Junior Hospital Doctor Years

It was January 1974, and the results were in. The good thing about Medicine is that you either pass or fail, and very few ever get "honours", certainly never when you played as much cricket and football as I did. I was about to learn that all that effort had not been wasted. The first house officer jobs were up on the Medical School notice board. To the complete surprise of everybody, I got the plumb house surgeon job working for Mr Leonard Cotton and Mr Hedley Berry. I would quickly point out that this was not remotely related to any surgical skill displayed in my training but purely down to the many hours of monotonously nurdling singles to fine leg over the last four years. It so happened that Hedley Berry was the greatest fan of Geoffrey Boycott and had always embraced everything that was fine about Yorkshire cricket. He was president of the Kings College Cricket and Football Clubs and had spent many hours watching me compile some of the slowest 50s in hospital cricket history. He was also a life-long Leeds United fan and clearly spotted a bit of Alan "sniffer" Clarke in my predatory finishing. The list had only been up for a day before a formal complaint had been lodged by a female honours graduate. In a measured response, Mr Berry commented that "If he were to be stuck in theatre with a house surgeon for five hours, then it would be much more tolerable to be able to discuss whether Geoff Boycott's mother could really have tamed the Indian pace attack with a stick of rhubarb or why Leeds United was the finest team

English football had ever produced". He also observed that "anybody who could get 11 lazy medical students to play cricket twice a week could certainly organise his operating list". To me, this was a complete vindication of the medical interview process five years earlier. Although in the words of JK Dudley, you could tell that Hedley Berry was a fine man by the way he played his cricket, there would be no place for his approach in modern-day human resources.

House Surgeon (Jan-June 1974)

I remember my first day as a house surgeon at Kings. The job was supposed to be 1 in 2, which means that you worked until about 7pm every day, and on alternate nights and weekends, you worked right, though. This seemed bad enough until I was greeted by Mr Cotton on my first day. He informed me that he liked to do a ward round each evening and every weekend, and he expected me to be there: no such thing as overtime then. Tell that to the youngsters today, and they do not believe you!

The young doctors of today don't know they're born.

The major task of a house surgeon is to make sure that operating lists run smoothly. This involved "clerking" the patients by taking a history and sorting out their investigations, medication, and blood tests pre-operatively. Most importantly, for a vascular surgeon, cross-matching several units of blood for the following day was crucial. Unfortunately for me, during the second week of my job, there was a national blood shortage. I received a phone call at 7am on the day to tell me that no blood was available for the major procedure. On my arrival in the theatre, the anaesthetist was sympathetic and left very quickly, "mmm, I think I will leave it to you to tell your boss!" To this day, I can remember watching Mr Cotton walk the entire length of the hospital corridor only to have to break the news to him. There was a pause of a few seconds; the blood surged into his neck veins, and what followed was the closest I had seen to the Incredible Hulk metamorphosis. I cannot remember his parting words as he turned and departed, but "imbecile" was somewhere in there. I realised that it was going to be very difficult to come back from this...but on my first weekend on call, things were about to get worse.

It was around midnight on Saturday when my bleep went after a very demanding day on duty following on from a chaotic first week. It was a call from the private wing. It was a surprise to me that we had a private wing, let alone that I was on-call for Mr Cotton's patients there.

I arrived on the ward to be summoned to the bed of a gentleman from Saudi Arabia who spoke no English. It was clear that he was in considerable pain in his foot and lower leg and was getting no relief from his post-operative pethidine injections. A review of the operation notes from Friday told me that Mr Cotton had performed a femoral angioplasty, a graft to bypass a blocked artery. What we now know is that this was not a very good procedure as these grafts frequently became blocked, and clearly, little or no blood was getting to this man's foot. He was heading towards gangrene with probable loss of his leg. It was now 2am, and there was no alternative but to ring Mr Cotton at home. I took several deep breaths and dialled the number. After around 10 rings, I heard the gruff tones of Mr C and started to tell him the story. To my surprise, he simply slammed the phone down on me. At this moment, I felt very lonely and isolated. I simply could not face ringing him again, especially if my judgement was wrong. I noted from the records that the anaesthetist for this man's operation, Dr H, was the same one who showed me sympathy a few days earlier. At 2.30 am, I rang Dr H, and he agreed with me and contacted Mr C. The result was that the patient was back in surgery by 5am. I looked in the next day, and the man's foot was looking "less blue", but I feared the longer-term outlook for his leg was not good. The next week in theatre, Dr H smiled at me and remarked, "Well done, young man, that took balls!" I received no comment from Mr C. This use of house surgeons to cover consultant's private patients as part of the NHS contract would not be allowed today.

Effectively, this job was virtually on-call 100% of the time, most often with the same senior registrar, Mr Charles Derry. I remember one crazy night on 13th March 1974 when we were struggling to deal with massive arterial blood loss, and things were clearly going rapidly downhill. Emergency blood was being sent from the transfusion centre, and at 3am, I was sent to find out what was happening. As I entered the main corridor, I saw a uniformed courier sprinting down the corridor with a large box. He tripped and went flying through a glass door. As he fell, the blood box went flying, and a couple of blood bottles smashed. As if this wasn't enough, he stretched his hand to break his fall; he severed his brachial artery on the glass. The spurting arterial blood hit the ceiling. Within seconds, it was like scenes from a double bill of Reservoir Dog and the Texas Chain Saw Massacre. I had to compress the brachial artery and shout for help. We had to abandon the case in theatre to deal with the courier, who was rapidly bleeding to death. Of course, we had to send for several units of O-negative blood as the samples he brought were incompatible.

On 15th March 1974, it was another busy weekend, and I was admitting another patient in casualty. I looked across at the duty board and the 3 surgical house officers for the weekend, and the choices for the patients were Drs Hackett, Cutting or Carver, a gruesome combination. David Cutting eventually ended up as a GP in a neighbouring practice in Tamworth

I was admitting a Mr Sylvester Brown, 42, from Trinidad, who had an indoor TV aerial rammed up his arse. In those days, TV aerials consisted of 2 long pointed prongs, and his story was that he spent many hours wandering around the house only to discover that the only decent picture was achieved by hanging out of the window. He claimed to have been watching his favourite programme, "till death us do part", in the nude at home when he slipped, accidentally sitting on the coffee table where he had placed the aerial for best reception. He was in some distress, and it was clear that he had perforated bowel and bladder, at least. His cover was blown when his hysterical wife, Princess, arrived later and proceeded to list the other various objects that she would shove up the next time she came home early and caught him on the job. This poor chap had extensive internal damage, and his case became the subject of a major paper in the Lancet.

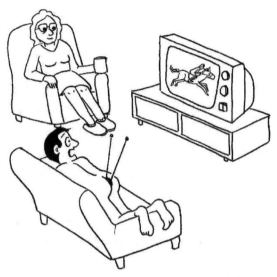

"Perfect picture, you've just rammed the aerial up my arse."

Patients in Accident and Emergency were assessed in bays divided by curtains, and in cubicle 1, David Cutting, still a mate today, was clerking in a deaf 82-year-old, Doris, with abdominal pain. She was accompanied by her older and, I suspect, deafer husband. David had to shout at the top of his voice, and, as usual, when patients do not understand, we shout even louder. "Where is the pain?", "Eh," she replied. "Is it Down here?" "Oh... yes". "Is it sharp... or dull?" "Eh", "IS IT SHARP OR DULL?" "Sharp, I think". It continued like this, and by now, everybody in the department was hanging on to every word. After about 5 minutes, he turned to the husband in frustration. "Any previous operations?" "Gall bladder 1965", the old man answered. There was almost palpable relief from David as he was now making progress at last. He piled on with his questions for a further 10 minutes, writing hastily in the notes. "Waterworks problems?" "No". "What age did the periods stop?" asked David. There was a sudden hesitation in the flow, "Oh, are you asking about the wife?". A sound of head banging on the wall was followed by the ripping of several sheets of paper. As David pulled back the curtains, he was greeted by a standing ovation.

I always prided myself on being a good communicator with patients. It was 17th March 1974, and Horace Potter had come in for a vascular bypass operation the next day. He had severely blocked arteries in the left leg. Having taken his history, I proceeded to draw detailed diagrams of his legs, explaining where the blockages were and how we would bypass these obstructions. I explained about dressings and drains, pain relief and how long he would be in hospital." Do you have any further questions, anything at all?" I asked. "No, I don't think so", was his reply. As I returned to the desk in the middle of the ward to write up the notes, I saw his visitors arrive. His wife asked, "Hello, Horace; what is it that they are doing to you tomorrow?" "Not a clue", he replied, "Nobody tells you a bloody thing around here".

I know that he must have done well, as two years later, as a medical registrar, I found a group of nurses laughing at drawings of the legs of a Mr Horace Potter in a set of notes. They were struggling to read the doctor's signature. I confess that I never owned up to those drawings. I may be a good communicator, but I have always had the artistic and handwriting skills of a 4-year-old. Luckily, most doctors have realised that illegible handwriting can often be a major advantage.

One of the important roles of a house surgeon was to arrange a second opinion from another specialist. On 21st March 1994, I had been asked to seek a cardiology opinion on an 80-year-old gentleman as to whether he was fit for surgery. I duly lodged to request with the cardiology secretary. Two days later, on the routine ward round, we arrived at the bed and introduced Mr Berry, my boss, to the patient and gently shook him to wake him from sleep. We could get no response as he had clearly passed away. We pulled to curtains, and I took his notes to the nursing station to make an entry. I noted that the cardiologist had been to see him one hour earlier and made the entry, "There is nothing that I can offer this man; he is dead!" I can only assume that he must have been in a hurry.

One of the interesting hospital characters in those days was Peter Mayhew, alias "Peter the Porter", who was 7ft 3inches tall and suffered from Marfan's Syndrome, a condition associated with giant stature and heart valve problems. He usually worked with another porter who was a little over 5ft, and they were usually on duty for the mortuary. They were quite a sinister pair. We were stunned when Peter announced one day that he was leaving the bright lights of Camberwell for a career in Hollywood. He went on to play Chewbacca in the Star Wars films until his death in 2019, aged 74.

I often think back to the surgical wards in the seventies. In those days, patients would remain on the ward for 7-10 days after an appendicectomy, gall bladder removal or hernia repair, procedures that nowadays are day cases or overnight stays. We used to conduct ward rounds on patients who were essentially just on prolonged bed rest. We even had convalescent homes in the country where patients could enjoy the fresh mountain air as they recovered; how things have changed.

As a penalty for a top surgical job, house officers were usually to be sent to some god-forsaken place for Medical placement. In my case, it was Isle of Thanet Hospital in Ramsgate in late 1974, working for consultants Drs Lillicrap and Cocking (I jest not). This job was full-on with virtually no time off, and only two games of cricket were possible in the six-month rotation. Almost every day, there were no empty beds, and I vividly remember a visit from Princess Anne. This involved several weeks of intense preparation, as nothing very exciting ever happened in Ramsgate. As the tour progressed, we were moving beds through corridors and back into the wards that she had just left to prevent her from seeing the chaos. The manoeuvre was conducted with military precision.

By now, I was still not certain where I was going in my career but had ruled out surgery in favour of medicine. I applied for a 2-year medical registrar rotation back at Kings, but although unsuccessful, I was offered a guaranteed post six months later. I accepted as it would give me some stability rather than moving around every six months. With a medical Registrar job sorted, I decided to take a convenient 6-month post-registration house officer job in Gynaecology back at Dulwich Hospital, part of the Kings group. This was a decision that was viewed later as being indecisive and subsequently worked against me.

The Gynae job for the late Mr John Studd was tough, with around 15-20 patients on every daily operating list. This was not helped when the other house officer announced that, as a conscientious objector, he could not be involved in terminations of pregnancy (TOP). It was never a comfortable subject for me either; still a Church going Catholic at this stage. To compensate, the other guy did read the daily newspapers for me while I did his operating list. To make it worse, the registrar at the time was also of the view that we needed to be doing TOPs only in exceptional circumstances. He had dared to question Mr Studd's decisions on a couple of occasions, advising against TOP in a few cases. The boss was furious, feeling that his authority was being undermined, and charged me with the duty of watching the registrar to make sure this did not happen again. This put me in a virtually impossible position and resulted in my having to do even more procedures. During the many hours in theatre at Dulwich Hospital, I got to chat regularly with the anaesthetists, alias "the gas men". Little did I realise that the "gas man position" would turn out to be my favourite sex position to recommend to my patients with premature ejaculation. For those unaware of this position, the major advantage is that in the gas man position you can stay in all day and nobody comes.

My regular anaesthetist was a particularly quiet registrar who had a reputation for not saying much and just getting on with the job. He ran into a bit of trouble when, after three years in post, one of the consultants decided that it was time that he made an upward career move, something he had previously resisted. It was only at this stage that he was required to produce his medical documents. It transpired that he was not medically qualified but picked up his skills watching anaesthetists whilst working as a hospital porter. He subsequently began to help them out with ever more complex tasks until it was assumed that he was one of the team. Despite three years without a single complaint, he ended up with a custodial sentence, creating a major scandal at the time.

Medical Registrar (Kings) July 1975 to July 1977.

It was July 1975, and I had the stability of a 2-year medical registrar rotation at Kings and Dulwich Hospitals. I was now much more in my comfort zone, where my skills were maximised. I now had house officers working below me and felt that I was making important decisions on the ward and in outpatients. The second 6 months were Geriatric Medicine at St Francis Hospital, which enabled me to have a hospital flat in the nursing home rather than the constant hot bedding of the last two years. I worked under a very senior lady assistant specialist, Dr Raybould, who taught me that for geriatric ladies, the weekly visit from the hairdresser was at least as important as the consultant ward round.

I moved on to three months at St Giles hospital and more general medicine. This was an old hospital destined for demolition shortly. I shared the staff accommodation with a rather strange psychiatry registrar, not that I ever met a normal one. Over the last few weeks of the summer, he had been abseiling down the wall of the hospital. I then realised that I had not seen him for several weeks. I subsequently learned that he had been building a Morgan car from a kit in the downstairs changing rooms and had completed the job without considering how he would get it out the door.

After 12 months of general medicine, I moved over to Kings and the Maudsley for a joint Neurology and Neurosurgery registrar post with Professors Marsden and Zilkha, two of the most brilliant men I had ever encountered. In those days, we depended on traditional examination skills and subtle signs rather than routinely requesting an MRI scan and working it out from there. The disappointing aspect was that treatments in Neurology were pretty limited, and some cynics commented that there were only two types of neurological conditions, amitriptyline responsive and amitriptyline nonresponsive. Amitriptyline is an antidepressant that blocks multiple neurological pathways, causing multiple side effects, some of which turn out to be beneficial if you can put up with the others. At this stage, as a centre of excellence, we were seeing some of the first cases of Creutzfeldt-Jacob disease, later popularised as "mad-cow" disease. I presented a couple of cases at the hospital grand round and felt that I was something of an expert. The importance of this will crop up later. The next three months involved work in the Neurosurgical Unit at the Maudsley Hospital under Mr McCabe and Mr Polkey. This was the toughest 3-month period of my life. Essentially, we were on duty all the time, unable to even sleep in the normal doctor's residence due to the number of high-risk patients. Nights were spent in a room next to the intensive care unit. Tell that to young doctors today, and they will not believe you.

Most nights, there would be a catastrophic head injury or intra-cerebral bleed admitted, which would mean an 8-hour operation, leading straight into a full day's operation list the next morning. As there were no house officers in neurosurgery, I was once again the lowest in the food chain. As the medical registrar on the team, my major role was in diagnosis and investigation, with surgical duties usually restricted to holding the retractor and managing suction. Eight hours of this during the night took its toll a couple of times when I fell asleep during operations and had to be "retired".

It was really around this time that I was able to afford to run a car in London, and my first car was a Reliant Robin, not the status symbol at the time that it is now. Not many people realise that you have a 50% greater chance of hitting hedgehogs in a Reliant Robin, which caused me great ethical concern. Another unique feature is that you can lock yourself out by simply closing the door and having left the keys in the ignition. Luckily, a trick one garage showed me was that the construction was so flimsy that you could bend the locked door to get your hand through and extract the ignition keys. I was driving the Robin when I met my future wife, Sally, at an infamous Kings disco and offered her a lift home. "So, you've got some wheels," she said, clearly extremely impressed. Luckily, she never asked how many.

Having experienced a few hairy drives over the Thelwall Viaduct on the M6, I decided to treat myself to the relative luxury of a Citroen Ami, only one step above the 2CV. We all make bad second-hand car decisions at times, but after three months, I decided to clean the front mats and discovered an expansive view of the road below. I was only slightly upmarket from a Fred Flintstone special. Imagine my surprise when the new American Senior Registrar, over six months secondment, offered to buy the Ami from me. My relief was tempered with concern that I still had to work with this chap for three months. I should not have worried. On the same day that the money and the documents changed hands, some desperate thief stole the car from outside the Maudsley Hospital and wrapped it around some bollards on Coldharbour Lane. Clearly, they had not worked out that the left foot needed to be firmly on the road when braking at speed. The SR was extremely apologetic that he might have contributed to my "pride and joy" coming to an abrupt end.

It was during this post that the other Registrar, a proper career neurosurgeon, wanted study leave for his FRCS examination. Shortly after, I made a similar request to help with my part one MRCP exam. Not surprisingly, his application was successful, and mine was not, although I was given a morning off to take the examination. Not surprisingly, with 14 days of continuous on-call, I was unsuccessful, achieving a "bare failure".

The final phase of the rotation was six months as Medical Registrar on Accident and Emergency at Kings. Essentially, I was the initial resource for medical rather than surgical emergencies that presented. This post made me realise that an A and E post should be compulsory in every doctor's training. The immediate attraction of this post was the flexibility of the work, meaning that after a night

79

shift, the following day was completely off duty. After three months at the Maudsley, this was bliss, and I was able to step up my cricket for 1977, which was one of the hottest summers on record. I played so many games that season I made over 1000 runs in several hundred hours at the crease. I managed to have my front teeth removed by a rather sharp West Indian quickie, which led to multiple attendances at the dental hospital over the next two years. Having resumed playing again, I was keeping wicket when a top edge removed all the impressive dental work, necessitating a full bridge and another 50 hours of dental work. I became a regular dental exhibit in the dental school for teaching and examination purposes. Remarkably 46 years later, the dental bridge is still in excellent shape. If my old mate and fellow footballer, Kevin Esplin, is reading this book, then I would like to say, "thanks, mate, a fantastic job".

Back at work, a couple of weeks into the job, a 6-year-old girl was brought into A and E, having been electrocuted whilst playing on the railway lines at Denmark Hill. This was extremely distressing for all the staff as there were severe deep burns on the limbs from the electric wires. After repeated efforts at resuscitation and multiple shocks to the heart, the team wanted to give up, but, knowing that electrical injuries should carry a greater chance of success, I pushed on. Eventually, we got a pulse, intubated her and, after several hours of work, transferred her to Intensive Care. Unfortunately, we had no idea as to how long her brain was deprived of oxygen. As I was still a Catholic Church goer, I ended my shift and headed off to the Catholic Church in Camberwell. To my surprise, the priest began the service with news about the young girl, who belonged to a staunch Catholic family. He extolled the virtue of the doctors who had worked miracles to save her, and the congregation united in prayer. I was reluctant to do so, as I feared the worse for the girl. Unfortunately, I never found out what had happened to her.

Six months on, and after lots of hard work this time, I went for the part 1 MRCP again, which is a multiple-choice examination with a low pass rate. I had never been good at multiple choice as I tended to overthink the questions, but this time, I felt much better prepared. Of course, I achieved a clear failure this time, meaning I had only one attempt left. If I did not pass parts 1 and 2, then I had no chance of a worthwhile SR job. I decided to try the Irish MRCP part 1, which consisted of a traditional exam with essays and case histories, rather than choosing a selection of answers. I was able to take this only two months later. Sally accompanied me to Dublin for the exam. We were on a very tight budget and stayed at the single-star Harcourt Hotel in Harcourt Square. The unwelcoming foyer belayed the hovel that greeted us on the 3rd floor. I decided to have a bath (not en-suite) after the ferry crossing, only for half the masonry to fall on my head. I retired to the bedroom. As I relaxed, my hand went down the side of the bed, and I felt an article of clothing. This turned out to be a mummified pair of string Y fronts. Luckily, we were only booked for one night. In case you are wondering, the underpants washed up quite nicely but always tended to hang a bit lower than I liked.

As it was a Sunday, I did not want to miss worship, so Sally accompanied me to the local Catholic church. The priest that day would not have been out of place in an episode of "Father Ted". He began by destroying the concept of church unity by announcing that Non-Catholics were not welcome in his church. I detected that Sally was on the verge of walking out, but I urged her to stay. The collection arrived, and I emptied a considerable number of coins (punts) from my pocket onto the collection plate – quite generous, I thought. The priest then announced, "It has come to my notice that some parishioners are putting coins onto the collection plate, may I remind you that they will answer for that in hell fire". Rather steep, I thought. At this point, we were both on our way. On that day, I think Sally was turned off from the Catholic church, and I think that my attitude also changed.

At the Royal College in Kildare St the next day, the exam papers arrived, and to my pleasant surprise, the long diagnostic case was clearly Creutzfeldt-Jacob disease, my pet topic. This was manna from heaven. It made me realise how much luck plays a part in our lives. I later learned that the pass rate for this exam was only 17%, and I was one of the lucky ones. Three months later, I returned to Dublin, not surprisingly choosing a different hotel. I passed part 2, first time as I realised that exams involving patient communication skills were to my advantage.

As I was waiting for the right job to arise, I spent the next six months doing locums around London, and there was plenty of work I could handle, Medical, A and E, and Gynae posts. It was interesting working in over 30 different hospitals around London. Some nights my bleep would go off, and my first thought was, "Who am I?" rapidly followed by "Where am I?" unsure of which specialist I was and where I was working that night. I remember an SHO Gynae post at the Prince of Wales Hospital, Tottenham, where I fell in with a couple of Australian anaesthetists over a very quiet weekend on-call and lost more money at poker than I had earned in locum fees.

I found myself on duty in A and E at St Stephen's Hospital, Chelsea, when an IRA bomber, Patrick Hackett, had planted nine bombs in central London. One exploded prematurely, causing him to lose a leg and part of an arm. It was very demanding having to do your best to save the life of a terrorist you had attempted mass murder, even one with the same name. I was hounded by the press all night, with repeated questions as to possible associations I might have with the IRA. Patrick was eventually sentenced to 30 years.

One night I was on-call Medical Registrar at St Mary's Hospital in London, and for the second time that day, I was with the crash team for resuscitation that was not going well. As I was giving chest compressions, I was looking straight into the eye of a patient across the ward, and I could see that he was just about to arrest. I made a decision to stop the immediate case and switch to the newly arresting patient. I doubt that he would have survived had we not been a few metres away at the very moment that he arrested. This was a case of the third time lucky that day.

In April 1978, I was offered a 2-week post as a medical house office at Bromley Hospital. I was taking jobs at lower grades as the money was still good. On my first ward round with the consultant, I already seemed to know more about the patients than the incumbent registrar. At the end of the round, the boss took me to one side and said, "You seem to be a smart chap; how would you like to be registrar?" He promptly dispensed with the services of the existing locum registrar, who had been appointed by hospital management. Three days later, he told me that he had been watching me closely and felt that I could be left in charge, as he felt that he could now take a long overdue holiday. Effectively I had been promoted from house officer to consultant in three days! There was little that I could do but accept gracefully. Four days into my promotion, I was presented with a very complex patient who was going downhill, and I could not work out a diagnosis. I decided to approach the other medical consultant for his advice. To my surprise, his response was, "You work for that b*****d. He and I haven't spoken for years; you're on your own", and he walked out. Luckily, I was able to ring a consultant at the sister hospital, who came over to help me out.

I was now applying for multiple further registrar jobs, focusing on top London Hospitals, along with Oxford and Cambridge. I was always getting to a final interview, but my decision to take a job in gynaecology was being singled out as a sign of indecision. It was clear that some of the jobs were already a "done deal" for the local applicant. I could not even get a job at Cambridge, which had come up early because the previous doctor had committed suicide. I decided to lower my sights and applied for jobs at two Manchester hospitals, and interviews arrived for the morning and afternoon the next Friday. I decided to combine the interviews with a trip home to see my father in Bolton. I must have been more relaxed for these jobs as I was offered both, but curiously both sets of consultants felt that I should really be setting my sights higher, say London or Oxford. They suggested that I might be taking a backward step if I accepted the Manchester job. I followed their advice and declined both posts. Both hospitals declined to pay my travelling expenses.

I noted that the BMJ was advertising a registrar post in Renal Medicine in St Louis, Missouri working for Professor Hubert Lubowitz, with interviews to be held in London. Why not go for it, I thought, now or never? The interview went well, and I was offered the job. There was even some confidence that Sally would be able to get a job in Physiotherapy. I had passed my ECFMG, which, as far as I was aware, was the only examination required for the US, but, unknown to me, two new exams, FLEX and TRAB, had just been introduced, but there had been no formal sittings for them. I was, therefore, in the ultimate catch-22 situation. Professor Lubowitz rang me at home a couple of times and threatened to "kick-ass" at his end. Inevitably the job fell through. I did one more interview at Cambridge, only to overhear two female applicants discussing that they already knew that they had the jobs, and for one, it would fill in four months before maternity leave. That was the final straw. I felt that I was travelling all over the country just to make up the numbers. It was the summer of 1978, and I think I finally realised that a career change was required. I turned to the BMJ general practice section and spotted a GP partnership in Cheshire, close to where my family had lived. I was also aware that in six months, three years of mandatory training in General Practice was about to become compulsory. It really was now or never.

I sent off my CV to the practice in Holmes Chapel, failing to realise that there were more than 200 applicants. Most of whom had perfectly planned careers compared with my recent knee-jerk decision. After about ten days, I had heard nothing, so I rang the practice, asking if I could come up and look around. I failed to realise at that point that I was being completely naïve. I clearly took them by surprise, and I arranged to go up the following week. In retrospect, I realised that my CV must have been rescued from the discarded bin. Once again, I was about to discover that the most important things in life are completely due to chance.

CHAPTER 6

The Sex Tsar in General Practice –
more art than science?

Rather like those confusing films that constantly flit between different historical films, I would now like to take the reader back to the very beginning of my "journey" (oh no, there I go again). I arrived in Holmes Chapel, Cheshire, in November 1978, having got the job as a GP partner after a series of demanding interviews, including trial by sherry. At that time, the doctor's wife (an actual demand in those days) was a crucial member of the team, meaning that interviews were very much for "the couple". Often out of hours calls from high-profile aristocratic patients came in while the doctor was out, and a cool head and polite voice were required. As Sally was, by this stage, a senior physiotherapist in intensive care and came from Woking, she scored 10/10 on both counts. I was taking over from the Senior Partner of more than 30 years, and some highly important patients were being entrusted to me. The expectation in those days was that once you reached 75, the GP would visit you at home. How things have changed, as nowadays they are all on the golf course. I was provided with a regular visiting list and noted that after each name was listed, such items as "case of Glenfiddich", "Christmas turkey", or "brace of pheasant". "What does this mean?" I asked. The list was hastily retracted and replaced with a simple list of names but without gifts. I soon realised that all these Christmas "bonuses" had been earned over several years and did not come as a matter of course. I soon managed to get the list trimmed down. After a gentle first 2-week acclimatisation, the surgery and visiting load got busy, and the 1 in 3 on-call was tough.

On my first weekend on call, one of our real VIPs (but unknown to me) attended on a Saturday afternoon after an incident with a chainsaw that flew off and badly slashed his neck. In those times, patients rushed to the surgery with all sorts of emergencies, even heart attacks. He was holding a large towel around his neck and making it clear that he had a strong aversion to hospitals. As I removed the towel, it was clear that the damage was extensive (rather worse than a bad shaving accident), but he seemed to have avoided major arteries and nerves. I have treated chain saws with great respect ever since. Having recently worked in a major A and E unit, I cracked on, matched up all the loose tissue, and was very pleased with the final result. I applied a dressing and sent him home. Five days later, I was called in by one of the other partners, who was astounded that I had attempted such a complex repair. The bottom line was that the patient was delighted. I learned that he produced limited addition pottery. I was given a piece, which I still have to this day.

The early days of home visiting were very tricky, and I had little idea where I was going. Often directions were passed on second hand, via Sally, if I was out on another call. This was, of course, long before the age of satellite navigation and mobile phones. One such set of challenging directions at night was, to "The Hollies Farm, halfway down the long drive. There is no name on the gate, and I am not sure what colour the gate is, but it used to be painted brown. You can't miss it!". There were many such wild goose chases.

On January 3rd, 1979, a call came from Sally whilst I was out on another visit. The message was that Mrs Sproston was having "trouble down below". I found the house and was greeted by a moderately confused elderly gentleman with bilateral hearing aids that seemed to be switched off. "Mrs Sproston, trouble down below", I said. I pushed past him as I could see an old lady in the corner. Mr S was equally deaf, so I decided to circumvent the story by rolling her over to get a good look. As I was peering up his wife's nether regions, the old boy asked, "And who might you be, young man?" "I'm the doctor", I replied. The old chap looked relieved and slightly surprised. I suspected that they might have been waiting for the gas man.

On 17th January 1979, Sally had handed me an address for an evening visit for Mrs Doris Twemlow at what looked like 16 Manor Lane. Of course, most night visits were made with no reference to any notes. The message said, "stomach pains". It was around 11pm that I arrived at the house. The husband greeted me at the door and showed me upstairs. The lady seemed pleased to see me and told me, at some length, about her pains. It seemed like long-standing chronic diverticulitis, and it was looking like a bit of a wasted visit. As the new doctor, I was very keen to make a good impression and not upset anybody, so I made reassuring tones and moved towards the door. Only at this point did she say, "It is very nice of you to visit, but we did not call a doctor". To avoid appearing foolish, I mumbled something about "conducting routine home checks and all part of the service!"

I glanced down at the paper and noted that the writing most probably said 18 Manor Lane. I shot out the door and next door to number 18. The man at number 16 watched me and seemed very impressed that the new young doctor was working his way along the entire street one house at a time at 11pm. Of course, Mrs T was in severe pain and required admission. I apologised for the delay in getting there.

During a busy morning surgery, a week later, I was called to an emergency at a private girls' boarding school as the violin teacher was short of breath. As I started to examine her, the head mistress chipped in with, "She has always been highly strung!". Luckily, it was only a panic attack, and she settled after rebreathing from a paper bag.

On February 24th, 1979, at 11pm, I was on call again with an address that I had taken down as being 42 Cedar Avenue, with the message, "pains in chest, please use rear entrance (!), door open, patient in bed upstairs". Unfortunately, there was also a Cedar Crescent, and I was headed for the wrong address. Luckily, I was very adept at using the rear entrance. I opened the door and entered the kitchen, only to be jumped upon by a large man who pinned me to the ground as his equally large dog sank its teeth into my leg. This time, the "I'm the doctor" story didn't seem adequate to get me out of trouble. I was learning the hard way to be more careful checking names and addresses, particularly over the telephone.

The first 12 months in general practice were tough, especially with having to work up to parity in three years. Sally had to give up her job in London, and we had insufficient income between us to get a mortgage in an area where housing and rents were expensive. Eventually, at age 30, I was able to get a two-bedroomed bungalow, and Sally had a physio job in ITU at North Staffordshire Infirmary. At one stage, the partners had paid themselves back some money that was owed, meaning that for one quarter, I received nothing. We were quite low at that stage, wondering if I had made the right decision. I applied for a job as a GP in Saudi Arabia and was successful. We hoped that we might be able to put something aside for the future. Unfortunately, Sally could not get a job in Saudi, meaning that we could not go. On reflection, this was a blessing as life for a woman in Saudi at that stage would have been very restrictive. I must have been pretty desperate to have considered such a move.

I was approached by another practice looking for a new partner, promising me a better deal, but on looking at it in some detail, they were also seeking to exploit the situation for the first three years. Nowadays, contracts with long periods of parity are unacceptable, and I made sure that new partners in the future did not have to go through the same experience. I remember then I eventually sold the bungalow; the estate agent described the garden as "A fine example of deferred maintenance." I stuck it out with the practice, and I was glad I did. I bought the second house at auction, which is not an experience I would be keen to repeat.

By January 1980, I had sorted out my own list of home visits, on the basis of need, rather than future Christmas presents, although I did regularly visit an old lady called Gladys, who was disabled and housebound but insisted on her daughter getting in some fish and chips from my favourite piscine emporium in Lower Peover. They would be by the fire to keep them warm, and we would have a nice chat. Gladys had a heart of gold, but life had not been kind to her. I frequently got into trouble with Sally if I did not devour my lunch. She knew at once if I had visited Gladys for haddock and chips.

July 1980, and I had been looking after Dick Long, aged 75, who lost his wife three years earlier and now lived with his son. He was getting worse and had taken to his bed. His main complaints were tiredness and lack of motivation, but blood tests had been normal, and I concluded that he was probably depressed. I commenced one antidepressant, increased the dose, and prescribed a second one. I had to visit every few days at his son's request. I approached the local psychiatrist, Dr Patel, for a domiciliary visit, and we arranged to meet at the house. The son greeted us, and we went upstairs. I entered the room, and Mr Long seemed asleep. I shook him, saying, "Dick, I've brought a specialist, Dr Patel, to see you, Mr Long, Mr Long. It was clear that Dick was dead. His son casually leaned forward and calmly delivered the statement, "I guess that the depression must have been more severe than you thought, doctor!"

Around the same time, I was having similar problems with Mrs Scraggins, a nice old aged 85. She was having dizzy spells and passing out, and there seemed to be no obvious reason. I had visited 3-4 times, taken blood tests, and seemed to be getting nowhere. Each time her daughter was present and seemed very attentive. I decided to sit down, but the daughter and her husband had the only other chairs, so I opted for a pouffe. As I sat down, I spotted the daughter gasp as I collapsed on the floor amidst hundreds of sherry bottles stacked under a throw and made to look like a pouffe. Mrs S would ask all her carers to just get her some eggs... and perhaps a wee sherry, then the next one, just a loaf of bread... and perhaps a wee sherry. The daughter had clearly piled all these bottles, knowing exactly what her mother was doing whilst watching the new doctor blunder along, trying to find a cause.

It was March 1981, and I was back looking for a country farmhouse in the dark at 11pm. This was Mrs Nora Cox, aged 36, wife of a local businessman. She was complaining of right-sided abdominal pain. The house had been beautifully renovated, and the message was that he was in bed upstairs and I should let myself in. Her husband was away on a shooting trip. She commented that he was rarely home nowadays and preferred shooting trips with his friends. Things were not especially good between them, as he was

91

jealous and, at times, dominating. The history was a little concerning; there had been difficulty conceiving in the past with a number of infections. Nora had given up on getting pregnant but was now three weeks late but had a few spots of bleeding and now pain on the right that was getting worse. These symptoms caused me some concern, and I was suspicious of ectopic pregnancy. She suddenly said, "I expect now you'll need to examine me." and threw off the duvet. She was completely naked. Rather than try to rescue the duvet from the floor, I decided to carry on examining her abdomen. I informed her that I would need to do an internal examination. Just after I had started, the bedroom door burst open, and there was her husband, Hugh, with a shotgun in his hand. He looked at me, and I looked at him, and time seemed to stand still. My first thoughts were, "Is this the way it ends for me?" and the only thing I could think of to say was, "I'm the doctor!" It did turn out to be an ectopic pregnancy, and she required surgery to remove the tube and ovary, which would not have been good for future fertility.

This case made me think of the insistence that many doctors have for chaperones. Of course, nothing could have been done here, as I had no idea what I was walking into. As a country GP on call, there just were not random chaperones around waiting for a call. I have never really worried about the issue and feel that the need to ask suggested a feeling of distrust. The patient might think, "why does he need someone else here?". It seems to be normal for a female doctor to get a female chaperone, meaning that a poor guy has two women ogling his bits. On the other hand, a male doctor and a male chaperone would seem unusual. Perhaps the most vulnerable situation might be a male doctor conducting an intimate examination on a gay patient? Would he want a female chaperone? What happens if you do not know his orientation? The bottom line for me is that I have had no issues in 40 years and intend to continue that way.

When I arrived in the practice, there were no female partners, and I was the one with all the gynaecology experience, especially contraception and IUCD insertion. These were lucrative sources of income for the practice. We soon had female registrars, and once I had trained them, I would lose most of the patients, suggesting that the gender of the doctor was far more important than clinical experience.

This brings me to my next case. Mrs Mandy Till, 35, was a checkout attendant at the village supermarket and a regular patient of mine in the contraceptive clinic. I rarely shopped in the village, but this time had popped in for some vegetables on the way back from evening surgery. It was quite busy, with a queue behind me, and Mandy was working flat out. Just as she had her hand ready to scan my particularly large cucumber, she suddenly looked up and said, "Oh, Dr Hackett, that nasty vaginal discharge still hasn't cleared up". Three customers behind me immediately moved to an adjacent checkout.

Sometimes in surgery, things slip out of the mouth unintentionally. In January 1984, Mrs Page Turner had come to see me with recurrent cystitis and had been awaiting the results of her most recent urine test. "Well, doctor, what have we found?" Page asked. I looked at the lab report and confidently announced, "There is no sign of active infection, but you have multiple orgasms". "Really", she said, "and you can tell that from a urine sample; that's amazing". I had to hastily explain the significance of multiple *organisms* in the urine.

A month later, *Mrs Nesbit was in surgery with her 14-year-old daughter, Phoebe, a nervous girl with bothersome asthma. Conscious of her anxiety, I was trying to make her feel relaxed. As she lifted her top and I put the stethoscope to her chest, I said, "Now Phoebe, big breasts". "Pardon, doctor", said the mother. There was really no way back from that one. The more you think that you must not say something, the more likely it is to slip out.*

Some patients have some names that make it impossible to focus when they come in. I remember Mrs Ivy Dick, who was always bringing her son into the surgery and usually commenced the conversation with, "I'm very worried about Everard". Then there was a South African Chap, who played for the village cricket team with me, called George Shaw-Twilly. There are just some names that should not be hyphenated.

It was back on call, and sometimes with holidays, it could be five nights on duty on the trot. I had been up most of the night before with a delusional schizophrenic who had to be sectioned. I waited three hours at the house waiting for a psychiatric social worker the sign the form. *At 3am, the phone went, and it was Mrs Bacon ringing about her daughter Megan, 16, with stomach pains. This sounded like another wasted trip. I had seen a man two nights earlier, rolling in pain. Just after I got there, he let out a huge fart and said, "Ah, better out than in"- problem solved. As I left the house, Sally mumbled, "I bet she's in labour". Megan was a very large girl, and her mother told me that she had been to the surgery twice in the last two weeks and had been given two different laxatives. A quick look at her abdomen gave me the diagnosis that she was, indeed, in labour. I told Mum to make a cup of tea and sit herself down as I broke the news. "Oh Megan, you silly sausage!" I explained that it had gone a bit further than that. It continues to amaze me how a young girl can get to full term without her or the mother noticing and how two doctors could miss a full-term uterus. Megan required a Caesarean Section, but both mother and baby did well afterwards.*

I had passed my MRCGP parts 1 and 2 first time in 1980, despite my previous problems with multiple choice. I was working as a research fellow in General Practice in Liverpool when in 1985, another opportunity presented itself. My father had been out to Brisbane and had been diagnosed with a malignant melanoma on his back whilst seeing a GP for a chest infection. The GP, Dr David Pincus, was a family friend of my uncle Tom and it seemed that this doctor was looking for a GP exchange in the UK, meaning a swap of jobs, houses, cars, pets, and everything except wives. As we had a child of 2, with a second on the way, this looked possible, and I thought that it was probably now or never. As I still had an Australian passport, it was straightforward, and so an exchange was agreed for June 1986 for four months. In the back of my mind was the possibility that, if all worked well, we might settle in Australia, as it would be much easier with very young children.

In September 1985, we returned from holiday to discover that we had been burgled. Luckily some friends had tidied the place up as it had been badly trashed. Those of us who have been through the experience know how devastating it is. Six months before, I had gone into my garden at lunchtime and interrupted burglars smashing through the patio doors of my next-door neighbours, saving them from a similar experience. It was straight back to work after the burglary, and I found myself visiting a 32-year-old woman, Robyn House, on one of the estates. She was a regular at the surgery. She suffered from panic attacks, and the prescribed tablets were not working. I sat there for some time, delving into her domestic situation. Her partner had been violent and manipulative, but she put this down to the great stress he was under, working all hours, especially nights. "What line is he in?" I asked. "He's a burglar", she answered with not a semblance of shame. I could not believe that, for the last 30 minutes, I had been sympathising with a woman over her partner's stressful life as a burglar. He was even possibly the one who had trashed my home. Shortly after this, another partner was burgled, and I remembered walking into the waiting room to hear a receptionist, in the full range of about 30 people, announcing, "Yes, Dr H is away for two weeks with his family and won't be back until February 27th". I suggested that these "friendly family doctor" announcements needed to stop or that the staff should add that "Dr H will be leaving his four Rottweilers in the house, and they are all fully trained to put out fires".

In June 1986, we set out for Australia with two small children on a "round the world" ticket via Vancouver, Hawaii, and Fiji, arriving in Brisbane. We stayed in an old colonial house in the suburbs, and my practice was in the Stafford district of Brisbane. Before starting work, I had to go before the Queensland Medical Board for a medical licence and had been studying the Australian Healthcare System. As I entered the examination, 3 doctors were trying out a new putter on the carpet. Once they realised that I played golf, the remainder of the assessment consisted of a discussion as to whether a weaker left-hand grip was the best way to deal with a shank.

My first patient in Australia was my Uncle Tom, who had come to discuss the results of his recent chest x-ray. I put the x-ray up on the screen, and to my horror, it showed moderately sized lung cancer. What a start! Uncle Tom survived my time there but died shortly afterwards.

My lasting impression was that the Australians did not tolerate waiting lists. Blood tests were done immediately with results were back the same day. The same went for relatively complicated radiology, along with immediate reports. Consultant referrals were usually seen within a matter of days, with admissions within a few weeks, even for routine conditions. GPs could earn a lot of money dealing with various forms of skin cancer. Payments for minor operations were related to the number of sutures. I became quite adept at squeezing the maximum number whenever possible. Virtually every patient would have some form of facial skin damage justifying biopsy, excision, or cryotherapy.

Although we enjoyed the trip, from the outset, there was no real chance that we would stay. Although there were some good points about the system, as it allowed for a basic "Medicare" system that ensured a good level of basic care, it allowed individuals to "top-up." This meant that the patient could pay to get a better room in the hospital or a GP practice allowing longer consultations. There was also a "Gold Card" service for war veterans, providing higher allowances. I felt that the UK could learn from the Australian system as we do not treat ex-forces personnel particularly well. Overall, I felt that we had more "clinical freedom" in the UK, especially with prescribing. Little did I know how much that would change in the forthcoming years. We returned via Singapore and Bangkok and resumed life in Holmes Chapel in November 1996.

I've often heard doctors say that patients never really appreciate when a doctor has done a good job. You can get things badly wrong, but if you do it with a smile, the patient will think you are great. In contrast, you can make a life-saving diagnosis, but if you come across as slightly arrogant, they will not have a good thing to say about you. The following case demonstrates this:

It was January 1987, and it was another emergency call to a lady, Rose Heffer, 65, at a remote farm. I was following some vague directions once again, but I was pretty confident where it was. I arrived to find a very distressed lady with chest pain, shortness of breath, and a very rapid heart rate. After contacting an ambulance, knowing it would be some time, I rapidly inserted an intravenous line and performed an electrocardiogram (ECG), which showed very fast atrial flutter. For certain, she was going to die unless I acted quickly. I remembered that I possibly had the right drug in my bag but realised that things were disorganised as I had not had the chance to check it since returning from Australia. I found the four ampoules of verapamil, a cardiac drug that I was looking for. I administered the first slowly into the vein and noted very little effect, so a few minutes later, two more, and the rate slowed significantly. Instantly she seemed to improve, and she squeezed my hands in gratitude. I slowly gave the fourth ampoule, and the rate was now down to virtually normal. At this point, the ambulance arrived, and the look on the face of the ambulance man displayed the fact that the patient did not look as bad as expected. "Where is the hospital letter?" he said disapprovingly. Clearly, I should have had my fountain pen out for an elegant referral letter whilst resuscitating the patient. I apologised and hastily jotted down a list of events as they carried her out to the ambulance. I went home, now wide awake, as I could never sleep again after the adrenaline rush of cases like these. Three days later, I noted the husband, Roger Heffer, on my surgery list. I contacted the hospital in the meantime to confirm that Rose was doing well. Her husband entered the room. I was getting ready for an emotional display of gratitude when he erupted, "What have you got to say about this?" thumbing an empty ampoule down on the table. I picked it up. Was he complaining about my lack of tidiness as I had missed an ampoule amidst all the chaos? "It's three months out of date". He shouted. He left in no doubt that his wife would have died without this drug, and he was very lucky to find a GP who carried a selection of cardiac drugs. From that day on, I was meticulous about checking the dates on the drugs in my bag, well, for a year or so, anyway. This became an issue a few years later when we began to carry "clot buster" drugs costing several hundred pounds, only for the majority to be discarded when out of date.

Such experiences persuaded us to carry a defibrillator when on-call. Often when you might have needed it for an emergency, it would be the boot of a partner's car at the golf club, but on one occasion, I had it with me and leapt into action. The patient was **Seymour Bush,** a mountain of a man who had passed out on his bed with no sign of cardiac output. Everything was good to go, and I was just about to discharge when I noticed that four family members were holding onto the metal bed frame, having failed to realise what the words "stand back" meant. I was remarkably close to recording a score of *minus five* for cardiac resuscitation.

General Practice is often defined as an art and not a science. As junior hospital doctors, we would tick every box on the blood form and order every x-ray possible on the basis that something would turn up. Primary Care would be impossible if we all did this, and the NHS would be bankrupted. We, therefore, had to rely on a "sixth sense" that something was not right. The following two cases demonstrate this.

Jennifer was 21 months old and had presented with reluctance to put her foot on the ground. There was little to find on examination, and the case had all the features of a difficult child playing up to anxious parents. I arranged an x-ray of the entire leg, which was normal, and I could see that the parents were just beginning to get slightly frustrated with me. After listening to the mother for some time, I began to realise that all was not right here. I picked up the phone and spoke to one of the paediatricians who saw her that day. Jennifer had a nasty form of leukaemia. For the next two years, Jennifer and her family bravely fought the disease, but she sadly died. During that time, I became very close to the family and to this lovely little girl. Sadly, as so often happens, it also takes its toll on the parents' marriage.

The second case was Bethan, a baby of 6 weeks brought to a Saturday morning surgery with feeding problems and being sick after most but not all milk feeds. Now, there are several cases presenting like this in the average GPs day. I gave the usual advice and advised some infant Gaviscon and moved on. For some reason, later the Saturday afternoon, I was doing a home visit in the same village and found myself going past the house. It was a lovely day, and work was slow. For some reason, call it "sixth sense", I pulled into the drive and knocked on the door. It was feeding time, and I walked into the lounge to see Bethan produce a projectile vomit of about three metres. The diagnosis of pyloric stenosis was immediately clear. I could feel a tight band of muscle at the lower end of the stomach. This can only be effectively treated by surgery. Bethan was admitted, had the operation, and thrived from then on. Unfortunately, many parents have picked up on the term "projectile vomiting" and use it routinely to impress. There is no doubt when you see a proper case. The family must have been impressed by this local doctor dropping in on a "gut feeling" when, in reality, it was pure chance. I am not sure that things like this happen nowadays.

One of the toughest tasks in general practice is managing patients who clearly need an operation but need to wait on long waiting lists. Some waited for years, especially if an orthopaedic surgeon had told them to "Go away and lose five stones".

Such a woman was Olive Green, 75, suffering terrible pain in her right hip. She had already waited nine months and still had not been seen in the clinic. At that stage, I was regularly going to Old Trafford with the Manchester United Consultant, who had carried out hip and knee surgery on high-profile sportsmen. I told her that I would "call in a favour" and get her seen sooner. She seemed extremely pleased. I rang the surgeon that evening, and he replied, "Seeing as It's you, I will fit her in at the end of clinic tomorrow". Unfortunately, helping a mate is totally out of the question in the modern NHS. I rang Olive with the news that evening. There was a long pause on the phone. I assumed that she might have been overcome with relief. After a few seconds, she replied, "Your chap can't be very good if he can see me tomorrow; I think I'll stick with the original specialist".

On Monday, 28th January 1988, I was last to finish surgery and found that I had been allocated an emergency call for a 52-year-old, Ivor Hardwick, with a bad back at the "Sun and Air Naturist Colony", at Allostock, near Knutsford. The practice manager felt, for some reason, that I was best equipped to handle the case. When I arrived at the gate, the attendant insisted that I would need to remove my clothes before entering, but I would be allowed to wear my stethoscope. As one, who has fortunately not required the services of the "Small Penis Clinic" at Sheffield, this caused me only slight concern. I asked where I should put my thermometer. Luckily, he *could not keep the joke up any longer and let me in fully clothed. It was quite daunting, wandering around this large campsite, being the only person wearing clothes. As the tents were not well numbered, I was heavily exposed by the time I got to the correct one. There was little room in the tiny tent for a proper examination, and I remember conducting straight leg raising on the grass, exposing Mr Hardwick's testicles to all passers-by.*

As I left, it was getting a bit nippy, and I found it strange that the naturists chose to wear a jacket to keep warm whilst leaving the bottom half uncovered. I must have gone down well as the manager of the site rang the practice later to ask if I could be their regular doctor. Subsequently, I visited a few more times, but I have never fully embraced the naturist philosophy, especially in winter in Northern England.

I managed my entire GP career without a formal complaint from a patient. I am convinced that the key was never to "lecture" patients or "patronise" them. I believe that whenever you do so, that patient "marks your card", such that the next time that your management falls short, that patient will probably complain.

The nearest I came to a complaint was in my weekly session in occupational health at the local hospital. A job applicant, Ernest Slack, had travelled up from Cardiff for a medical in relation to a possible job. Our excellent nurse, Jean, had uncovered some poor performance issues and a pattern of drug abuse leading us to a decision to fail him on medical grounds. On this day, I had brought my 3-month Labrador, Lucy, into the clinic as Sally was working, and Jean, the clinic nurse, wanted to see the puppy. Not only was the gentleman not happy at coming all that way, only to fail a medical, but he realised that my Labrador had sneaked into his changing.

cubicle and eaten his socks. We knew this as one had been regurgitated on the clinic floor. I remember suggesting that the good news was that his "lab tests" were all normal, but he did not see the joke.

Ernest looked like a sorry sight walking away down the corridor with bare ankles showing above his shoes, a fashion statement well ahead of his time. The second sock appeared a few days later. Lucy bit off more than she could chew when she ate my lucky underpants. They had to be removed surgically by the vet and never quite fitted as snugly from that day onwards. Sadly, Jean passed away in 2022, but we were able to return for her memorial service in Knutsford.

In April 1990, I was invited to be the doctor for the making of the Robin Hood movie filmed at Peckforten Castle in Cheshire. Unfortunately, this was not the "Hollywood style" Kevin Costner version but a more traditional version starring Patrick Bergin, a young Uma Thurman, and Edward Fox. Although it might sound glamourous, the work mainly involved a few of the Sheriff's men with bad backs and the after-effects of mead and Wenching orgies. Although I did not get official recognition, I did make an unscripted entry stage right in one of the fight scenes. It might be worth getting a copy from the archives now that "Blockbuster" is no more. Blink twice, and you will miss my brief entry. I don't think it made the "Directors Cut".

In June 1990, there was a case that still haunts me today. I was called late a night by a mother, who I knew to be a nurse at the local learning disability unit. Her 3-year-old had a temperature and cough. I visited at around midnight and diagnosed a simple viral illness, avoiding an antibiotic as the practice pharmacist had commented that I had the highest prescribing rate, a badge of shame. The mother was clearly struggling to cope, but who wouldn't with a 3-year-old and a small baby? I noticed a cot and asked about the infant, who I believed to be 12 weeks. I remembered the mother from a couple of years before I had switched her to a "mini-pill". She made the strange comment, "Can I sue you if it fails?" The following morning, I was on my way to Keele University and would be going past the house. I promised to drop in and check on the child. When I arrived, the 3-year-old was better but sleeping, and the baby boy had been placed on the chair whilst the mother answered the door. I played with him, tickled his tummy, and made him chuckle. He was the picture of health. I then carried on to the hospital for a morning clinic. Later in the day, I returned for evening surgery to learn that, at 10.30 that morning, one of my partners was called out as the baby was found dead by the mother. My partner diagnosed a cot death syndrome. I was totally shocked. I did not visit the mother afterwards as she had taken a liking to one of the female partners. I next saw her 12 months later about a minor matter, and I asked how she and her family were coping. She was now active in the "Sudden Infant Death Association," offering counselling to other parents. She suddenly looked me in the eye and said, "You don't know, do you?". I asked what he meant, and after a few seconds of hesitation, she said, "Never mind," and left. Over the next few years, I became aware of the work of Professor Southall, described elsewhere in this book. I wonder to this day why she came to check what I knew or suspected and what she was very close to telling me.

Many GPs will recognise the "Absent Relative Syndrome", a familiar occurrence on bank holiday weekends. In this case, it was August Bank Holiday in 1990. This usually involves a long-time absent son or daughter, often a "high-flier", who decides to visit Mum or Dad after an absence of several years.

In this case, 80-year-old Archibald, with terminal cancer of the pancreas, was being looked after at home by Daphne, 78, assisted by the practice nurse. This was well before the days of regular visits from McMillan nurses and shared hospice care. My partner had been visiting at least once daily and was administering regular morphine injections to keep him comfortable. A nasogastric tube was helping Daphne to get some fluids down. Archibald's son, an investment banker from London, had visited on the bank holiday Saturday and was shocked to see the decline in his father from a year earlier when he last visited. He decided that things needed to be "sorted," and he demanded an urgent visit from the duty doctor. I arrived to find Archibald clearly distressed with a "bubbling chest" and a matter of hours to live. I sat the son and his wife down and gave them a long explanation of the extent of the cancer and how the palliative care programme was working. I stated that I would give him a further injection to relieve his distress and return that evening. I told them to prepare for the worst and that we were looking at hours rather than days. I thought that the son had taken all of this in when suddenly he announced, "Would it make a difference if we went privately?"

A few weeks later, I was called to Maud Ward, 90, who was in the late stages of palliative care for cancer of the oesophagus. She had long since been unable to swallow, and nutrition was provided with liquids through a narrow tube inserted into her stomach. Although Maud was unconscious, brewing terminal pneumonia, her husband, Claud, was trying to crush her statin tablets and blood pressure tablets and force them down the tube, but now the tube was blocked. I explained to the family that Maud had a matter of hours to live and that treating her cholesterol and blood pressure was now pointless. I advised that they stop the tablets, and I unblocked the tube. Her daughter, visiting from Surrey, then announced, "The Heart specialist said that she must always take these tablets; otherwise, some serious, like a heart attack or stroke, might happen". I attempted to explain that something a lot more serious than that had changed the circumstances. I later learned that one of my partners was called back later that evening and restarted the cholesterol and blood pressure tablets. Maud died comfortably the next morning.

In August 1991, I was late arriving back for evening surgery, pulled into my parking place, and headed for the front door. Out of the corner of my eye, I noted a Ford Fiesta performing some elaborate manoeuvres in the car park, when to my horror, I spotted that he seemed to be reversing into the "doctors" bay where I had just parked. I noted the car was driven by an elderly gentleman, who was looking straight ahead as he reversed. I shouted loudly, but he continued, crashing into the rear of my car. He got out of the car and inspected the damage. I politely asked why he was not looking and why he had not responded to my shouting. "Terrible arthritis in the neck and deaf as a post nowadays", he replied. Not much you can say about that. He then turned to me and said, "I must say that you're taking this much better than most people I crash into". He then produced the card of his preferred garage, saying £450 should just about cover it. Ultimately his estimate was within £10 of the final price. I excused myself, as I was late, and five minutes later, I was starting my surgery with an elderly driving medical assessment, a great chance to catch up on time. "Mr Reginald Molehusband", I called. Who should appear, but the man from the car park incident. He explained that he only used the car for local shopping and to pop out to the doctor or pharmacy for prescriptions for his housebound wife, Sybil. Reginald, 89, was unsteady, totally unable to turn his neck without going dizzy, deaf, and failed the eyesight test miserably. Despite these findings and the earlier events, he seemed totally surprised and devastated when I broke the news that he had failed the medical.

In September 1991, I was approached by a rich businessman, MN, from Pakistan, who had recently moved to a mansion in the area. He had a much younger English wife, who had been a very promising tennis player who had appeared at Junior Wimbledon. He had selected me to look after both of them, including his newly pregnant wife's maternity care. He seemed charming and made some generous donations to the practice over the next few months. They took Sally and me out to restaurants, such as La Belle Epoque in Knutsford, which is not normally affordable for us. All went well, and the successful delivery of a baby girl resulted in even more donations.

I was on duty on the August bank holiday in 1992 when I was called out at 2 am in the morning on Saturday as the baby had a high temperature. The father was wearing a silk dressing ground, and their master bedroom was magnificent. As the baby vomited all down the front of his gown, I thought to myself that life was a great leveller. I diagnosed an ear infection, prescribed an antibiotic, and promised to look back in the morning. The baby was much better when I checked at 10 am in the morning. In the daylight, I was impressed by the magnificence of the estate. He had his own landing strip, and I spotted at least two planes on the runway. I was also struck by the tight security. I wondered how anybody could have made so much money by the age of 40.

The rest of the weekend was hectic, and on the Bank Holiday Monday morning, the morning papers arrived, and I collected them as I took Sally her usual breakfast in bed. The front pages all had coverage of a huge undercover police raid on the mansion of a Cheshire millionaire, exposed as a major drug dealer and fraudster.

107

They had acted on a tip-off that a major consignment was arriving in the middle of the night via his private airstrip. I certainly had my answer as to how he was that rich by 40. The extent of his corruption was revealed over several pages. He received 15 years and, of course, lost his wife and daughter. I later realised that MN was released after nine years but was killed shortly afterwards, flying a light aircraft. There was a strong suspicion of suicide. The mansion was purchased by a former Aston Villa and England footballer, who subsequently played for Manchester City, Everton, and West Bromwich Albion. At the current time, it is on the market at £4.2 million.

By 1992, I was finding things tough. One partner had been off long-term sick, and the out-of-hours was stressful, often five days on call 24/7. I was also faced with two sets of private school fees, with a third to follow. I was doing routine visits in the evening simply because there had been no free time in the day. Sometimes I had to wake the patient for a visit they were expecting earlier in the day. Administrative meetings dominated, and we had become heavily involved in fundholding. We had taken on a finance manager, and a decision had been made to negotiate packages with different hospitals to save money. I was never happy with the concept of fundholding, with practices making money by restructuring referrals. Of course, the concept was dismantled by the Labour government two years later. It is questionable as to whether the multiple reorganisations of the NHS have moved us any further since.

I was also developing my interest in sexual medicine after my "Road to Damascus" moment with Mr Mike Heal at Leighton Hospital when I discovered that we had the power to restore a man's erections. I had tried to treat some patients in my surgery but was told that "The receptionists were concerned about what you were doing with these men behind closed doors" and that "This must stop, and you should send them to the Psychiatrists where they belong". I was now working for a private clinic at weekends and was seeing the great possibilities that we now had to treat these men. The final straw was Sally calling me in and saying, "Geoff, may I introduce you to your 2-year-old son, Dan?" Things had to change. It was now clear by 1993 that I needed to make some major decisions.

CHAPTER 7

GP Pastures New

The six months that followed my decision to move on from Cheshire were very difficult. I felt guilty because I had always seen myself being in one practice for my whole career, but partnership can be very difficult. There cannot be many jobs where the expectation is that a person will arrive at 27 and do exactly the same job day in and day out for 40 years, just getting older alongside their patients. I found that each partner had developed their talents and expertise in such a way that this invariably created strains on the core work of the practice. There was no way that six people could share exactly the same philosophies in terms of work-life balance. No matter how much a partner might bring into the practice kitty, their partners would still expect them to be doing an equal share of the work. How could the motivation of a male partner with three children to pay through private school have the same motivation to get up for multiple night visits as a female partner married to a highly successful husband with four children of her own at home? For such reasons, the traditional concept of GP partnerships simply does not work very well in the modern day. The final straw was fund-holding which encouraged an entrepreneurial approach from practices, where contracts could be moved to other hospitals, potentially saving large amounts that the practice could reinvest in various ways. I saw this scheme as divisive between primary and secondary care, and as it turned out, I was right, and it was reversed by a Labour victory at the next election. In the meantime, I had been perceived as not being a "team player," which was probably correct as I did not believe that the team was playing the right game.

Essentially, while I was working out the last six months of my notice, I did my own surgeries and drank coffee, and had lunch in my own room with little contact with the other doctors. At age 42, making the right move was not straightforward. There was certainly no "head-hunting" in general practice in those days. Luckily, I spotted a potential job in Lichfield, about 50 miles away, equidistant from Keele University, where I was working as a Senior Lecturer. I was completing an MD in Sexual Problems in Men, which I eventually achieved in 2000. The Lichfield advertisement was for a half-time partner, which would allow me more time to develop my interest in men's health. I later discovered that they were looking for a female partner to replace one who was leaving. Even at this time, advertisements could not be that blatant, so I was probably shortlisted as the nominal male. A couple of consultants at Leighton Hospital gave me excellent references. One, in particular, John Felmingham, a consultant gynaecologist, went out of his way to help. I don't think that this would happen nowadays, where contacts are few and far between. The heady days of the medical conferences abroad have long since gone. I remember John making a controversial statement at a meeting in Spain when he suggested that a women's sexual satisfaction might be related to the size of her partner's male member! Dr Bollinger was not amused and mounted a robust defence that would have been reassuring for all attendees at my or Professor Kevan Wylie's "small penis clinic"!

When I attended an interview in Lichfield, I was told that they had several more to see, but on return home, I received a call to say that the job was mine. We even managed to sell our house in Cheshire and move into a place in the country near Lichfield on the same day I started work. The saving grace was that state schools in Lichfield were much better, and we were able to save on long-term private education. With the support of Mike Heal and a business plan to run a "stand-alone service," I convinced Good Hope Hospital, Sutton Coldfield, that a men's health clinic was needed. The good news was that I would be starting with the title "Consultant Urologist" as I already held a post as University senior lecturer. Things fell into place very quickly, and I started on 1st July 1993. This caused something of a furore some years later when I was invited to speak regularly at BAUS (British Association of Urological Surgeons). One surgeon complained to the president of BAUS, who came up with the diplomatic decision to change my job title to "Consultant in Urology," and seemingly, this solved the problem!

There were other excellent benefits from the move. The new practice looked after a GP maternity unit, with GP beds in the community hospital, where out-of-hours patients were also seen, with the assistance of trained minor injuries nurses. We were also responsible for the local hospice and renal unit. The work was varied, challenging, and rewarding, and I had escaped all the ethical issues around fundholding. Within 18 months, fundholding was abolished, and all the ethical issues vanished. I often wonder how many practices might have broken up because of the divisive effects of fundholding. Let us hope that future Conservative governments don't seek to reinvent the concept.

One of my earliest on-call experiences in the new practice came in September 1993, when I had to attend the death of a 3-year-old who had been tragically strangled by a cord on some lounge curtains simply by slipping off a chair. It was incredible to think that such an event could happen because of a simple set of lounge curtains.

Soon after this, another night of psychiatric mayhem arrived. I was called to a house on one of the estates where the local police had an emergency situation. I rushed to the address to be met by about a dozen armed police offers with batons and riot shields gathered in the kitchen of the house. A 23-year-old man, Shaun, which a known psychiatric history, had threatened his mother with a large Arabic sword. She had escaped to safety, but Shaun was now isolated in the lounge with a collection of swords and was threatening anybody who tried to enter. The senior police officer had a cunning plan, "Shaun, we're sending in the doctor, ushering me to the door. Suddenly, I was pushed through the door armed only with a Gladstone bag. I hoped that I had not unknowingly upset him at some stage without knowing. While he was distracted by my arrival, the armed police charged him, pinning him to the ground. I wondered whether the police believed that GPs were surrounded by an impermeable force shield or were simply collateral damage. The rest of the night, until 6am, was spent with the emergency psychiatric team, deciding whether to section him. The eventual decision was that, with weapons removed and a regular nurse visit to ensure compliance with medication, then he would be fine.

I have always found dealing with suicide very difficult. In my last practice, I had seen three, all men. I was always struck not only by the lack of warning but how the victim often plans the visual impact of the scene, presumably to leave a lasting impression on those left behind. Certainly, the memories of these events will remain with me for life. My first was a local undertaker who dressed in his old military uniform before hanging himself. I remember being asked to visit the house and peeping through the letter box to see his pristine polished military boots suspended in mid-air. The second was an eminent Lord of the Realm who was facing dishonourable exposure. He opted for a minimal dress but impaled himself on his masonic sword in an immaculate white bedroom. The third was also a businessman facing financial ruin, who dressed up in his best pin-striped suit.

On this occasion, it was a 19-year-old who was brought by the mother, saying that the boy was threatening suicide. The warning sign was that his father had committed suicide five years earlier. I tried my best to get the crisis team involved immediately, without success, but there was an appointment for a couple of weeks. Three days later, he attended to see a partner, complaining of infected rope burns to the neck and was prescribed antibiotic tablets and cream. This worked beautifully, as a week later, the wounds had healed well enough to complete the job properly a day before the crisis appointment. Around the same time, a local farmer rang me expressing negative thoughts. As I was in the middle of a busy surgery, we fitted in an appointment at the end, but he promptly went to the stable and shot himself in the head.

On the brighter side, in June 2001 came one of my greatest successes. I was on call one weekend and was just visiting a patient of mine on the ward when I was summoned to the delivery suite where a new-born baby was struggling to breathe. There was a weak pulse, so we cleared the airway and ventilated the baby with oxygen through a mask. It had been many years since I had intubated a new born baby, and I did not think it was worth the risk of trying now. I took the baby in an ambulance to A and E at Burton Hospital with continual ventilation and repeated suction. I feared the worst when the paediatricians struggled to insert the tube. After a stormy couple of days, the baby did well. It was gratifying that the parents went out of their way to track me down and sent me a card on her birthday after several years. The important learning point here was that this had been classified as a very low-risk delivery and identified as suitable for community delivery. In effect, there is no such thing as a "no risk" delivery.

In 2003, came my nearest thing to a complaint. It was 10pm one evening, and I was called to the roughest area in the practice to a man of 62 with low abdominal pain. The house was badly neglected, with minimal lighting. He had been seen by another partner twice, and it was unclear what, if any, diagnosis was made. I checked his urine, and it contained white cells and blood, so I diagnosed a urine infection and gave him an antibiotic. I was woken at 2am, as he was now worse. Rather than revisit the house, I called for an ambulance to take him to the GP hospital, arranging a bed for him. I told the ward to ring me when he arrived. The phone went at 5am, as ambulances had been busy that night, so I headed to the GP hospital. Now that I could do a proper examination, it was clear that he had peritonitis and was very sick. I immediately contacted the surgeons. He turned out to have necrotising colitis, a so-called "flesh-eating infection". He lost a large piece of his bowel but fortunately survived. Around six months later, the solicitor's letter arrived with all the doctors in the practice named. The report went on, "It was only the prompt action of the doctor at the hospital that saved his life". I don't think he had realised that the doctor who visited him at home was also the one at the hospital. When this was pointed out, the case against me was dropped.

By 2005, my NHS clinic, private work, and research were growing. I was also doing appraisals and had two sessions as Medical

Adviser for the Primary Care Trust. It was becoming difficult to fit in a lot of international travel. I was confident that I was pulling my weight in practice, but an event was about the change things. Over the years, all the partners had immediately passed all the "men's problems" to the practice "expert" whilst still expecting me to see all the routine stuff. Things were moving away from personalised lists by then, anyway.

The Primary Care Trust (PCT) pharmacists had identified me as a "significant prescribing outlier", seemingly to them the ultimate badge of shame. It seemed to surprise them that if one doctor sees 100% of patients with a problem, then they are likely to be a high prescriber for that condition. Claiming that you might be offering a better service than the rest would be dismissed as arrogance and a request to justify the statement, essentially implying criticism of colleagues. No wonder innovation is stifled in primary care.

There is always much discussion about patients who call out doctors unnecessarily. I have never seen a patient admit that they had requested a visit unnecessarily. Every serious debate I have ever heard on the subject fails miserably when a tragic case is raised when a patient dies as a result of doctor not visiting. I always tried to visit when requested, but sometimes the body was not capable. In March 2005, the practice had a problem patient, Millicent Rogers, who had chronic chest disease related to smoking. She was requesting home visits on a daily basis. At the practice meeting, we agreed that requests to visit in the future should come through her husband and carer, Roy. I was on call the next evening when I received a call from Millicent requesting a visit as she could not breathe. She clearly had no trouble speaking. I asked to speak to Roy, who confirmed that he did not think a visit was necessary. Roy found Millicent dead in bed the next morning.

In May 2005, I was coming to the end of a busy evening surgery when Mr Richard (call me Dick) Cumming arrived. He was concerned about some urinary symptoms and a slightly raised PSA. I concluded that a digital rectal examination was required. I was acknowledged to have the most educated digit in practice. As he was rambling on a bit, I put him in a side room while I saw another patient. I had been on call all day and was running well behind. I entered the room, and Dick started wittering on again. I told him to roll over on his left side, pull down his pants and draw up his knees. At that precise moment, there was a knock on the door, "Dr Hackett; we have an acute emergency; a patient has collapsed in the shopping precinct". I quickly said to Dick," "Stay right there until I come back". I grabbed my bag and shot out the door. The collapsed patient in the precinct came around but seemed to have been out for some time. I had to wait around until she was safely in the ambulance. I returned to the surgery, and the receptionist greeted me with the words I wanted to hear "The others have seen your last couple of patients, get yourself home and put your feet up". An hour later, I was relaxing with a nice glass of wine when the phone went. It was one of the cleaners who had entered my side room to find Dick still in a perfect pose, presenting his rectum for digital examination. I was impressed that he had followed my instructions precisely. I returned to the surgery and completed the examination. This case took me back to a story of an elderly senior partner who had firmly told a patient to remain on complete best rest until he returned. Unfortunately, the GP collapsed and died suddenly a few days later. The woman was found two weeks later still in bed waiting for him.

I had been looking after a man with mesothelioma, the worst form of lung cancer, usually due to asbestos exposure. In his last few months, he wanted to be able to make love to his wife and "be a man" for as long as possible. Strictly speaking, this dreadful condition does not make a man eligible for NHS therapy unless he suffers severe distress! Clearly, an imminent nasty death would be severely distressing and putting him on a waiting list for me to refer to myself at the hospital just to make the decision was just daft. I rang the pharmacist at the PCT, who essentially told me, "rules are rules". Luckily, I remembered the reasons I went into medicine, so I gave them a liberal supply of tablets to enjoy what time they had left. They told me something that I have heard many times, preserving the ability to make love is a vitally important part of terminal care. He burst into tears when he explained what it meant to them. Unfortunately, his wife later came to the clinic for more tablets a few weeks later, and another partner in the practice refused to prescribe them, stating that he did not qualify and that I had acted in breach of the rules. The woman was in an emotional state and said some very strong words to the other partner. The primary care pharmacist was later asked to perform a detailed search to find other cases where I might have circumvented the regulations by not referring to myself at my hospital clinic.

I remember around this time, one of the partners informed me that "I was the greatest patient advocate that he had ever come across". I thanked him, but he replied, "that wasn't a compliment". It is often said that GP practices are like "marriages", but being married to one person is hard enough, but with five or six, it can eventually become impossible, especially as individuals develop and their career progression almost inevitably leads to conflict.

After 28 years as a GP Principal, I felt the time had come to be a full-time Sex Tsar.

CHAPTER 8

Testosterone – the true story!

Testosterone deficiency (or Hypogonadism as endocrine doctors prefer) is one of the most controversial issues in medicine, and alone, the topic could fill a book three times this size, but I will try to keep it as simple as possible. In fact, along with my good friend and colleague, Professor Mike Kirby, I have written a textbook on testosterone therapy and men's health, published in September 2022. I realise, however, that this will have little effect on the dogmatic medical views in the UK, which is why, ultimately, the patient is going to have to take control of their own health.

Unfortunately, a bit of science is required at the outset. I have just one request for the reader. Do not seek out the internet for your knowledge on this subject, as there are sites out there to trap you into expensive long-term treatments. There are doctors with the proper training, and *some* of these have an empathetic approach; your GP should be able to refer you if you specifically ask. Most importantly, you need to find a sympathetic GP. Everything else you need will be in the following chapters based on evidence from my 2022 textbook, "the role of testosterone in diabetes and other diseases".

The difficulty here is that the subject of low testosterone crosses many traditional medical specialities, especially endocrinology, urology, sexual medicine, and even cardiology and psychiatry. This means that doctors compiling medical guidelines will be focused on the issues, practicalities, and workload associated with their own specialism. For example, the largest study on low testosterone clearly found that erectile dysfunction (ED), loss of morning erections, and low sexual desire are the three most common symptoms of low testosterone (hypogonadism), so surely it is logical to send patients to a specialist in sexual medicine. This rarely happens as few health commissioners will have access to sexual medicine services. The choice will lie between a urologist, who will follow his European Urology guidelines and perform three rectal examinations in the first year, or an endocrinologist, whose guidelines state, "we are not very good at rectal examination, so don't recommend it, as it may be dangerous!" When offered the choice of three non-recommended and potentially dangerous digits per year versus no educated digits at all will lead to a patient choosing the endocrinologist, who has no training in sexual medicine and may be more interested in the intellectual exclusion of some very interesting but obscure syndromes. These may have little relevance to the three bothersome symptoms that brought the patient to his doctor in the first place.

The patient will then enter the miasma of confusion around repeated blood tests that have to be taken in the morning, fasted, with seasonal variations and endless discussion on which test kit is available, when, in reality, the doctor is stuck with whatever the local laboratory uses. There is even considerable variation between laboratories as to what they accept as "normal". The net result is that hospitals can drag the whole process out for years by endless navel gazing and procrastination.

The other problem is terminology. Endocrinologists prefer the term **HYPOGONADISM**, which will mean nothing to the patient, when, in reality, the term means under activity of the testicles, which have cells producing testosterone (Leydig cells) and sperm (Sertoli cells), but the patients we are usually treating only have problems related to testosterone. Hence the term **TESTOSTERONE DEFICIENCY** more accurately defines the clinical problem and, more importantly, is understandable for the patient. This intellectual argument continues to rumble on. It is no wonder that many men give up on the medical system and turn to the internet, which is the modern strategy for dealing with most problems.

Testosterone deficiency is divided into **PRIMARY**, affecting 2% of the male population, **where the problem lies in the testicles**, which are failing to produce testosterone, and **SECONDARY**, affecting 10%, **where the problem lies at a higher level, usually in the pituitary gland,** situated just below the brain. The pituitary gland can be affected by several chronic diseases, such as diabetes, and medications, such as painkillers, antidepressants, and so-called "recreational" drugs.

PRIMARY causes include some very rare genetic conditions that most family doctors will never see, but more importantly, can be due to conditions such as trauma to the testicles, infections such as mumps, or tumours in younger men that might require surgery or chemotherapy. Young men are often seen as "cured" only to pop-up several years because the "normal" tissue left behind is unable to cope or when fertility is expected. It seems incredible how many so-called "cured" patients state that they were never warned about problems later on, usually for fear of causing "anxiety".

What we do know is that having a low testosterone level is bad news. There is a 3 to 4-fold increased risk of developing type 2 diabetes mellitus (T2DM), and several studies have shown strong associations with early death. Many doctors decline to measure testosterone, feeling that it is better not to know for fear of opening "Pandora's box". The most common reason for checking testosterone is ED. ALL men should be checked as low testosterone is a potentially treatable cause of ED and a reason why conventional tablets (such as Viagra) might be less effective. If a doctor tries to tell you that this is not necessary as you seem to have a "nice beard" or are "well developed", do not accept this and insist on a blood test, usually best done before 11am in the morning, ideally fasting. Just as women fought for many years to have menopausal symptoms taken seriously, it is only by standing our ground that we will get medical attitudes to change. Unfortunately, with men, there is often one chance, and if a poor consultation happens, then the patient does not return after a bad experience.

Do not accept that your testosterone level has been checked and is "normal." Always ask what the value actually is. So-called normal values are, in fact, the "reference range" drawn from the manufacturers who took 100 samples from healthy volunteers. They then classified the top 2.5% and the bottom 2.5% as abnormal and the other 95% as normal. These values have no relationship to who might benefit from treatment. Being in the top or bottom 2.5% for cholesterol, blood pressure, or blood glucose has no relevance to who needs treatment. If we think about obesity, the heaviest 2.5% of the population may well be totally immobile with too many health problems. It is likely that better results will be obtained by concentrating on the slightly less obese.

International Expert Guidelines recommend that a level of above 12 nmol/l is accepted as normal. Tests should be done in the morning and preferably fasting. Healthy young men usually have levels between 18 and 30 nmol/l. As levels fall, more symptoms appear. Below 15 nmol/l, men might feel that they have less sexual desire, less enjoyment of life, and less "get up and go". As levels fall below 12 nmol/l, tiredness, loss of strength, reduced morning erections, poor concentration, poor sleep, weight gain, diabetes, and depression appear. Below 10 nmol/l, ED and sweating occur. These variable thresholds for symptoms explain why there are diverse views on when to treat.

The reality is that whilst you might be concerned that you have lost interest in sex or lost your "mojo", this is unlikely to be a priority for the NHS, especially as treatment is relatively expensive. As Frank Dobson,

Health Secretary in 1998, famously said in a provocative statement, "the NHS is not about helping middle-aged men to strut their stuff in discos"!

Apart from the above symptoms, low testosterone is associated with increased obesity, with a 3-4 times greater risk of T2DM and earlier death from multiple causes associated with increased frailty. They also have an increased risk of more aggressive prostate cancer. Several special groups are at increased risk of low testosterone and so-called **SECONDARY TESTOSTERONE DEFICIENCY**, those with:

- Obesity (especially men from South Asia)

- T2DM (especially men from South Asia)

- Long-term painkillers, such as co-codamol, tramadol, or opiate abusers. These are usually medically prescribed with the best of intentions.

- Heart Failure, Heart Attack.

- HIV.

- Chronic Kidney Disease (CKD).

- Current or past users of anabolic steroids, especially for body-building purposes.

- **And most importantly, COVID-19 infection as an acute and chronic problem (see separate chapter)**

Implications for the future following the pandemic

Multiple guidelines already recommended that men in the high-risk groups above should be checked and that low levels of testosterone should be treated (see below). In the UK, we have not been following this guidance. We rely too heavily on NICE, who have yet to publish any guidance. All we have had so far is a "Clinical Knowledge Summary on Erectile Dysfunction" in 2019, which was a straight copy of the BSSM (British Society for Sexual Medicine Guidelines) that I had published a year earlier. When I pointed this out to them, their response was to remove the document and do nothing further.

The message from this pandemic is even more clear. All men in the above groups should ensure that their testosterone level is checked. If the level is below 12 nmol/l, this needs to be treated to improve symptoms and quality of life and to reduce vulnerability to future pandemics.

In spite of this logical connection, there has been more interest in the UK as to why HRT might be protecting women. In fact, as of 2022, women are able to get HRT from pharmacies without a prescription, whereas men struggle to get any measurement of testosterone levels, even if they fall into the high-risk group with diabetes. Whilst emergency measures and vaccine development are vitally important, during the pandemic, reducing the risks for vulnerable patients is equally important in the long term.

The bottom line is that men need to be aware of the problems of low testosterone themselves and not rely on doctors to make the diagnosis for them. These issues are often considered "lifestyle problems" and not part of general NHS care. Men need to accept that they need to be proactive and seek investigation, diagnosis, and treatment in the private sector. There are many private laboratories that arrange home diagnostic testing, but these are often linked to a requirement for expensive ongoing private medication.

Some men can have features of primary and secondary conditions and are termed **MIXED TESTOSTERONE DEFICIENCY.**

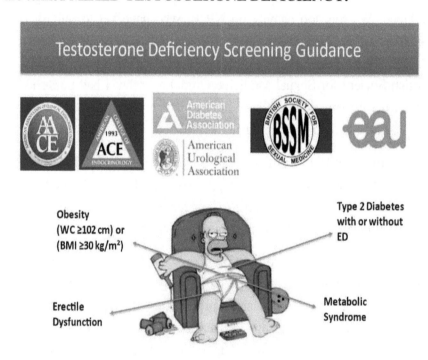

Dealing with Myths

Testosterone is an emotive topic, and most people have a view on the subject, often based on faulty premises. The first myth to deal with is that testosterone therapy causes prostate cancer. In fact, evidence suggests the opposite, as older men get prostate cancer, and those with the lowest testosterone levels get more aggressive prostate cancer. Recently studies suggest that men who have been treated effectively for prostate cancer have fewer recurrences if their low testosterone is corrected. Of course, many will want to wait for the perfect long-term trial, but it is unlikely that this study will ever be done.

The second myth is that testosterone therapy increases heart attack or stroke risk. Multiple trials have shown that restoring testosterone levels to normal reduces death due to all causes, including heart disease. The confusion arises from reports of increased cardiac events in the Anabolic Steroid (AS) community, where doses several times higher than those required for replacement are commonly used in an unregulated fashion. It should be obvious that choosing to take ten times the recommended dose of any medication is a bad idea. Just consider the results of taking ten times the required dose of diabetes or thyroid medications.

Replacing testosterone to normal levels is not usually associated with baldness or acne but can be associated with a slight reduction in testicular volume and infertility. These issues can usually be managed by subtle changes in therapy.

Possible benefits of testosterone therapy

After 40 years of medical practice, I continue to be surprised by the benefits of testosterone therapy *for men with low levels*. Likewise, treating a man with normal levels is unrewarding, however much he might want it to work. In these cases, there is usually another condition causing the symptoms. Such men will be disappointed if they see it as a panacea. I usually prefer to adopt the Ed Miliband (remember him) approach of under-promising and over-delivering. In my own study of nearly 1000 men with T2DM, we have shown numerous health benefits and reduced mortality over a 10-year period. To date, we have published over 14 peer-reviewed papers from this research. Men with T2DM also have high rates of ED, up to 75%, and up to 40% have low testosterone. The benefits of screening and treating these men are well-established. A 10-year study from Germany has shown that testosterone can halt the progression and reverse T2DM. Doctors routinely screen for an underactive thyroid in men with diabetes in fear of litigation if they miss the diagnosis, even though the pickup rate is around 1%. In contrast, they do not routinely measure for low testosterone (40% of cases) and would not remotely fear a complaint for a missed diagnosis. In fact, I have had complaints from GPs that I have complicated the management by making the diagnosis.

A large study of 1007 men from Australia (termed T4DM standing for **T**estosterone **F**or **D**iabetes **M**ellitus) published in 2021 has shown the benefits of treating overweight men with borderline testosterone with testosterone injections versus placebo (both combined with a lifestyle programme) for two years. In the men on placebo, 21% developed diabetes versus 12% on T therapy, a 41% reduction overall. This has a potentially huge effect on the population as diabetes levels have continued to increase despite all the lifestyle advice and exercise programmes introduced by the NHS over many years. Currently, 3.5 million UK men have pre-diabetes, with 40% (1.4 million) with low testosterone. T4DM suggests that potentially 23,000 cases of male T2DM could be prevented every two years merely by following the current BSSM guidelines. Despite this massive study published in the Lancet, the word "testosterone" is not mentioned on either the Diabetes UK or NHS Diabetes website. Neither has NICE been stimulated to even consider guidelines. The only strategy to prevent this progression is more "lifestyle and exercise", completely missing the point that men with low testosterone lack the physical strength and motivation to exercise. The approach to low motivation is usually the prescription of an anti-depressant. Surely the definition of insanity is to constantly repeat practices that have previously failed. Of course, diet and exercise are important, but no other treatment has been shown to have such an impressive effect, but unfortunately, elements of the NHS seem to be unable to accept that lifestyle change alone is clearly not working and that it is relatively expensive to deliver. T4DM also demonstrated a considerable reduction in fat, increased muscle and physical performance, correction of anaemia, and increase in bone strength. There were also symptomatic improvements, such as improved sexual function. These multiple benefits are likely to motivate men to continue not only with the medication but also with lifestyle changes.

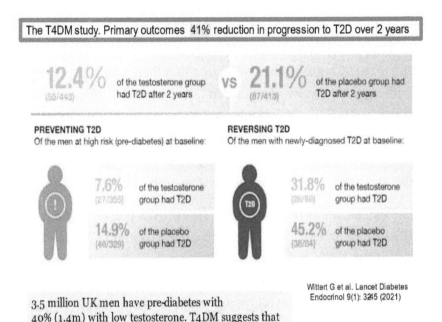

The T4DM study. Primary outcomes 41% reduction in progression to T2D over 2 years

12.4% (55/443) of the testosterone group had T2D after 2 years **VS** **21.1%** (87/413) of the placebo group had T2D after 2 years

PREVENTING T2D
Of the men at high risk (pre-diabetes) at baseline:

7.6% (27/355) of the testosterone group had T2D

14.9% (49/329) of the placebo group had T2D

REVERSING T2D
Of the men with newly-diagnosed T2D at baseline:

31.8% (28/88) of the testosterone group had T2D

45.2% (38/84) of the placebo group had T2D

Wittert G et al. Lancet Diabetes Endocrinol 9(1): 32–45 (2021)

3.5 million UK men have pre-diabetes with 40% (1.4m) with low testosterone. T4DM suggests that 23k cases of male T2DM/2 years could be prevented

Results from our own BLAST study, which involved 857 men with T2DM from seven general practices in Burton, Lichfield, Atherstone, Sutton, and Tamworth, endorse these findings. These men on the GP diabetes registers were screened for low testosterone, 40% were found to have low levels, and 200 patients entered a trial of testosterone therapy. After four years, 19.7% of the untreated men with low testosterone died, compared with only 3.6% of treated men. When we looked at the 175 men who were started on testosterone therapy, of the 78 who were still taking testosterone after four years, there were NO DEATHS, whereas, in the 97 who had stopped, there were 6 deaths (6.2%). In the 362 men with low testosterone who remained untreated over the four years, 61 out of 362 died (16.9%), and in the men with normal testosterone levels, 36 out of 320 (12.5%) died. This study clearly showed that in men with T2DM, low testosterone is linked to early death, and treating low testosterone significantly reduced mortality. Having followed up with these men for four years, I am sure that will agree that there can be no doubt as to whether patients were alive or dead, and we had absolute certainty about medication as the practice nurses were giving the injections every 12 weeks. Perhaps the reader can understand my frustration when years later, I have to answer the question, "is testosterone safe?" and the inevitable conclusion, "more long-term studies are required"!

The real shame here is that four years on, the prescribing advisers identified these practices as "high prescribing outliers," which might prevent them from reaching "quality standards". This resulted in therapy (and presumably death rates) being reduced to "normal" national levels, so everybody was happy once more! This was probably the last straw for me, and I decided that, after 30 years, it was time to leave the NHS and try to offer the best care that I could in the private sector.

There are around 2.5 million men with T2DM in the UK, and if 40% have low testosterone, this is 1 million men. We showed that men with low testosterone (hypogonadal) were significantly more likely to die in the next four years than those with normal (eugonadal) testosterone levels. Our study in men with diabetes suggests that untreated, 197,000 would die in four years, versus 36,000 with treatment, a potential saving of 161,000 lives over four years!! Whilst it is not practical to expect that ALL men with diabetes will be screened and treated, even if we only targeted the men with very low levels and treated 10%, this would amount to 16,000 fewer deaths over 4 years.

We took out the men who were prescribed tablets for ED as these medications further reduce the risk, but more of this is in the next chapter. These figures, of course, make several assumptions, but perhaps the reader might see why I feel reassured to treat these men. I believe that these figures truly make the point that we need to take our health care into our own hands.

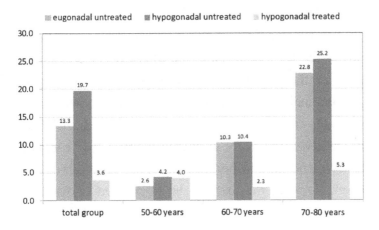

Mortality Data of Men with Type 2 Diabetes mellitus not receiving PDE5 Inhibitors followed for approximately 4 Years (n= 682)

Hackett G et al. Int J Clin Pract 70(3): 244 -253 (2016)

Pain Killers and Testosterone Levels.

In the US and UK, we face an epidemic of pain-killer abuse. In many cases, these drugs may be prescribed for legitimate reasons such as chronic back pain, but low testosterone levels will be seen in 40-50% of men, and they are at higher risk of early death. US and UK studies have shown a huge reduction in mortality when low testosterone is treated. The advice must be to try to wean off opiate products, even codeine and tramadol, switching to safer drugs such as paracetamol or ibuprofen. This group of patients with low testosterone definitely benefits from testosterone (replacement?) therapy.

By far, the most difficult group is men who abuse anabolic steroids (AS) either currently or in the past. All men might have been tempted to try shortcuts in that search for that perfect body that they think women desire. They probably intend to use them for a short time but soon get trapped into ever-increasing doses by the rebound symptoms as the levels fall. As some of the doses are several times more than the therapeutic dose, problems can arise very quickly. Acute dangers include thickening of the blood and heart attacks due to raised cholesterol and direct toxic effects on the heart. There are a few very sad cases. The major problems appear a few years later when the pituitary gland fails to bounce back once the high-dose steroids are stopped. By now, the man might be married or want to start a family.

Often the problem is difficult to diagnose as the man denies past use because of intense shame or fear of being blamed as a "cheat". This is often compounded by endocrinologists who tell men to be patient and wait years for things will recover, even at the cost of their marriage and the loss of the best years of their lives. It is very difficult for these men to access sympathetic treatment from recognised specialists, and they often drift back into their habits. These patients can be very demanding but often rewarding. They often expect the immediate "highs" that they experienced from their previous rapid-acting injections, but with patience, they can usually be established on safer medications that maintain levels in the normal range, plus, of course, daily tadalafil to treat their ED as shown in later chapters.

There are often associated infertility problems with past AS use or the controlled T therapy now being given. Often, they require regular injections of a drug called hCG (human chorionic gonadotrophin) or an oral drug called clomiphene, previously used to treat infertility in women. Frequently we need to work with fertility specialists to retrieve sperm from the testes of these men and then later proceed to IVF.

If only men commencing AS for that perfect body knew what was waiting for them down the road! Often the real victims are the innocent partners of these men. Unfortunately, the desirability for the "hench" body and the shortcuts taken to get there are trends that are difficult to reverse as they are ingrained in our culture. Sometimes that new year resolution of a gym membership is the first step on a slippery slope.

The advice here is clear – Don't take AS not prescribed by a physician.

Dangers of Prescribed Medications.

In addition to the widespread abuse of pain-killers leading to sexual problems in men and women, two frequently prescribed medications in young men can be associated with major sexual problems, as these two cases will demonstrate:

Rupert was 21 and suffered from severe acne, which had made him a recluse, constantly feeling that everyone was staring at his pustules. The vicious comments on Facebook then destroyed whatever self-esteem he ever had, such that he had never really had a proper relationship. Multiple courses of antibiotics and creams from his GP had not solved the problem, so he was referred to a specialist dermatologist, who prescribed Roaccutane (Isotretinoin) reserved for severe cases. He had two courses of 3-4 months over the next year, and the effect on his skin was pretty good. He then complained that he now had no desire to go out and find a girlfriend, and, on questioning, he stated that he had lost all his morning erections. Unfortunately, this is a question few doctors ask, as they mistakenly believe that erections are of no interest to men who are not in a relationship. The trouble with this drug is that it affects many steroid pathways in the brain leading to severe, often irreversible sexual dysfunction in a few young men. The bottom line is that Rupert had very low testosterone levels, despite the misconception that acne must be related to high levels causing greasy skin. We commenced him on testosterone injections, hCG injections to preserve fertility, and later some clomiphene tablets to lower his oestrogen levels, which caused some breast tenderness. Of course, he takes tadalafil 5mg to restore morning erections, as, without these, there would be confident to start a relationship. I am prescribing the hCG and clomiphene "off label" as the GP practice abdicates responsibility.

Five years later, he is still on this complex therapy regime and in a long-term relationship, with fertility shown to be preserved. The bottom line is that he has had to fund all these medications privately (around £180 per month) despite my writing several letters explaining that his problems are related to NHS-prescribed medication.

It is also of interest that despite many papers on this subject, doctors still do not warn men of these complications, nor are they mentioned on any website. It is all too easy to dismiss these young men as "insecure" because of concerns about appearance. I get regular emails from a mother who has strong views about what should be done to the dermatologists who prescribe them. Of course, it could be argued that Rupert's acne could have severely impacted his social life and caused additional permanent scarring if poorly treated. This just goes to show that, in medicine, sometimes the doctor is between a rock and a hard place!

The other common culprit is finasteride, prescribed at a 5mg dose in older men for enlarged prostate but at 1mg for young men with premature hair loss. Whereas men with prostate disease will usually be under the care of their doctor, younger men with hair loss will usually be seeking treatment from private clinics or even online. Most importantly, young men are far more likely to be severely affected by this than older men, who probably already have erection problems associated with their enlarged prostate.

Tristram was 19 and had noticed thinning hair for two years and tried several hairstyles and preparations to reduce the loss. He felt self-conscious and had not been in a relationship. He contacted a clinic and was sent finasteride 1mg tablets (Propecia) to take daily. After six months, there was a minimal change, but he noticed that he had lost morning erections. Eventually, he summoned up the courage to see his GP, who had been to one of my seminars, who stopped the finasteride and prescribed tadalafil 5mg daily (of course). Tristram has his morning erections back but still lacks the confidence to start a relationship. He is working with a sex therapist to improve his confidence. We hope that the effect of the finasteride will wear off, but it has been over one year. He accepted an offer of counselling but found it of little value.

These two young men are sad examples of how the system has let them down badly and the long battles that they have fought to access therapy.

Misunderstandings about testosterone

Over the years, I have been approached several times regarding media and TV programmes about testosterone. Invariably I try to point out the important associations with ageing, diabetes, obesity, heart disease, early death, and depression, but invariably all they want to talk about is "hench" toned physique and sexual endurance records as they presume that this attracts viewers. Invariably the interviewer was under 30, and the concept of "old people" over 50 still having sex seems "gross" and of no public interest. Testosterone, therefore, becomes perceived as some form of "recreational" drug. There is a similar reaction in the sporting world. We are all aware of high-profile athletes permanently "disgraced " or labelled as "cheats" after a positive test. Fortunately, most sports do not feature the over 50s described above. A notable exception is golf. I have been involved as a medical adviser to the European golf tour for the past 20 years. In fact, golf is unique as there are lucrative over 50 seniors' tours (and now rebel tours), and many players actually earn as much after they hit 50 as in their prime. Many may have put on some weight and developed diabetes or blood pressure with the resulting detection of low testosterone levels. Many may have remarried, with younger wives, a feature of tour golf, which puts great strain on marriages and relationships. Testosterone therapy would be entirely appropriate for these men. In theory, treatment might assist weight loss and increase muscular strength, giving him an advantage, but so would treating an underactive thyroid or diabetes. Unfortunately, as even senior golfers are subject to routine drug testing, they are likely to be picked up and branded as "cheats," whereas they are merely seeking licensed treatment appropriate for a troublesome medical condition. Unfortunately, the sporting world does not see it this way due to all the media hype around testosterone, but more about this in a later chapter.

The politics of testosterone

Unfortunately, the press coverage of all issues concerning testosterone, especially the obsession with bodybuilders and the zero tolerance in sports, has made it virtually impossible to treat patients (and couples) appropriately. It has also been difficult for doctors to help patients who might have made mistakes when they were younger and taken hormones but now realise the error of their ways. This often happens when as a result of their sculptured enhanced physique, they attract a stunning "babe" and then want to start a family in their 30s. This couple will often encounter a frosty response from the medical world as this problem is of the man's making, especially as he may have been "cheating". Some would say, "once a cheat, always a cheat".

I vividly remember the case of Paul, aged 32, who had taken AS for several years and won a number of power-lifting competitions by managing to pass random tests by the many techniques known by such professionals. He was now settling down with Roxanne (30), but she had not managed to become pregnant after two years of trying without contraception. Paul had erection problems after stopping his AS and felt dreadful with low energy and motivation. I treated him with clomiphene, a drug that stimulates the body's natural testosterone production and sperm production but then had to add in some low-dose testosterone gel to improve his symptoms without affecting his sperm levels. At the outset, I made him promise that he would not be involved in any more competitive weightlifting. I even wondered if I had a duty to inform his previous regulatory bodies that his previous titles were won through performance-enhancing drugs, but I felt that this potentially breached patient confidentiality. He reassured me that his lifting days were over. The effect of clomiphene and gel was modest, so I added a depot testosterone injection (more about that later), maintaining the clomiphene to preserve his fertility. I reviewed him six months later and not only was his partner now pregnant, but he presented me with several cuttings of the long-distance golf driving competitions he had recently won!

My heart sank. I thought that I had done so well to get him out of competitive weightlifting, but he had now converted to the sport that I was actively working as a medical adviser to the European Golf Tour and PGA. He had already won several large cheques, and one glance at Paul's physique ripping into the golf ball and sending it 400 yards would lead to only one conclusion! He did share some recent photos of his "clean and jerk" regime, designed to reduce the risk of a wrist injury. More detailed workout regimes can be found in the appendix of this book.

The politics of testosterone will feature heavily in the remaining chapters due to the perception of bodybuilders and athletic enhancement, but the 10% of men in the general population with genuine deficiency associated with important medical conditions such as diabetes and painkillers are suffering because of media hype and misconception. In contrast, women have fought successfully for HRT on the NHS for menopausal symptoms, associated with a "natural" process that affects 100% of women, albeit that suffering can be severe for women suffering abrupt menopause. HRT is now provided free on NHS prescription and, as of 2022, from pharmacies without prescription, following intense pressure on the government. It is becoming easier for women to get testosterone therapy off-licence than it is for men with a clear deficiency detected by blood testing.

Men will usually be declined treatment by their GP, often with some "man-up" comments, leaving them to seek help from the "dark web", usually leading to misinformation and exploitation.

CHAPTER 9

The Viagra Years and Beyond

It was the summer of 96, and the first patients from the sildenafil studies had returned for assessment. It was clear that at least half of them (50% had to be on placebo) were showing profound effects. It was becoming impossible to get them to return the unused tablets. This was a problem that I had never encountered before. I arrived home and stormed into the house, "Where is the number of that stockbroker?" Suddenly I realised that this might be considered "insider dealing", although things were less clear at that stage. There had been no problem whatsoever recruiting men for these trials, as only painful injections were available previously. I was always aware of the vast difference between men and women in relation to drug trials. In the case of women, their bodies are *temples,* and they need thorough information as to the absolute safety of anything being put into their bodies. In the case of men, merely telling them that, to date, only five rats had ever taken this medication would be sufficient if at least two of the rats had survived. The trials involved being provided with unlimited medication to be taken prior to sexual attempts and then completing a "Sexual Encounter Profile" (SEP), with explicit questions about what happened to the penis before and during penetration. There was also an "International Index of Erectile Function" (IIEF) Questionnaire to be completed at each visit. Later on, there was much criticism, as these questionnaires, developed in middle America, only addressed issues in heterosexual couples.

The Nineties were a golden age for clinical research, and it was a privilege to be involved right from the beginning in the development of a Nobel prize-winning drug that not only changed clinical practice forever but is now a household name. We were also doing studies on Invicorp, an injectable drug for ED, and I was still a full-time GP partner in Lichfield. Work was great fun then. There were frequent clinical trial meetings, usually at pleasant venues in the UK, plus regular international meetings in Urology and Sexual Medicine. I often wonder why medicine has lost its attraction for so many doctors in recent years

Based on the development of sildenafil (Viagra) and similar drugs that followed, a new speciality developed. Initially, Professor Alan Riley had set up the British Erectile Disorder Society, aptly named BEDS. I was treasurer and was charged with organising the inaugural meeting. I chose the Victoria Hotel, Stratford-upon-Avon and handled all the negotiations with the hotel. Having recently attended a meeting on "Revascularisation of the Penis" in Madrid, where the huge banner outside the hotel had caused public consternation, I was concerned that nothing similar happened to the delicate residents of Shakespeare's Birthplace. I dealt with a lovely girl, Sharon, and rang a couple of days before the meeting in May 1997 just to check that there were no issues related to our "special" group. "We have had all sorts here", was her comforting reply. I was greatly reassured as we had about 80 delegates attending. Imagine my surprise when I parked outside the hotel in Stratford to see a huge sign outside saying:

"The Victoria Hotel, Stratford-upon-Avon, welcomes the British *Reptile* Society,". Perhaps her major concern was that delegates might be keeping snakes and iguanas suitably moist and cool in the bathrooms.

BEDS only lasted about 18 months before being renamed the British Society for Sexual Medicine (BSSM) in line with the

European Society for Sexual Medicine (ESSM) and the International Society for Sexual Medicine (ISSM). Dr Bollinger was now a rising star in the Sexual Medicine world, displaying all the finest qualities of British Diplomacy to keep the rival Italian, Greek and Turkish factions in order. Whilst I was a hard-working, "serious" researcher, Dr B's flamboyant, eccentric, larger-than-life style meant that he was destined for greatness.

By September 1997, the genie was out of the bottle, and patients were aware that a "miracle" tablet was available. The clinic was becoming busy. This was excellent news for clinical trial recruitment for the trials as this was the only way to gain access to the new treatments. Although 50% received a placebo, after 3-6 months, all patients received active treatment for up to 12 months. Trials were also just beginning for tadalafil (Cialis) and vardenafil (Levitra) as members of the same class of drug, PDE5 inhibitors. As a "key opinion leader", I was also able to obtain medication directly from the manufacturer prior to the UK licence of Viagra in 1998, which gave the Good Hope clinic a significant edge. Things were going to change in September 2018 when the Department of Health brought in some draconian regulations to restrict NHS prescribing to contain expenditure on the miracle blue pill.

A "miracle" drug will also be associated with unrealistic expectations. Despite all the best advice, older men were still seeking to "surprise" their partners after several years of inactivity. They would take a tablet just before Match of the Day and expect a rustling in the trousers even during the dullest of 0-0 draws. If we could persuade them that both parties needed to get their kit off first and that they needed to rediscover the concept of foreplay, then they might have a chance.

By May 1998, the clinic had developed a bit of a waiting list as none of the patients on tablets could be discharged back to their GPs. To save time, I asked the nurses to get the patients to complete an IIEF score to assess the severity of ED, An Ageing Male Symptom Score (AMS) and the International Prostate Symptom Score (IPSS). I am a big fan of questionnaires as they get the patients to do a lot of the work, and if I forget to ask a question, then I know that the answer will be there in one of the questionnaires when I come to write the letter. I used to look at these before referring to the GP letter to see how well they predicted the patient's problem. Sometimes the process let me down badly. Horace Stapes was 73 when he saw me on 23rd May 1998. His questionnaires looked surprisingly normal, so I went back to basics,

"Now, Horace, what has brought you along today?"

"I'm having trouble with a buzzing in the left ear." he said. "Is it worse when you get an erection?" I asked.

"No, but sometimes I am a bit deaf, and I feel blocked up. I can't sleep". "Any trouble with libido or ejaculation?" I was now having to ask direct questions to make progress. "No, that's fine, but sometimes the buzzing turns to a ringing noise". Out of desperation, I decided to read the GP letter:

142

Dr Benjamin Hardwick. MB.BS. MRCGP
The Bell End Surgery, 23, Bell End Lane, West Midlands, B65
9LP
Tel: 01562 623489
Fax 01562 632492

Dear Doctor,

Re Mr Horace Stapes, 14/12/38.

14 Crotch Crescent, Bell End, Worcestershire B65. 9LS.

Please assess Mr Horace Stapes who is being troubled with a severe bout of tin nuts.

Dr Benjamin Hardwick

GP Registrar

Not only had the GP's practice spell check badly let them down, but somebody in the hospital appointment department had a strange idea of my clinic workload.

Many men thought that Viagra would make them instantly attractive to women. Some believed that every erection must end with sex, and many thought that Viagra would roll back the years. Many women thought that it would turn their husbands into sex maniacs. In reality, there were probably marriages only held together by the man's ED, but that was no excuse not to treat him. Some women in the US tried to sue Pfizer for their husband's infidelity after they had been treated with Viagra.

Archibald Johnson, 63, presented in late 1998 following a series of heart attacks and a couple of failed cardiac stents. It took him nearly five minutes to walk the 20 metres from the waiting room, and he was breathless for a full minute after sitting down. His wife, Cynthia, was 15 years younger, and he found her very attractive but feared that he would lose her if he was unable to satisfy her. The great cardiologist Graham Jackson showed us that sex is a physical activity equivalent to walking a mile in 20 minutes and climbing two flights of stairs. Clearly, Archibald's heart was not capable of the effort involved in sex. We discussed the issues, but he seems unable to comprehend that sex is dangerous for him. If he is walking and gets chest pain or shortness of breath, then he can stop, but at the height of erotic frenzy after a large meal and a bottle of Claret, he is likely to push on beyond his limit. Men often comment, "What a nice way to go!" without realising the impact on the partner of such an event. Men in this situation often say that "Without sex, life is not worth living". Although the proper answer is to tell such men to forget sex, this advice will not be taken. In such cases, I believe that it is possible to negotiate with the couple some form of limited sexual activity, where most of the work is done by the partner. It is crucial that the partner fully understands the risk and that this is documented in the notes. The paradox is that these drugs that we use for ED are actually very good drugs for the heart.

Sex after a heart attack is rarely discussed by cardiac rehabilitation nurses. Comprehensive advice is given about a date when hoovering can be safely resumed. I can assure nurses that none of these men in coronary care are thinking about when they can next get behind the controls of their Dyson Big Ball. In fact, in common with most men, I have spent most of my life trying to have as much sex as I can whilst doing as little hoovering as possible. Every week in my clinic, I see a man referred after a recent heart attack. In nearly every case, the ED commenced 3-5 years earlier, and many chances were missed. Despite all the evidence, this situation has not changed significantly over the last 20 years.

Nicholas Dingle, 70, was a former Barrister with a high sex drive. He had developed Parkinson's disease and had been drinking more heavily since giving up work. His glamourous wife, Annette, at 52, usually attended with him. Penile Injections had been largely unsuccessful, but he now wanted to try the tablets. By trial and error, he worked out that two tablets and one injection did the trick. I constantly looked at Nicholas with his shaking hands and drooling from the mouth and could not really imagine the two of them together. Annette told me that, every night, Nicholas would book a taxi and head to the red-light area of Birmingham, returning home after 3am, usually drunk and often shouting and unsteady. Her major issue was that her previously high-flying husband was now a complete embarrassment. I was aware that a common side effect of drugs for Parkinson's disease was hypersexuality, and this was clearly the problem here. He was totally fixated on sex, but neither his GP nor neurologist were interested in any discussion about changing his medication. It was obvious to me that Annette was having a relationship with somebody else, but I had to explain that Nicholas was my patient and that my duty of care was to him, and this was the life that he had chosen.

I remember an 85-year-old lady on multiple drugs for Parkinson's disease in a nursing home. She was frequently found on top of elderly gentlemen, having wandered into their rooms at night. I still remember visiting the home and catching her on top of this poor old chap, pulling at his todger whilst he was screaming and pressing the panic button.

The range of referrals to the clinic was rapidly changing. This was usually driven by the development of effective treatments. GPs were pragmatic and did not see the point of referring patients when they knew that there was nothing that could be offered. We knew for some time that a lot of young men with ED did not respond to tablets because their testosterone was low. Nobody wanted to go on to injections in the penis, and we were finding that restoring the testosterone levels to normal not only stiffened the erections but also improved their libido, energy levels and much more. We now had very effective testosterone treatments in the form of gels and long-acting injections. Things were getting very exciting. GPs realised that sending these men to Endocrinologists was largely a waste of time as patients were seen by junior doctors who just repeated blood tests until the doctor moved on to his next job, and then the new Doc could take over and request further tests. Many of these men with low testosterone were belated referred with infertility. In the NHS, a couple who are not conceiving will be referred to an Infertility clinic, usually in a Gynaecology clinic, run by doctors who may not have treated a man for several years. The role of man is often regarded as a mere sperm donor. His medical and psychological problems are rarely considered.

Sean (35) and Sarah (34) Goodfellow had been seeing Mr Bender, Private Gynaecologist in Harley St for infertility for two years. I had treated his ED well with daily tadalafil giving him frequent morning erections. They were having sex twice daily. Previously their GP had been rationing Sean to one tablet per week on the basis of NHS guidance from 1998, based on a "No sex please, We're British"

Survey from the 70s and 80s. Sarah brought a letter from Mr Bender that seemed to have identified the problem:

Mr Hugh Bender. MB.BS. MD. FRCOG

The Infertility Clinic. 147 Harley St, W1G6AQ

Re Mrs Sarah Goodfellow 03/07/75

3rd April 2009

79, Minge Lane, Upton-on Severn, Worcestershire. WR8 0NN.

Dear Dr Hackett,

I believe that Sarah's infertility is due to allergy to her husband, Sean's semen. She therefore needs comprehensive prick testing, which I have personally administered today. I will see her again in two weeks.

Yours sincerely

Hugh Bender.

Certainly, Mr Bender's personal prick test had done the trick, and it was smiles all around, although I suspect that the daily tadalafil was also crucial to success.

Despite the CCG embargo on accepting female referrals, my experience in research into female sexual dysfunction led to a limited number of referrals, often when I had Identified that the major sexual issue was with the woman. The immediate problem in treating woman is that the predominant problem is a lack of *sexual desire*. This is common around menopause but causes much more distress when it arises in younger women. The problem is often related to hormonal contraception. The high dose of oestrogen in oral contraceptives increases the production by the liver of "sex hormone binding globulin" (SHBG). The function of SHBG is to lock onto the oestrogen, rendering it inactive, and transport it around the body. The problem is that the SHBG has a stronger affinity for testosterone than oestrogen. Women have roughly 10% of the male level of testosterone, so the rendering of this SHBG-bound testosterone as "inactive" produces significant symptoms, especially a lack of sexual desire or libido. This can be treated with low-dose testosterone patches and gel, but these are not licensed for women. Treating a woman with low-dose testosterone is very rewarding, and I have been treating many women since 1999.

Rose was 59 and had been treated with bilateral mastectomies for breast cancer and hysterectomy and removal of ovaries for ovarian cancer. I had been treating her husband, David, with diabetes and low desire by prescribing testosterone gel and daily tadalafil with limited success, mainly because of the problems Rose was experiencing. The addition of a tiny amount of testosterone gel for Rose had an immediate effect and transformed their relationship. Their only problem then was that Rose was now more interested in sex but found difficulty in getting aroused and reaching orgasm. The addition of daily tadalafil to her regime made a huge difference. After six months, the dynamics of their relationship had changed, Rose was now initiating sex, and David was having difficulty keeping up.

I saw a very similar effect with Janet, 68, and Peter, 66. They both had T2DM, and I was having moderate success with Peter, but he was aware that Janet seemed to be getting little pleasure from sex and was extremely dry, a common problem for women with diabetes. The addition of a tiny amount of testosterone gel was effective, but it was only the addition of daily tadalafil that changed the picture. Peter commented that, by three months, Janet was a different woman. She had stopped her anti-depressant and become much more mentally alert, contributing much more conversation. She just seemed a much happier person. I have followed them up for 10 years, and they still have an active sex life. In fact, Peter now struggles to keep up with her.

I was becoming very positive about treating more women and approached the hospital management. An immediate problem had cropped up. Because both testosterone and tadalafil were "unlicensed" for women, the pharmacy and the GPs were refusing to continue prescriptions. I had been issuing private prescriptions, as I was aware of this issue, but it was pointed out that hospital policy did not allow the issuing of private prescriptions, so this had to stop. I have managed to transfer a few patients into the private sector to maintain the treatment.

On reviewing my medical insurance, the following year, I discovered that my premium had been *doubled* as I prescribed *off-label* medication! This became a real problem when I went part-time but was actually getting lots of referrals from other doctors for tricky cases that required innovative interventions, often with off-label medication. It was actually reaching the stage where NHS income barely covered my medical insurance and professional society fees. Any litigation in relation to the prescription of off-label medication potentially risked financial ruin!

More prescribing issues were emerging. The NHS was still restricting men to one tablet per week of the drug with the lowest acquisition cost, pharmacist jargon for "cheapest". This was based on a UK lifestyle study from the 70s, which revealed that married couples over 50 had sex once per week. They included the 50% who would have ED, which meant that those who could have sex did it twice per week. They applied this rule to all and made no allowance for younger, single, gay, or bisexual people. In 1998 they also introduced a restriction that only men with diabetes, Parkinson's disease, and a few other rare conditions could get medication on the NHS. The rest had to pay inflated private charges irrespective of age or financial means. They also introduced a category of "single gene neurological disease", which was a mystery to all of us. The only disease of this type I knew was red/green colour blindness, so curiously I introduced sight testing in the ED clinic. The most bizarre rule was that men suffering "severe distress" could be treated on the NHS, but this totally new disorder could only be diagnosed by a consultant in a hospital, and all drugs must be prescribed (indefinitely) by the hospital. When we operated in line with these guidelines, the Primary Care Trusts would impose fines on the hospital for failing to discharge patients within a reasonable period. Any sane person would see these rules as complete "bonkers", but we have been stuck with these for 22 years. Although these rules were later relaxed to allow cheap generic prescribing to all comers, they were left in place for the other medications.

I mention this as on 5th April 2009, my first four referrals of the day included a line from the GP, "I think that his problem is causing him severe distress". My comprehensive test for this was to say, "Mr Donger, do you think your problem causes you severe distress?" Almost always, they had been primed to answer, "My God, yes, doctor, every minute of the day". The diagnosis was now clear, and this man would now be visiting the hospital pharmacy (at huge additional cost) indefinitely. Occasionally some patients had not been primed properly and answered, "I'm not happy, but severely distressed... probably not". "In that case, Mr Pike, here is a private prescription that will cost around £60 per month". Invariably the response was, "You know, doctor, on second thought, I am severely distressed, and the wife, she was so distressed, she was in tears when I left the house today". At this point, I would tear up the private one and issue an NHS script.

If the reader thinks all this is rather strange, the last of these patients was actually referred by myself from my own practice. Yes, I saw patients in my own practice and wrote a referral letter to myself. Six weeks later, I would greet them at the hospital and confirm that I totally agreed with their GP (me) that they were suffering from severe distress and provide an NHS prescription so that they could make the regular 30-mile round trip to pick up their tablets from the hospital, indefinitely. I would then dictate a letter to myself "Dear Doctor Hackett, Thank you for your excellent referral letter; I totally agree with your diagnosis..." Occasionally I commented that I was so impressed with the standard of the referral that I suspected that I must have had additional training!" My secretary expressed concern when she read some of these letters, strongly suggesting that I might be losing the plot.

Restoring a couple's sex life can be the most rewarding thing a doctor can do. As a GP, I remembered many diagnostic successes, but no matter how well you controlled blood pressure, cholesterol, or diabetes, this was rarely appreciated. In contrast, restoring a man's erections makes him a friend for life. Not only that, but his wife would hug you if she saw you in the street. Never have I had a wife shake my hand and say, "Lowering my husband's cholesterol has changed our lives".

Unfortunately, some cases are not straightforward, as in the case of Aaron Schmuck, 28 and unemployed on long-term benefits. Taking a full sexual history is vital in all patients. Aaron had never had a sexual partner but was complaining of ED based on considerable masturbatory experience. Without being cruel, it was difficult to imagine that he was likely to have much success as there was little that I could see that would make him attractive to women. Five visits in, the daily tadalafil (under severe distress regulations) was giving him morning erections, and he was successfully masturbating several times per week with the use of some heavy pornography. I decided to have an open conversation with him as to what more he expected from me. It was clear that he had hoped that his morning erections would attract women from near and far, but tactfully, I tried to explain that this was not going to happen unless he was proactive. Clearly, as an NHS consultant, I cannot arrange dating or escort services or even provide a number that I might have seen in a local telephone box (if you can find one). I hoped that he might have gotten the message, but he left, stating that he would still like to see me again. Reluctantly I relented. Three months later, Aaron was back and still seeing success with regular masturbation. My advice had been partially successful as he had been visiting a local prostitute on three occasions and felt that there was some form of connection. He was seeking my advice as to whether I thought he should ask her out on a date. Of course, his idea was likely to be a complete disaster, but I did not want to destroy all his hopes at one foul swoop, so I answered, "Well, it certainly worked for Richard Gere". Strangely, I did not see Aaron again. I would like to think that he carried his "Julia Roberts" off into the sunset.

As the clinic and GP work had been demanding, I was looking forward to teaching at a GP course in the West Country and an overnight stay with the Bollingers the night before. Dr B was always the most generous host, fine chef, and sommelier. We arrived at their country estate after the long drive and were greeted at the gate by Hector, their exuberant but friendly schnauzer. Mrs B greeted us, and we adjourned to the lounge for a drink as Dr B was delayed at work. As the conversation was flowing, Hector climbed onto my head from over the back of the sofa. I was used to boisterous dogs at home, so I saw this as a sign of affection. By now, Hector's teeth were just by my left ear, and the familiar whiff of canine halitosis was evident. I noted that Mrs B was stroking Hector's testicles fondly. "Geoff, would you just mind checking Hector's left testicle," asked Mrs B. I spluttered on my gin and tonic, catching site of Hector's glistening fangs in close proximity to my left cheek. I contemplated how he might react to a strange hand exerting pressure on his left epididymis. I politely declined, reminding her that whilst vets can treat humans, strictly speaking, physicians should not treat dogs. Conversation continued until we noted that Hector was repeatedly scratching at his ears. I made the big mistake of asking if he was OK. Jan (Mrs B) informed me that the Vet had diagnosed eczema, but after 3 visits and 3 different creams, it was no better and had cost a fortune. She showed me the tubes of cream, and it was pretty mild stuff. Sally then interrupted, "One of our Labradors had the same problem, and Geoff prescribed a strong cream for me on prescription, and it worked a treat. This was a big mistake, as 5 minutes later, I had issued a private prescription for Mrs B. When Dr B arrived home, we enjoyed a massive fillet of beef on the BBQ and several fine bottles of Claret and retired to bed rather late. As with most meetings after a night with Dr B, I was just about coherent by 11am, the following day, a pity as my talk had been at 9:30am. A week later, I decided to ring and thank them for outstanding hospitality and politely enquired how Hector was getting on. "Well," answered Jan, " I took the prescription to the chemist as you suggested, and the pharmacist came out and said *the usual instructions are that, if you are using this on the nose, put a small knob on a cotton wool bud and gently apply in each nostril. For the ear, put a small knob on the little finger and gently insert it into the canal"*. "Actually, I'm putting in on my schnauzer", answered Mrs B. The Pharmacist replied, "*In that case, I would recommend loose-fitting underwear and no sexual activity for at least 48 hours"*.

In recent years, the clinics were full of health-conscious IT

"Hector seems to have a lump on his left testicle, would you mind just checking it while you're here?"

"consultants" who arrived with spreadsheets of symptoms and blood results on their iPads. They approached problems in their sex life in the same way as they approached software issues, failing to realise that, where women are involved, no app had ever been devised to solve such problems.

154

Adam Rutter, 38, was a fitness fanatic and ran his own website design company. *He had suffered anxiety problems, and multiple relationships had failed. He refused to believe that somebody running 100 miles a week could possibly develop ED. At his last visit, I had commenced him on tadalafil 5mg daily, and within a week, he had noticed firm morning erections and multiple spontaneous ones during the day, especially when working with attractive girls. His first question was, "Is it dangerous to go running when I have such a strong erection?" "Only if you run the 4x 100m relay". I replied. "No, more of a middle-distance man myself", he answered. Yet another piece of fine satire had missed the mark.*

"I knew I shouldn't have taken a second Viagra this morning."

The first patient in my clinic on 25th June 2012 was Roger Shakeshaft, who was 34 and complaining of a sudden loss of libido. I asked about his wife and family, and he proudly announced that he and his wife Tracey had six children aged 3,4,5,6,7 and 8. One might be tempted to think that a loss of libido might be long overdue. I was intrigued as to how he managed to afford six children in six years and inquired as to his occupation. "I'm a precision grinder", he replied.

In July 2012, a hospital doctor popped into my clinic to ask for a box of Viagra as it was his mate Steve's 40th birthday soon, and he was planning a cunning stunt. He planned to leave a box of Viagra, with two tablets missing, in his bedside cabinet, in anticipation that his wife, Jane, would find it. I declined to cooperate and tried to persuade him that this was a bad idea. He ignored my advice and got hold of the tablets elsewhere. Things did not work out well. Jane found the tablets and confronted Steve, who denied ever using Viagra, even when Jane challenged him with her discovery. What the pranksters did not realise was that Steve and Jane had not had sex for a long time, and Jane was highly suspicious that Steve was having affairs, no matter how many times he pleaded his innocence. Jane proceeded to become obsessional and constantly checked his phone and email accounts. Steve asked the prankster to tell Jane about the stunt, but this was the final straw. Jane thought that Steve had sunk so low as to persuade a friend to lie to get him out of trouble. Steve came home to find his clothes shredded and his suitcase by the door. A salutary warning for anybody prone to such cunning stunts. Luckily, having been kicked out of the house, Steve was able to move in with his girlfriend.

In 2013, I was approached by the University of Bedfordshire with the offer of a Professorial post in the Department of Diabetes in Older People. There was actually a very small salary which was a pleasant surprise. The appointment was based on my research and publications around testosterone and diabetes. I soon realised that the real reason for this offer was my ability to potentially generate funds from outside sources. It was no accident that I had recently secured the promise of a substantial grant. From my point of view, it was far wiser for the University to administer the grant, even if they took 20% for themselves. Little did I suspect that the accounting processes of the university were unusual. They were spending my budget on salaries for other projects in the hope of generating future income. This effectively left nothing in the pot when vital payments were needed for my research. The Head of the Department concerned moved his unit to another university shortly afterwards, and my position was terminated.

In 2014, a case demonstrated the difficulty of dealing with myths and misconceptions. Alan Tickle, 72, and his wife Tess, 73, attended with ED, that had not responded to his GPs prescription for sildenafil. The letter stated that their daughter was the assistant manager of the hospital's Patient Advice and Liaison Department (PALS). Alan seemed fit, apart from some long-standing back pain treated with co-codamol intermittently for five years. My routine questionnaires suggested that Alan had symptoms of an enlarged prostate and possible low testosterone. His GP had checked his testosterone which was slightly low, and I rechecked it and found it lower still. A rectal examination was normal. I ordered a PSA (prostate) test as I would for all men of his age with low testosterone or prostate symptoms. I suggested that the GP commence some testosterone gel and daily tadalafil 5mg daily. I told them that the tablets would only work if his testosterone was treated at the same time, explaining that the low testosterone was likely to be related to all the painkillers he had taken. The couple told me that an active sex life was a high priority for them both. I returned from holiday three weeks later and found that his PSA was slightly increased at 4.5 ng/ml, and this was confirmed on repeat testing. Alan had only just received the prescription from the GP and used it twice. I advised that he stopped the gel and referred him to a colleague, who did a prostate biopsy which confirmed cancer confined to the prostate. He was successfully treated by a radical prostatectomy. Despite all the trauma, Alan and Tess seemed delighted that I had picked this up early and that he was effectively "cured" of his cancer, although he now had severe ED after the operation.

I was shocked when a letter of complaint arrived from the daughter, suggesting that I had prescribed testosterone inappropriately and that the treatment (two doses only) led to prostate cancer. The myth is that testosterone therapy causes prostate cancer when all the evidence, as in this case, is that low testosterone is associated with an increased risk of more aggressive cancers. Because of her important position in the trust, this complaint was treated seriously. Not only were her parents not informed prior to the complaint being made, but the daughter was totally unaware of the couple's request to treat the ED as a very important issue. Many daughters do not even consider the remote possibilities that parents in their 70s might still be having sex. The daughter had totally missed the point that prostate cancer develops over many years and his raised PSA tests predated testosterone therapy. The reality was that, had this couple not had the ED investigated with a testosterone level, the PSA would not have been done, and the prostate cancer may well have been diagnosed much later. Six months later, Alan went on testosterone therapy, which enhanced the effect of the tadalafil, and they resumed an active sex life. Alan and Tess advised their daughter to withdraw the complaint.

One particularly sad case I remember very well involved a retired army captain, Drew Peacock, aged 72. Drew had sadly lost his first wife, Flo, five years earlier. He had given up any hope of ever meeting

158

another partner but had recently met Miriam on a mature dating site.
He thought that there was little future for a long-term relationship, as
she lived in rural Somerset and he lived in Erdington. Miriam was 64,
very attractive and Drew clearly felt that he was "punching above his
weight". He was aware that little had been rustling "down below" for
some time. He had bought some Viagra over the internet and achieved
moderate success. The problem was that Miriam was expecting a
repeat performance the following morning, and he was unable to
oblige. She had also made pointed comments as to how much she
disapproved of older men who needed "performance enhancement".
He felt that his lack morning of morning tumescence was potentially
threatening the relationship. In short, he was desperate. I quickly
spotted that he was on a morning tablet to help with his "prostate
symptoms". I suggested that if we changed him to daily tadalafil, then
this would be equally good for his prostate and restore his erections
spontaneously. I confirmed that he was suffering from "severe
distress" and issued regular prescriptions from the hospital
pharmacy. He returned six weeks later with a broad smile on his face.
Not only was he regularly managing a regular morning "repechage",
but Miriam had commented that "she was concerned that he might
have been taking Viagra, but now she knew he did not". All she knew
was that the hospital specialist had changed his daily prostate tablet
to a better one, and his "waterworks" were much improved. There
was now no need to confess to anything, as his bedroom prowess was
merely a welcome "side-effect of his prostate tablet. He then delivered
the bombshell that he was selling his house, moving down to Devon,
and he and Miriam were getting married. I shook his hand and left
the clinic that day, thinking that I had the best job in the world.
Imagine my surprise when nine months later, Drew appeared in my
clinic. He was now back in Erdington and living with his daughter.

He told me his sad story. He and Miriam got married and had a wonderful honeymoon in St Lucia. He had sold his flat and moved into Miriam's bungalow in Devon. About six weeks later, he registered with the local GP for a new patient appointment and requested his prostate tablets. The GP had refused to prescribe them after checking with the CCG pharmacist and had put him back on his old tablets. When Miriam found out the reason for the immediate decline in his performance, she told him that she felt "betrayed". The relationship had quickly deteriorated, and he felt that he had no choice but to move out and was now back with his daughter. Of course, I put him back on the daily tadalafil and can only hope that he managed to find happiness again.

In July 2015, Peter Wood, 58, a past local major, attended the clinic, having previously been under the care of a urology colleague who had recently retired. Peter had severe ED and had failed with all medical treatments. Having been on the waiting list for a penile implant for two years due to a lack of funding from his CCG, he was expecting more bad news. The week before, I had been discussing the lack of local funding with a good friend and senior consultant at a London Teaching hospital. He informed me that they had a special training budget and they were keen for more cases. I told Peter the good news. He was seen on the following Saturday in London, and the operation took place a week later. He and his wife, Kate, have been delighted with the results. We often use them as a teaching case at meetings.

In the last few years, more funding for trans patients requesting full gender reassignment has been made available as this has been a hot political issue. A penile implant is the only solution for a full female-to-male transition.

Not all cases have worked out as well as Peter, the previous case. George Nobbs was 79 and married to Norah for over 50 years. All medical treatments had failed, but they were desperate for a solution. As George had been treated with radiotherapy for prostate cancer and also had diabetes, my colleague in London was reluctant to use an inflatable implant. George was offered a malleable implant that works like a "bendy toy" that is bent upwards for sex and then downwards for the remainder of the time. The procedure was performed as a day case under local anaesthetic, and all seemed to be going well. George and Norah seemed very pleased. Unfortunately, one morning he forgot to tuck it away after some morning activity, as he was in a hurry to drop his grandchildren at school. The bulge was noted by some of the mothers at the school, and a complaint went to the headmaster. Subsequently, a letter was sent to Norah's daughter. George and Norah were absolutely distraught.

Body image problems are an increasing problem, especially concerning penile length. In the last 25 years, I have yet to hear a man, as he gets undressed by the couch on a cold day, state, "I'm afraid it's rather large". Despite showing them a mould of a "normal" flaccid penis at 4.59-inch and 3.66-inch girth, these men are never convinced. The usual problem is that the length is completely normal but just concealed in fat. The solution is not what they want to hear. The usual reason for presentation is a new partner, who might have had a well-endowed former lover. One wrong expression or a comment such as "Is that it?" is enough to cause a complex for life. I often point out to the man that there must be a reason why the other chap is an ex-partner whilst he is the current partner. The other culprit, contributing to body image problems, is the well-hung donkey in a packed locker room who insists on going through his 10-minute arse-towelling ritual at every opportunity.

On 25th January 2017, Will Ankers, a 58-year-old bank manager wearing a 3-piece-suit, had presented with ED. He was accompanied by his wife, Ruth. A final-year medical student was sitting in on the consultation. Hugh disappeared behind the curtain and undressed. I became aware of some strange "clunking" noises as he removed his trousers. On pulling back the curtain, I was not only presented with a collection of full-body tattoos and nipple piercing but a set of five Nobrium rings running the length of his penis and connected by a long silver chain. I glanced across at Ruth, who was trying to distance herself from the embarrassing situation. The student and I managed to keep a straight face, and we decided to administer an injection into his penis as tablets had previously failed. This involved removal of the five rings, all of which pierced the penis through separate holes. He had a good result, and he left cock-a-hoop, although Ruth seemed less certain.

These cases made me realise that I needed to keep up to date with body image trends by watching all three series of "Naked Attraction". Luckily, Sally records this on series link for me, so I never miss an episode. I recommend this programme as essential viewing to anybody with body image concerns. Couples of all sexual orientations choose would-be partners on naked appearance alone. I now know how to appreciate a "nice tidy growler" when I see one. A more recent must-watch programme, "Naked Beach", invites vulnerable people with body image issues to live on a Greek Island with naked people of all shapes and sizes. The objective is that they will strip off in public on Naked Beach after seven days.

On 6th March 2008, a young man of 29, Paul Gherkin, presented in my clinic. He complained to his GP about ED, loss of libido, tiredness, and poor sleep. The GP prescribed four sildenafil which *were ineffective. Paul did not have a girlfriend. The GP diagnosed depression and prescribed two different antidepressants that were ineffective. Very quickly, we picked up that he had been treated for testicular cancer aged 16, his left testicle was removed, and he was treated with chemotherapy. We found his testosterone was very low at 4 nmol/l. The normal level should be at least 12 nmol/l. He responded very well to testosterone gel plus low-dose clomiphene tablets to preserve fertility. It was a pity that there was a lack of continuity in care, as low testosterone was an inevitable consequence of his earlier cancer therapy. The treatment for depression was inappropriate, and he effectively lost what should have been the best ten years of his life. Unfortunately, symptoms of low testosterone are frequently misdiagnosed as depression and treated inappropriately with medications that have severe adverse effects on sexual function. The tragedy of cases like this is that we can never give those men back the years that they have lost.*

Over the years, I have seen many doctors and health care professionals who have self-referred to me, as they felt too embarrassed to go through conventional channels. I wrote up ten of these cases, entitled "a tale of 19 testes", in a medical journal. In case you are wondering, one of the doctors had only one testicle. I now present a few of these cases to demonstrate how sexual problems impact the quality of life, even for doctors!

Mahmood was a 38-year-old registrar in diabetes who attended my clinic as part of his training. After sitting in on cases, I noted that he was nodding off, which is not a common experience during a dynamic session with the Tsar! On questioning, he reported the symptoms of tiredness, poor concentration, reduction in physical strength, ED, loss of libido and relationship stress were being reported by many men subsequently diagnosed and treated for Testosterone Deficiency Syndrome. He arranged for a total testosterone (TT) level to be taken, which was 7.1nmol/l, and was pre-diabetic. He had a strong family history of T2DM. After two years on long-acting testosterone undecanoate (TU), his symptoms had resolved, he had lost weight, reduced his waist circumference by 6cm, and his work performance improved, with promotion and a research award at an international meeting. He subsequently took up a consultant post in India, where he is one of the few specialists treating men with low testosterone.

Alan was a 60-year-old GP with well-controlled diabetes who attended a former colleague's practice. He had never been asked about or mentioned ED in more than six years. He felt that since retirement, he was ageing prematurely. Diagnosis was confirmed with levels of 8.4 and 9nmol/l, and he commenced long-acting testosterone injections, which he initially funded privately, but after several months he persuaded his GP to issue prescriptions. On contacting him two years later, he confirmed that he was fit and volunteered spontaneously that he was peeing much better. He described his testosterone replacement therapy (TRT) as 'life-changing". The daily tadalafil also improved his bothersome prostate symptoms as well as his ED. He had been able to reduce many of his diabetes medicines. He was subsequently able to return to work part-time. Recently I presented his case at a GP meeting to demonstrate the point that Alan managed to secure a prescription that greatly improved his health because he was an intelligent, articulate healthcare professional. The average patient was highly unlikely to have such success.

George was a 59-year-old doctor from Africa visiting on holiday and attending a teaching day on men's health. He suffered from T2DM, hypertension and chronic kidney disease and was investigated for anaemia in Africa with upper and lower endoscopy plus bone marrow biopsy, with negative findings. We found that his testosterone was low, but no other doctor had performed a blood test. He had attended with his 43-year-old wife, Jasmine, and it was clear that they had stopped sex more than five years ago because of his ED. This had caused her much distress. After commencing testosterone therapy (he obtained supplies himself), he contacted me to say that his anaemia had corrected within three months, he had lost weight and reduced his insulin and that sex, aided by oral medication, was now possible.

Raman was a 46-year-old neurologist with mild ED but reduced enjoyment of life and his sex life in particular. He felt that his marriage was at risk, and his wife was constantly accusing him of having affairs (they have three small children). He tried sildenafil and tadalafil, but both caused headaches, even at small doses, with no improvement. He self-referred to my clinic, and we found that his testosterone levels were marginally low. A six-month trial of testosterone gel was suggested based on his symptoms. He noted improved morning erections and spontaneous sexual activity returned with no need for ED medication. His follow-up email stated that he was certain that TRT had saved his marriage.

Rashid was a 58-year-old consultant psychiatrist with T2DM who was putting on weight and becoming tired, lethargic, and depressed. He consulted a fellow psychiatrist, who prescribed several antidepressants with moderate effect, and eventually advised retirement on health grounds. Only at this stage did he mention low libido and ED to his GP, despite suffering for five years, as the GP was a 'good friend'. He was referred as an NHS patient and found to have a testosterone level of 5.8nmol/l. Response to testosterone therapy was dramatic, with 8kg weight loss, 5cm from his waist. Sexual function was restored with the help of daily tadalafil. He now had no regular job but returned to locum work as he felt "sharper than for several years". His major regret was that, over his psychiatric career, he must have missed several patients complaining of similar symptoms but who had only been treated as suffering from depression.

Ajaz was a clinical research scientist, aged 46, with well-controlled T2DM, body mass index of 23.2, and long-term epilepsy controlled with medication. He went to his GP with low libido, tiredness, profound fatigue, and ED unresponsive to sildenafil. He was a regular long-distance swimmer and was forced to give this up. His GP took two testosterone levels which were very low, at 5.4 and 7.2nmol/l. He was referred to an eminent professor of endocrinology in Birmingham. The letter he received from the professor stated, 'we see many diabetics like this'; 'we suggest lifestyle modification through diet and exercise'. He was appalled, feeling that his sexual problems were ignored. He commented that the professor looked as though he was usually at the front of the queue for the buffet. Ajaz subsequently arranged a self-referral to the Tsar, having read one of my papers. After two years of long-acting testosterone injections, his sex life was far better than before (now three times per week), with improved orgasm and ejaculation. It required considerable pressure on his GP to agree to prescriptions for testosterone and tadalafil. He was back to swimming, feeling much fitter and is working to a higher standard. His diabetes was even better controlled. He had intermittently suffered from acne on his back and chest, which required treatment while on testosterone therapy, but he saw this as

166

a small price to pay. During the COVID-19 lockdown, when he was unable to swim, he recently ran his personal best for a half marathon.

David was a 64-year-old retired GP with T2DM whose wife, a sex therapist, had seen me speak at a meeting. Not surprisingly, one NHS tablet of sildenafil did not satisfy their requirements, and the headaches were the final straw. He had recently been diagnosed with severe neuropathy with painful, tingling feet, keeping him awake at night. As suspected, his testosterone was very low, and the combination of daily tadalafil 5mg and testosterone gel not only solved his erection problems, it cured his neuropathy and sorted out his prostate problems meaning that he could stop the prostate tablets from the urologist that prevented ejaculation. He remained very well for six years until he returned with a loss of strength in his erections and cramps in his legs. The urologist had recently added finasteride for his prostate, and this had reduced his libido. He was now on an ACE inhibitor and a beta-blocker for blood pressure. I suggested that increasing the tadalafil to 10mg a day would mean that he could stop the finasteride. I also suggested a switch of beta-blocker to nebivolol, as this is the only one that improves erections as the others make them worse. Unfortunately, top cardiologists are too busy to bother about erections unless prompted. Within 2-3 weeks, his erections were back, the prostate was behaving, and the cramps in his legs were gone. A junior partner in the practice told him that he could not have the tadalafil 10mg daily, as, according to the practice pharmacist, this dose should only be taken within 36 hours of anticipated sexual activity. David replied that he always anticipated sex within the next 36 hours and that it was only the tablets that the practice now prescribed that seemed to prevent him from getting it. The young partner buckled under the pressure and handed him the prescription. I reliably informed David that, in my experience, men who are not anticipating some form of sexual activity in the next 36 hours are usually in need of resuscitation. Unfortunately, a non-medical patient would not have achieved the desired result from that particular GP. I spoke to David recently. He is now 75 and remains very well, having survived COVID-19 without needing hospitalisation. He now checks with me before accepting any new medications.

Reflecting on these cases, I wondered about the huge benefit for the patients of these doctors as a result of restoring their physicians to full function in their work. Clearly, if diagnosing and treating doctors with low testosterone results in such clear benefits for all their patients, we should appreciate that many of our patients have equally important roles in society.

On 5th April 2018, Peter Wang, 24, was seen by my colleague Dr Cole, with some very strange results with very low testosterone levels and no clear cause. I was reduced to saying, "The only possible explanation for these results would be extensive use of anabolic steroids over many years. I know that Dr Cole asked about this but is it possible that you might have forgotten something?" Only after a long pause did he admit to many years of injecting anabolic steroids. I concluded that the job is hard enough without the patients making it totally impossible by withholding crucial information. Peter was living in fear that we would be judgemental and refuse to treat him. He was petrified that the truth would get back to his GP and, ultimately, his family.

By February 2019, I thought that I had heard every name that a man could possibly give to his penis when Ernest and Alice Slack, both in their 70s, appeared, complaining of problems with "Big Ben". On examination, I was puzzled as to how they arrived at this name, as "Big Ben" had clearly seen better (and bigger) days. I summoned up the courage to ask how they had decided on the name for him. "Well," replied Alice, "He always has 2 hands on him, he's only cleaned properly every 15 years, and he hasn't seen any ding-dong since 2017".

By March 2019, I had over 1200 men attending the pharmacy on daily tadalafil 5mg under severe distress regulations and was the leading prescriber in the country, a title I saw as a badge of honour. Dr Milledge's old practice in Coleshill was the highest prescribing General Practice in the country. In every clinic, I would see men for 6 monthly follow-ups as required by pharmacy regulations. All these men had failed with the traditional method of taking Viagra 1 hour before sex and were now essentially "cured" by taking daily medication. Most were having sex 3-4 times per week with total spontaneity. Many attended with their partner, and the consultation went something like this:

"How are the tablets going?"

"Great."

"Any new medical problems?"

"No."

"Any other questions?"

"Can I have more tablets, please?" I would hand him the prescription; his partner would hug me, and off they would go to the pharmacy. There can be few more satisfying experiences for a doctor than 2 people totally satisfied with the results from 1 tablet per day.

Unfortunately, the Clinical Commissioning Groups did not see things this way. I was effectively being told that I must stop treatment that was highly effective and switch patients back to regimes that had failed repeatedly. This was the first time in my life that repeating a cycle of failure had been suggested to me as "best practice". Many of these patients had been surgically treated for prostate cancer. Getting sexual function back in these men can be extremely challenging. All my efforts and protests that this approach was not ethical were ignored. The response from senior hospital managers was, "This is hardly a matter of life and death". Another pharmacy advisor suggested that I might be getting too involved with my patients and needed to "Chill out". More about that in the final chapter, "Your doctor won't see you now".

The regulations in relation to TRT were even more chaotic. The hospital catchment area included five different clinical commissioning groups (CCG), all with different prescribing guidelines. These ranged from full cooperation with GPs taking overprescribing to no prescribing allowed at all. The rest included different variations in "shared care protocols" as to what prescribing was allowed. One CCG insisted that the hospital must administer all medication until the patient was on a stabilised dose. This essentially meant that I would have to be at each patient's house as they rose and showered in the morning, ready to enter the bathroom to apply four pumps of gel to his inner thighs before returning to my normal job. When I tried to explain this to a community pharmacist, her response was that this was not her problem. To make it worse, it was the postcode of the GP practice and not the patient that decided which set of regulations prevailed. If we applied the regulations from one CCG of taking on all the prescribing duties, we would then be hit with a fine for failing to discharge the patient according to a protocol agreed upon elsewhere.

Barely a week would go by with a letter arriving from a CCG threatening some sort of action against me for breaching one or other protocol. Invariably the patient was caught in the middle of this pantomime, totally unable to get reliable access to the therapy that they needed. I concluded that being classified by the NHS as a "rogue prescriber" is not far short of a double conviction for axe murder!

At this time, the trust had been shattered by the repercussions of the Ian Patterson case, as most of his work was carried out at Good Hope and Heartlands Hospitals. Ian Patterson was the "Rogue Breast Surgeon", jailed for 20 years for 17 counts of wounding with intent in May 2017. This had led to a culture of "mistrust", and I felt that the annual appraisal at the hospital had become more of an interrogation process rather than constructive career development. As I was prescribing a number of costly medications "off label" and for perceived "recreational purposes", I felt vulnerable and under such intense scrutiny. It had become virtually impossible to deliver a progressive service under these circumstances.

In 2017, my excellent clinical assistant, Dr Nigel Cole, had to retire due to a severe health problem, and management decided that I could manage without the need for a replacement.

A final straw was a letter from one GP practice who picked up a comment that I made when a retired partner and good friend had returned to part-time practice. As he had attended many of our educational meetings, I wrote in a letter that it was great to have a "Men's Health Champion" back. This triggered a complaint to hospital management from the practice senior partner that I was being "unprofessional" for inferring that the other doctors in the practice were not interested in men's health!

Since my departure from the NHS, I have been unable to escape the workload, as barely a day goes by without a desperate patient getting hold of my home phone number to seek help. It is very difficult to tell them that it is now inappropriate for me to be advising them.

COVID-19 lockdown has been detrimental to sexual relationships. I would use the following three cases as examples:

Stanley, 75, had been widowed in 2018, but in February 2020 had met a new lady friend but was seeing no sign of erection. He suffered from an enlarged prostate, treated with surgery. He also had moderate chronic kidney failure. A recent scan of his aorta had demonstrated a small aneurysm, but no action was required. His GP suggested that tablets might help his erection, was wanted a specialist appointment to check if it was safe. Due to COVID-19, all routine appointments had been cancelled, and with ED being an example of the "most routine", he waited from March to June to find that waiting times were now over 26 weeks. This effectively means that Stanley would have to wait nine months for a simple assessment as to whether a tablet was safe. He would spend this time in solo isolation, and it is highly unlikely that the new relationship would survive this time. Stanley has a limited life expectancy, and he was being deprived of the possibility of developing a relationship that would be potentially life-changing for two lonely people.

Patrick was a 76-year-old man with diabetes, widowed for five years. After a lot (or number) of investigations, I eventually sorted out his ED and loss of desire with a 3-monthly testosterone injection and daily tadalafil. He met Rose in late 2019, and they moved in together in early 2020. Due to COVID-19, his GP practice stopped all non-urgent treatment which included testosterone injections. As a result, his low sexual desire, tiredness, and low mood returned, and his tadalafil ceased to work for his erections. Unable to see his GP, as only "urgent" cases were being seen, and with the cancellation of his annual hospital follow-up, he stopped daily tadalafil altogether. His change in mood and frustration with sexual failure was too much for Rose, who moved back into her own flat. Both Patrick and Rose remain in isolation.

Stephen, 28, was a very handsome young man with an excellent physique who developed ED and a complete lack of sexual desire after he was treated for six months with Roaccutane, a drug used for severe acne. He was treated with multiple antidepressants for 2-3 years until he found his way to me, having read a paper I had written on the side effects of these drugs. He had attempted suicide twice. After developing a complex regime of hormone manipulation, he wrote me a Christmas card in 2019, telling me that "I had changed his life" and that, for the first time in five years, he felt motivated to meet girls and that a new relationship showed promise. In early June 2020, he informed me that the effect of the lockdown and enforced separation had caused the relationship to fail. He had been unable to get his medications from the practice and admitted to feeling some suicidal thoughts. A GP on telephone consultation had put him on an anti-depressant, meaning that we were repeating the cycle of the previous failure.

The obsession with "R" numbers and COVID-19 death statistics, to the exclusion of all other health-related outcomes, will have considerable long-term implications, even beyond the cancer delays that are already being highlighted. Of course, as administrators frequently told me, "sex is hardly a matter of life and death". In the famous words of Bill Shankly, in relation to football, "It is far more important than that!"

In 2018, colleagues felt that my work merited a current Professorial post rather than being "emeritus", a convenient term for a "has been". I duly attended an interview with the Dean of Aston University Medical School, with the exciting prospect of teaching at the new medical school opening shortly. Perhaps it was time for medical students to be taught something about sex by the Tsar? The interview went well, and the Dean seemed to be well in tune with my research and offered me the post, with teaching duties commencing when the first students arrived in September. He put me in touch with some of his research team, and we began working on a project involving mice treated with tadalafil to assess changes in body fat, but unfortunately, research funding was not granted. Unfortunately, the impact of the pandemic has been a disaster for such new initiatives.

Recently I heard from Aston University, and my position as the professor has now been ratified, and the Tsar will hopefully be able to pass his experience on to future doctors.

CHAPTER 10

A Drug

of Limited Clinical Value!!!

Right at the start of this chapter, we need to get rid of your preconceived views about "the little blue pill" that you take before sex on a Saturday night after Match of the Day. The reader needs to realise that if you have lost your morning erections, or are unable to manage an erection during sex, then you have a medical problem affecting your blood vessels 24/7, and this needs to be addressed as an important medical condition associated with increased risk of heart attack within the next 2-5 years. The solution is NOT with a quick cut price 4-pack from the internet. Thankfully qualified pharmacists are aware of this strong link between ED and cardiac risk and will direct men to the appropriate healthcare professional when they wander into a pharmacy with that "lost look".

The Viagra (sildenafil) Story

The little blue pill, Viagra, might just be the most famous drug in the world, and the scientists who developed it, quite rightly, won the Nobel prize for medicine. But Viagra (sildenafil) was developed to treat heart disease, but improved erections were noted as a "side-effect" because the men were refusing to return the pills during clinical trials. Pfizer, for obvious reasons, decided against having "yet another" heart drug, opting for the first pill to treat erectile dysfunction, and the rest is history. We should never lose sight of the fact that these drugs are still very good for the conditions that they were designed to treat.

The Cialis (tadalafil) story so far.

Time moves on, and the major problem with Viagra was that it only worked for four hours and so was only going to be useful for heart disease if taken three times daily. Four years later, Lilly released Cialis (tadalafil), which is active for 36 hours, as a smaller daily dose, which meant that couples' sex lives could be normalised, back to the way it was and with the return of spontaneous morning erections, which, as you will read at multiple points in this book, is a "barometer" of men's health, showing that multiple blood vessels are working 24/7. In comparative trials, 79% of men and 80% of partners preferred Cialis (tadalafil), which is effective for all that matters, as older couples are usually having sex for pleasure, and the preference of the partner is at least as important. I find it incredible that NICE can consider the response of two people as being of "limited clinical value"! There can be no other drug in Medicine where 80% of people get an improvement in their quality of life when the medication is actually taken by somebody else!

Taking a lower dose daily also reduces the side effects of headache and flushing, which were due to higher doses being taken previously in an attempt to force a rapid increase in blood flow within 30-60 minutes. I often liken this to drinking one pint of beer daily, compared with drinking seven pints in one evening.

More importantly, the NHS imposed a restriction of one tablet of sildenafil per week, meaning that none of the cardiac benefits would be seen in UK men, whereas taking one low dose of tadalafil per day would achieve these benefits. Remember that the scientists knew at the outset that these drugs were good for the heart, and this is exactly what has transpired.

A Dilemma for the NHS

In 1998, Viagra was £5 per tablet, but after 15 years, a drug patent ran out and "generic versions" sildenafil could be produced by multiple companies, so prices fell to around 5-10% of that price by 2013. Cialis was four years behind, becoming generic in 2017 as tadalafil, the name we should now use. The problem is that "Viagra" is the word that has become synonymous with this class of drug, just as we all go out to buy a "Hoover" and come back with a Dyson, showing our new "Hoover" to our friends. When Viagra was £5 per tablet, with 50% of men over 50 suffering from ED and lots of media hype, the NHS quite rightly saw impending financial doom for the NHS if all pensioners sought passionate sex several times per week, so they restricted NHS prescribing to once per week *for certain defined condition, most notably diabetes and prostate cancer*. In this way, they maintained the principle of *free healthcare at the point of access* while controlling costs. When daily Cialis came along four years later, they were presented with a real problem as the cost of 28 x 5 mg tablets was £55, and they had already defined "normal" sex for Brits as once per week, based on a "quasi" study they found from the early 80s, which, in reality, showed that couples without ED had sex twice per week, but by including men with ED in the calculation, the average came down to once per week. This is rather like including non-smokers in a calculation of the average number of cigarettes smoked. The additional problem was that daily Cialis was also licensed throughout Europe for enlarged prostate, a significant problem in around half the male population over 60, with considerable overlap with ED; hence Lilly seemed confident that they had the perfect drug for two common distressing symptoms in men. This left the NHS and NICE in a difficult position, as demand was likely to be high to treat both problems with one drug when there were already cheap drugs for enlarged prostate. As Lilly were aware that Cialis was no better than these old drugs for prostate but clearly likely to be the first choice by the men when they noted erections perking up, they felt that NICE was attempting to "stitch them up" by only assessing the prostate effect, so refused to co-operate. NICE were stunned by this, so placed a "drug of limited efficacy" classification on Cialis, which remains to this day, despite the price per month falling from £55 per month to less than £3 per month for generic tadalafil since 2017. In this time, prescription charges have risen to around £10 per item, meaning that patients get better value from a private, as opposed to an NHS prescription. Ten years since this fallout, UK men are still suffering from this dispute between NICE and Lilly. Many doctors feel that engaging in this discussion in some way breaches their terms of conditions in working with the NHS, when in reality, their greatest duty is to ensure that their patient has access to therapy that the doctor feels is in their best interest. Please remember, however, that I was once referred to as "the greatest patient advocate that he had ever seen, and this was NOT a compliment!"

The multiple benefits of daily tadalafil, a drug of "limited clinical value"

Men taking daily tadalafil have been consistently shown to increase their exercise time on a treadmill by 10-20% due to the dilating effect on coronary arteries. This should not surprise anybody as it was developed as a cardiac drug.

Three recent studies have shown very consistent cardiac benefits (see below). A 2016 UK study in nearly 6000 men with T2DM showed a 31% reduction in deaths over a 7.5-year period in men who took a PDE5 inhibitor (sildenafil or tadalafil). There were similar reductions in all non-fatal events. A 2017 Study from Sweden looked at 43,145 men after previous heart attacks and found a 38% reduction in mortality in men over just 3.3 years of taking a PDE5 inhibitor. They also found that the effect was dose-related and that men having a heart attack were 40% more likely to survive the heart attack if taking a PDE5 inhibitor. Our BLAST study involving 857 men with diabetes showed a 40% reduction in mortality in men taking PDE5 inhibitors. These studies showed that the benefits were greater the more doses were taken, and yet the NHS restricts UK men to one tablet per week. Remember that these are drugs of "limited clinical value"!

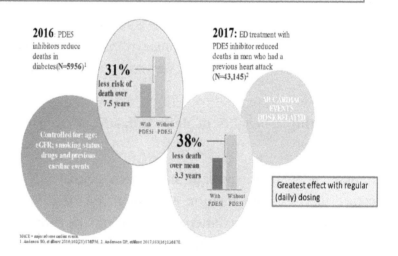

Erectile Dysfunction drugs reduce mortality in Heart Disease

2016: PDE5 inhibitors reduce deaths in diabetes(N=5956)[1]

31% less risk of death over 7.5 years

With Without
PDE5i PDE5i

Controlled for: age; eGFR; smoking status; drugs and previous cardiac events

2017: ED treatment with PDE5 inhibitor reduced deaths in men who had a previous heart attack (N=43,145)[2]

ALL CARDIAC EVENTS DOSE RELATED

38% less death over mean 3.3 years

With Without
PDE5i PDE5i

Greatest effect with regular (daily) dosing

MACE = major adverse cardiac events.
1. Anderson SG, et al Heart 2016;102(21)1750716. 2. Andersson DP, et Heart 2017;103(16)1264 70.

Blood flow to the lower limbs correspondingly improves, an important finding for smokers and men with diabetes who run into trouble with narrowing blood vessels to extremities. These drugs are effective in Raynaud's disease and patients with cold hands and feet in winter. Tadalafil increases blood flow to the kidneys and large muscles, where many of the problems of glucose metabolism and insulin resistance are seen. Trials show consistently that insulin sensitivity and hence diabetes improves, interestingly more so in women, and that the inflammation tests associated with heart disease also improve.

Recent studies have shown that tadalafil increases blood flow to the brain, improving tests of cognitive function and suggesting a possible preventive role for age-related dementia. They also improve mild to moderate depression. Cynics try to dismiss their findings as being secondary to "perky erections", but frankly "who cares" as long as the patient (and partner) feel better. In fact, I have never heard a wife say that she is feeling much better since her husband went on cholesterol tablets, usually the opposite, as men often moan about side effects.

A study from Sweden evaluated 4600 men at risk for colon cancer being followed up with a colonoscopy. Men taking an erectile dysfunction tablet had a 40% decreased rate of colon cancer. There are possible complicating issues with these studies, as, in many countries, men need to pay privately for ED drugs, meaning that potentially they might be of higher socio-economic status, potentially biasing the findings. Unfortunately, the perfect placebo-controlled studies required to answer these questions will never be done for cost, commercial and logistic reasons. Likewise, we will not see any of these benefits in UK men as long as they are restricted to one tablet per week by the NHS. There is preliminary evidence for a reduction in prostate cancer, which should not be surprising as increased blood flow is good for most organs.

Over the past 15 years, I have seen several men with advanced diabetic neuropathy, with reduced numbness in their feet and, not surprisingly, the penis, as virtually all of these men will have ED. It was only when I started treating them with daily tadalafil 5mg that we made three important discoveries that have been since verified by other studies:

- The first is a significant improvement in diabetic neuropathy, which is due to an improvement in blood supply to the small arteries,

- The second is an improvement in insulin sensitivity, meaning that diabetes medication can be reduced and,

- thirdly there is an improvement in testosterone levels due to a direct improvement in blood flow to the testes.

All these points can be demonstrated by the following patient, Randy Bentwick (not his real name, but you will see why it is appropriate):

Randy, 45, came to see me in 2010 with severe pain in his feet, preventing him from sleeping, walking, and working. He had recent erectile dysfunction for 3-4 months and had been diagnosed with T2DM two years earlier and was on tablets. He was moderately overweight. His father had severe diabetes and required an amputation. He had been treated with multiple painkillers, and antidepressants was brought by his wife as he was confused and unable to drive. I commenced him on daily tadalafil 5mg for erectile dysfunction and informed him that I had seen some patients who had seen a marked improvement in neuropathy in the lower limbs. Within four weeks, he had stopped all his painkillers and antidepressants, and the feelings in his feet had returned. He was back at work and had actually played golf for the first time in nine months. Over subsequent years, he has increased the dose to 10mg, as he had complained of curvature in the penis, frequently found in diabetes, and tadalafil has now become the first-line treatment for this condition through improving blood supply and tissue healing. I saw Randy last week, and 14 years on, he is pain-free, working full time and playing some of his best-ever golf. His initial testosterone level was borderline, but 14 years on, it is completely normal. His diabetes control is excellent, and his wife struggles to keep up with him in the bedroom. This is probably the most dramatic response I have seen.

A study in 2018 showed a 50% improvement in testosterone levels in 40 men treated with daily tadalafil for three months. A similar study showed improvement in diabetes control over 12 months with daily dosing. Unfortunately, whilst the NHS, apart from Durham, cling to outdated views that UK men only need sex once per week, then we are doomed.

Having convinced you that treating your penis with a daily tablet allows for the return of morning erections and the ability to have sex spontaneously when both of you are in the mood, the way it used to be, I would like to expand the argument. Several studies show that partners dislike orchestrated sex once per week, especially in new relationships when a man might be too embarrassed to mention that he takes medication. A brief patient story will demonstrate this point:

Mike was 50 and suffered with blood pressure. He travelled a lot with work and discovered that, in his absence, his wife had been having an affair, and they subsequently split up. For three years, he could not face another relationship but eventually met Debbie through internet dating. He was aware that he had poor erections, so he ordered tablets from the internet. When the big night came, he took one, and sex was pretty good, but the following morning Debbie made advances on him, and he had to pull away as he knew that he would fail. Her attitude changed immediately, and from that moment, he feared that the relationship might go no further. He consulted with the Tsar and was prescribed daily tadalafil. A week later, he stayed with Debbie for the weekend. They had sex the first night, and then Debbie initiated sex two further times over the weekend. After the second time, she said, "I really thought that you must be taking Viagra, but now I know you don't!" The relationship flourished from that day. He chose to tell Debbie that he took some tablets for his heart, which, of course, according to my early paragraphs, is completely true.

From now on, I will refer to Cialis as **tadalafil** 5mg as it is the only licensed treatment for daily use.

Tadalafil is also licensed to treat pulmonary hypertension, a very serious condition associated with raised pressure in the arteries of the lungs. This has led to it becoming a standard treatment for altitude sickness.

We need to move away from this concept of taking a "little blue pill" and then hoping that the mood is right in an hour, as in many cases, the moment of passion has passed, and one of the parties might be asleep. In these cases, sex can become dysfunctional to the detriment of the relationship.

I have seen several couples where George, the man of the house, has told his wife that "the weekly blue pill has been taken", usually followed by a "wink" (no typo here). Shortly after, the phone goes, and Doris gets some bad family news and is on the phone for some time. George interrupts to tell her that the pill might be "wearing off soon". Doris is not feeling remotely "sexy" by this stage and replies, "if you must, but get on with it and be quick!"

Just imagine if George had been taking daily tadalafil, he could have given her a cuddle and made a cup of tea, and Doris would probably appreciate her wonderful, thoughtful husband the next morning. It also becomes impractical for the woman to initiate sex when her husband takes the "blue pill", and her role can become passive, which might be a solution that the couple is seeking. Those of us who have been treating couples for years always consider what is best for two people and the importance of relationships. Unfortunately, too many "rules" come from bureaucrats who do not see or understand the patient.

I hope the reader will stop using Viagra as the generic name for these drugs in the way we talk of buying a Hoover, even though we have purchased Dysons for the last 10 years.

If tadalafil was developed to treat heart disease, it should surprise none of us that such a drug actually turns out to be very good for precisely that indication. Subsequently, it has been licensed to treat pulmonary hypertension, a very serious condition where the inflammation of the lungs causes an increase in pressure in the arteries, leading to high mortality rates within a few years. The effect of tadalafil is to relax the walls of arteries and reduce inflammation, allowing increased blood flow and tissue recovery. This process of pulmonary hypertension has been shown to be particularly important in patients who recover from COVID-19 infection. Studies currently suggest that many of these patients will be subject to fibrosis in their lungs, causing long-term breathing problems. This is likely to emerge as a major late consequence of the COVID-19 epidemic, and the early use of daily tadalafil as a preventive strategy could significantly reduce this chronic disease burden.

What about the Prevention of ED?

The vitamin and supplement market in the UK are worth £1bn per year, up by 13.8% over the last 5 years. Most vitamins are taken for their ant-oxidant properties, aimed at reducing oxidative stress and inflammation that damage the walls of arteries. The evidence for most of these effects suggests mild or tenuous benefits, whereas the findings in relation to daily tadalafil have been published in multiple placebo-controlled studies in peer review medical journals. This raises the question as to whether we should spend our hard-earned money on compounds that "might" work or a drug established to work based on evidence-based research. When we are ill, we choose to consult specialists using tried and tested therapies rather than visiting a herbalist, so why should it be different if we are trying to prevent serious disease? If we know that we have a 40% chance of ED by age 40 and 50% by age 50, isn't a problem that is common worth preventing? It might be a good idea to save your first marriage rather than wait for your second. Likewise, if we have a 30% chance of requiring surgery for enlarged prostate, is not the miserable prospect of waking several times at night worth preventing, as the benefits of daily tadalafil treatment for these conditions are beyond any dispute? The possibility of preserving kidney function and reducing heart attack and cancer risk makes a compelling argument for taking a small daily dose of daily tadalafil.

185

Daily tadalafil has been found to be highly effective in treating chronic prostatitis, a condition associated with persistent deep pain felt between the legs, often worse in passing urine and ejaculation. This has proved difficult to treat over the years. Men are often treated with multiple antibiotics, pain killers and antidepressants, often with little benefit. Using daily tadalafil by improving blood supply to the prostate relieves pain and promotes healing. Recently, I asked two of our top urologists to write a chapter on prostatitis for a textbook, and they mentioned 24 drugs that had been used. They did not mention tadalafil even once. When I questioned them, they both answered, "yes, I use tadalafil first in most of my patients!" When I asked one of them why they had not mentioned it in their chapters, his answer was that it was "off licence", and his training was never to mention "off licence" medication for legal reasons. Unfortunately, once patents expire and drugs become cheap, nobody will ever fund the tens of millions required to obtain a new licence for each of these important conditions, as they will never see a return on their investment. Surely doctors should be allowed to offer their patients treatment that they feel is in their best interests without fear of legal implications?

Cancer Prevention

Studies show a reduction in prostate and bowel cancer with regular tadalafil daily use due to its specific effect on the enzyme cytochrome P19a1, an important factor in cancer development. One very large review has suggested that daily tadalafil should be repositioned as an anti-cancer agent.

Other health benefits

Other studies have shown benefits in terms of weight loss, diabetes control, heart failure and reduction in osteoporosis by stimulation of the androgen (testosterone) receptors in bone.

As if the case wasn't strong enough for all these conditions, recent studies have shown improved mental function and reduction in dementia with daily tadalafil, even supported by scans showing increased blood supply to important regions of the brain after only eight weeks. As dementia is probably everybody's worse nightmare, if a man gets ED, does it not make sense to take a cheap daily medication with all these potential benefits, especially dementia prevention, rather than the occasional "little blue pill" on "special" occasions.

Tadalafil – the decathlon drug!

Hopefully, I have demonstrated the multiple benefits of daily tadalafil. It is <u>licensed</u> to treat 3 medical conditions, ED, symptoms associated with an enlarged prostate and pulmonary hypertension (men and women). For all the other conditions, although there is excellent evidence from multiple trials, submitting an application for each and every condition would have been prohibitively expensive, and, for each of these, there would have been at least one other drug licensed and with years of experience. This is why I use the term "decathlon drug". The decathlon consists of 10 athletic events, but it is unlikely that decathletes would have been selected or achieved qualifying standards in *any of the individual events,* yet they will probably be regarded as the best overall athletes, such as Daley Thompson or, in the case of women, the heptathlete, Jess Ennis. The problem in medicine is that each of these conditions will be managed by a group of experts who publish guidelines that look exclusively at that one indication to the exclusion of all others outside their narrow remit. I have tried for years to get medical experts to put themselves in the patients' shoes and think outside the box, but they are locked in the traditional medical paradigms that are often not patient centred. The "rules" do not allow them to consider the bigger picture, as that would be a matter for another expert panel. Patient reference is rarely considered to be high-level evidence. In a similar way, we may choose to buy a car which is not *first in class* in any road tests by the likes of *top gear* experts but just ticks a lot of boxes overall.

THE DECATHLON EFFECT

What about "natural" products?

In terms of "natural" supplements that men might consider, high dose L-Arginine (3g daily) and Carnitine are amino-acid precursors that may have some additional benefit on ED, along with saw palmetto, ginseng and Foti. Commercial products using combinations of these drugs continue to be produced, claiming "miracle" benefits for ED and the prostate. Unfortunately, the doses in commercial products are usually too low to produce any benefit. The effects are slight at best, yet there is little control over the sensational claims that can be made. In contrast, a licensed pharmaceutical product is subject to strict regulation, and a breach would attract potentially huge fines. Certainly, a man should take Vitamin D if he has a low level, especially Afro-Caribbean or South Asian men, and Folic acid 5mg daily in T2DM or men taking certain drugs for epilepsy.

The problem is that pharma companies would be heavily fined for making claims not supported by thorough research, and doctors were warned against ever making such claims, irrespective of years of personal experience. In contrast, manufacturers of "herbal" or "natural" products can claim "may improve" everything from baldness to halitosis without fear of prosecution, banking on the fact that, if thousands of people give it a try for a few months, profits will be pretty good.

In summary, I would advise that all men take daily tadalafil 5mg if they have T2DM or heart disease, even if they don't have ED (yet). I would advise all men to take it daily at the first sign of ED rather than wait for spontaneous resolution, as the longer that ED is ignored, the more difficult it will be to treat. Using daily tadalafil is treating *the medical condition,* meaning that, with time, results continue to improve progressively, whereas taking a tablet before sex just treats *a symptom,* meaning that eventually, they will stop working because the process of deterioration of the arteries will have continued, effectively untreated.

ED and loss of morning erections are early warning signs of cardiac events in the next 2-5 years. I would also recommend that all men over the age of 50 consider regular dosing for all the clear multiple benefits listed in this chapter. If we wait for this advice to become mainstream, it will be too late for many men who are over 50 now. It is highly unlikely that NHS funders and GPs would ever view the concept of ED prevention as a top priority, even if you can manage to find a GP. The reality is that, just as the NHS would not be expected to fund vitamin supplements, or indeed gym memberships, the burden of drugs to prevent ED will fall on the patient. As we already have Viagra over the counter, daily tadalafil will follow very soon. It can already be provided very cheaply by GPs on private prescriptions for less than the cost of a pint of beer or a cup of Costa per month.

Daily tadalafil is extremely safe and eminently suitable for direct-to-public sale after 20 years of experience in millions of men (and women), despite being classified by the National Institute of Health and Care Excellence as "drugs of limited clinical value", definitely the medical understatement of all time...NICE one!

CHAPTER 11

Media Triumphs and Disasters.

In Chapter One, I explained how I was first awarded the title "Sex Tsar" by Men's Health magazine in 2005 when I was approached for a telephone interview whilst waiting at Sydney airport. A couple of these studies are worthy of more exploration. My all-time favourite paper was the Caerphilly Cohort study which appeared in a Christmas British Medical Journal (BMJ) in 1997, showing men in the Welsh town who had *more than two orgasms per week* halved their risk of death from a heart attack. This paper suggests that the female (and male) partners of Welsh men hold the key to longevity. You are probably wondering whether masturbation counts and the good news is that the orgasm is key. It gets even better as previous research showed no increased risk of blindness. Even moderate sex twice per week will shed 20,900 kilojoules per year, the equivalent of running 80km per year. This might seem irrelevant to any serious athlete, but it comes with minimal stress to the knees and zero chance of being hit by an articulated lorry. In the case of women, it seems that the quality of sex is more important, but for men, it is the quantity that matters most.

Researchers at Rutgers University in the US found that regular sex acts as a painkiller, increasing blood flow to all parts of the brain during orgasm. As a sufferer of frequent migraines, I suggested this to my wife, Sally, as part of a clinical trial. She became suspicious after a month and terminated the study early. Although the activity was providing relief within a minute, she was becoming suspicious of the increased frequency of migraines, as they were now occurring

192

daily. She suggested that I might try a regime of self-intervention in the spare room.

One of the most powerful pieces of research of all time came from the Royal Edinburgh hospital, which examined 3500 people aged 18-102 (!). They found that those having sex three or more times per week looked, on average, 10 years younger. If ever there was a study that should change human behaviour, surely this is it.

My first excursion into the media was a readily forgettable appearance on "Kilroy" in 1999. This was a very popular daytime show in front of a live TV audience. James Kilroy Silk was a smooth silver fox who also had a controversial political career. The subject was low testosterone in men. The show was filmed at Teddington Studios in London. After a standard class rail trip to Euston, five of us were squeezed into a taxi for the hour-long journey to Teddington. After a few minutes, the slightly dishevelled man next to me, having overheard that I was a specialist, began telling me his life history. Five minutes into the journey, I was fully aware that he had a very limited sexual repertoire and suffered from ED, low libido and retarded ejaculation. "Do you think it might be related to all the drugs I take for my paranoid schizophrenia?" he asked. I suddenly realised that displaying any sign of indifference to this man might be a bad idea. Seldom have I been so relieved to reach a destination.

The experts were taken to a different room before the show, and Kilroy primed all the specialists as to when he would turn to us and what question we would be asked. I was very comfortable that I had 30 minutes to relax until my question. Soon after the live show started, it became clear that this was a complete set-up. There were several "plants" in the audience. They were there to report great responses to treatment received in a Harley St practice run by one of the experts.

Fifteen minutes into the show, as I was just nodding off, having been on-call the night before, Kilroy suddenly turned to me: "Dr Hackett, it sounds as though the NHS is letting these men down badly; what is your response?". I woke suddenly, my first reaction being to point out this was not my pre-prepared question, but I garbled a response that was incoherent nonsense. Strangely Kilroy decided not to go back to me for the planned question. My wife, Sally, had recorded the programme and still brings out the tape at dinner parties when she wants to subject me to yet another ritual humiliation.

Just when I thought my day couldn't get worse, things went rapidly downhill. The return journey to Euston at rush hour took nearly two hours and no prizes for guessing who was sitting next to me. Even worse, the stress of the day or missed medication meant that his anxiety levels had increased. He seemed impressed by my performance, which suggested to me that he was almost certainly becoming delusional. On reaching the station, I bid him goodbye as I could see that the train to Birmingham was leaving in five minutes. "What a coincidence", he said, "I'm going to Birmingham; we can travel together". As we reached the train, I was getting pretty desperate; "I'm in first class," I said and proceeded to turn right. Ten minutes into the journey, having been relieved of £85 for the full price of the first class ticket (money well spent, I thought), I was setting down to a gin and tonic and feeling soporific. I had drifted off into a relaxed sleep. I thought I was dreaming when I heard the announcement, "Person on line at Rugby". My first thought was that it might be somebody who had found today's Kilroy too much for them, but then the reality set in. We were being taken off the train at Milton Keynes and put on a coach to Birmingham. Fifteen minutes later, those of us in first class had the benefit of being first onto the coaches and suitably spread ourselves around the seats. There was a certain inevitability as to who was going to sit beside me for the 90-minute journey to Birmingham. This was possibly the worst day of my life. Twelve months later, I received a phone call from Thames television inviting me back on "Kilroy" for a follow-up show. Without a second thought, my response was, "I'm afraid I'm cleaning the parrot's cage on that day". Strangely I was not invited again.

After the Kilroy debacle, I decided it was time for some "Media Training" as it seemed that a couple of the pharma companies had seen my performance and decided to sponsor my attendance at a 2-day course. The "experts" seemed to be ex-TV interviewers charging £5k a day to teach doctors how" not" to answer any direct questions – perfect training for a would-be Conservative politician but not the Sex Tsar. I decided that I could develop my own flamboyant style.

My next opportunity came on Valentine's day in 2000, which seemed to be a prime time for sex phone-in programmes on the radio. My one take-home message from the media training videos was that I had the perfect face for radio. The first of these phone-ins was an afternoon slot on Capital Radio when I was paired up with a high-profile TV agony aunt and barely got a word in for two hours. I felt somewhat patronised, and my views were dismissed because "as a man, I could not possibly understand a woman's feelings". This was followed by "men with sexual problems much prefer to see a woman as they are non-judgemental". I began to wonder if my whole life had been wasted inside a man's body.

The evening session on Talk-Sport looked much more promising – surely this would be an audience of real men who talk footy and drink lager. The evening was taking a similar pattern with a traditional sex therapist, with twinset and pearls, preaching avoidance of porn and more concentration of sensate focus. I concluded this must have been going above the heads of most of the macho male listeners. She made a couple of outrageous comments like "I'll only treat men with nice legs" and "I' wouldn't recommend Viagra for an older man unless he has a much younger wife". We seemed to have more women phoning in. Martha from Cockfosters was complaining that for the last 20 years, her old man had tweaked her nipples as if he was tuning the TV". Much female laughter followed. Of course, as a man, I could not possibly give advice on the seductive caressing of the nipples. I decided to fight back by recounting the story of a 50-year-old farmer I had seen the week before, who complained that his wife continually yanked his todger as though she was milking a heifer. I still believe that as the possessor of a dick of my own, I have more personal experience of the way it should be handled. As I left the studio, the technicians all thanked me for their memorable moments of the evening.

I would like to say at this stage that I love sex therapists, especially Trudy Hannington from Doncaster, the sex capital of GB, known in the tabloids as "Bonkaster". Men in Doncaster officially have more sex than anywhere else in the country. I remember once sharing the platform with Trudy, who put me firmly in my place. Fairly early in the discussion, she stated that "only a woman can possibly understand the feelings of a female patient."

My other favourite is Angela Gregory from Nottingham, a "mistress of masturbation". There are other therapists who are easily offended. I remember, after one meeting, getting raspberry reviews for using a comment that I had seen a 60-year-old woman with a vagina "as dry as the Gobi Desert". I had taken the comment directly from the woman on one of the vaginal lubricants stands, but somehow, the statement became inappropriate coming from a man.

Colleagues still remind me how I died on the podium that day in the midst of gasps from offended therapists.

I remember a very senior Urologist, the late Clive Gingell, starting a presentation to the annual sex therapist (COSRT) with his favourite cartoon slide of a huge penis on a drawbridge being carried by several soldiers. Whilst this was usually greeted by riotous laughter from medical students, this time, there was stony silence – he realised that all was not going as expected. At the end, the lady chairperson thanked him with, "We all greatly enjoyed your presentation, Mr Gingell, apart from the first slide, which we found absolutely disgusting!".

On the afternoon of September 11th 2001, I was working from home, catching up on some football on the TV, when a female journalist from the US rang me for an interview on a vital issue that must have caused mental torment to all of us at some stage "the female prostate, does it exist?" Frankly, I had given up the search for the female prostate long ago, but I humoured her. The conversation drifted onto "G spot orgasm" when I suddenly noted on the TV vivid pictures of planes flying into the twin towers in New York. I tried to explain the magnitude of what was happening, but she reacted as though this was the lamest excuse for terminating a discussion that he had heard. Eventually, I made my excuses, trying to digest what I actually saw on the screen. They say that we all remember what we were doing at the precise moment of historical events, but I guarantee that nobody else was locked in an intellectual discussion on G-spot versus clitoral orgasm at the exact time of 9/11.

By 2003, the story was beginning to get around that ED was strongly linked with heart disease and that men should be encouraged to see their doctor at an early stage, and I was phoned by the Victoria

Derbyshire radio show for comment. During the interview, she made an important observation, "I suppose that many men consult their doctor about a trivial matter and then reach the door and turn around with a *by the way* comment". Remembering my determination to adopt a flamboyant style, I quickly replied, "Yes, this is very common. We call this the" *hand on knob* consultation". There was absolute silence and the producer cut in, saying, "Time for a traffic bulletin". During the break, he told me that they were all glad that there was a lot of traffic chaos that day.

I now seemed to be the "go-to" man for most tabloid journalists and barely a week went by without a random phone call from a freelance journalist at the Sun or the Daily Mail contacting me about some banal publication in an obscure journal. Invariably this was pre-publication, and I had no idea what it was all about. Rather than hanging up, I always tried to give them a strapline for publication. In the Summer of 2005, I was in the middle of a busy surgery when a call was put through from the Daily Mail, and for some reason, the new receptionist thought this must be put through instantly. The Journalist wanted some quotes on a new study on the increasing popularity of anal sex. I looked across my desk at a concerned mother hoping to have a discussion on the pros and cons of adenoidectomy for daughter Charlotte. I thought that the timing could have been better. Rather than be rude, I quickly replied, "A colleague of mine, Dr Bollinger, has spent the last five years researching this subject. He is a world expert". I could sense the enthusiasm in her voice that, at last, she had found a specialist passionate about anal sex. I think that Dr Bollinger was at a fundraising session for the village church organ when she rang him that evening. Although a fountain of most knowledge, I believe that Dr B also had only fleeting thoughts about anal sex. I think to this day, he has never forgiven me for this one.

A call to send shudders down the spine came from a lady at Maverick Television, a company that was beginning to push back the boundaries of taboo subjects surrounding sex. The lady was assistant to the producer of a programme airing that week on Channel 4 on the topic of "The role of furniture in sex through the ages". Once again, it was in the middle of a busy surgery. An escape strategy immediately came to mind as I replied, "This is not my area of expertise, but I can recommend an excellent sex therapist who likes nothing more than to get her hands on a nice piece of Chippendale". I gave her the phone number for Angela Gregory. The lady had missed the subtlety of my response and rang Angela, immediately repeating my comments about her love of a nice piece of Chippendale. Luckily Angela seemed to take it in better spirits than Dr B. I think her performance on that show led to an appearance on a special X-rated episode of Antiques Roadshow.

"There's nothing quite like getting your hands on a nice piece of Chippendale."

199

My major media debacle came on Sunday morning of 14th February 2007. I remember this well as it was my son's 21st birthday, and several of his friends had slept over after a successful attempt to totally empty my cocktail cabinet the night before. Sally and I had gone to bed at about 3am when the phone woke me from a deep slumber at 7am. It was the producer of BBC news asking if I would appear live on the 9am news as a story had broken that Boots were going to make Viagra available in their stores. They could have a taxi to my home within 30 minutes. For some reason, I will never understand, I accepted, only to realise that I had the mother of all hangovers once I assumed the vertical position. I slept throughout the taxi ride and the obligatory make-up session. For some reason, I needed more than usual that morning. At home, my son had woken all his friends, and they huddled around the TV while Sally made bacon sandwiches. The BBC 9am news started, and as I was in a later slot, I was struggling to stay awake. Suddenly on came the lights, and we were live. "My god, look at the state of him. Is he asleep?" Sally shrieked at the TV. The questions were quite straightforward, such as "How does Viagra work" and "Is it safe" questions that I could readily answer in my sleep. Suddenly, the newscaster asked, "And can you get it over the counter?" I paused for a couple of seconds, thinking that rarely does one get a moment like this on BBC live. At home, Sally shouted, "Please, please, no!" as she saw a twinkle in my eye. I had decided to go for it. "You know, I think I probably could". Strangely, not only was that the last question of the day but my last BBC appearance for several years. The good news was that I achieved instant "Legend" status with all my son's mates.

At this stage, I should formally apologise to my sons Nick and Dan, as life must have been tough for the spawn of a Sex Tsar. Dan has endured at least three detentions at school for repeating some of my wise words or choosing a project based on my work. Worst of all, at his recent wedding, he chose to remind me that he and his brothers were 12 and 15 and both promising sportsmen; I chose to sit them down for some tips on excellence in sportsmanship. I stated, "now, boys, you have both reached important stages in your personal careers, and I have two names to always bear in mind as role models, Lance Armstrong and Ryan Giggs!" Luckily, they have both had excellent sporting careers and work as junior school headmasters educating small children to maintain the high standards defined by the Tsar.

As President of the International Society for Sexual Medicine, Dr Bollinger popped up on our screens on "Dawn Goes Lesbian" on BBC 3 on September 6th, 2008. This was a 4-part series featuring journalist Dawn Porter. The series commenced with "Dawn gets Naked", then "Dawn goes Lesbian", then "Dawn gets a Baby", and finally "Dawn gets her Man". Dr B was the specialist who helped Dawn set strict rules, enabling her to move in with lesbian housemates, work in a busy Soho Lesbian bar and culminating with the big question, "was she up for a full-on lesbian snog!" Dr B was clearly addressing some of the most important ethical issues of the day. In an interview in 2013, Dawn listed this programme as the biggest regret of her career. She stated that "she cringes when she sees it, the programme was based on a false premise, and she did it at a time when she didn't know how to say no to people". After speaking to Dr B, he clearly felt the same, but if you think that this was as low as one could get for Dr B, read on.

In 2009, Dr Bollinger and I were the only UK doctors to be involved in trials of a drug, Flibanserin, to improve sexual desire in women. We were invited to the company Headquarters in Berkshire for a media day, along with several other "thought leaders" in the field. We were split into groups for "brainstorming" sessions. The only problem was that Dr B and I had been out for dinner at an Italian Restaurant the night before with a few libations before and after. Although I had learned the hard way on several occasions that I was lightweight in his company, and so, once more, I was struggling for the first hour of the meeting. Comments were made that I was "unusually quiet". The task for my brainstorming group was to identify the "perfect mature woman" as the "image "for Flibanserin. I was in a group of six that included Dr Dawn Harper, well-known as one of the presenters on "Embarrassing Bodies" on TV. The rest of the group was coming around to choosing Kate Winslett as the marketing face for this drug when I decided to strike a blow for common sense. For many years I have been enchanted by Fiona Bruce, such that I watched the 9pm news each evening merely to see what she was wearing. I never missed Antiques Roadshow, and more recently, I delight in her weekly appearances on Question Time and my personal favourite, Fake or Fortune. Only a week before, I had been watching her incredible cameo performance on Top Gear. I now thought that I would choose her as my specialist subject on Mastermind. Having contributed little to earlier discussions, I decided to make a robust case for Fiona Bruce above Kate Winslet. Dawn Harper prompted me with, "Come on, Geoff, tell us all why we should choose Fiona Bruce". "Well," I replied, "She was born in Singapore, educated in Milan, has a double first in French and Italian at Oxford, a further degree from Paris, happily married for 15 years, has two children, Simon and Mia, drives a Citroen Xara Picasso, goes to the gym four days per week and won Rear of the year in 2010…". "Woah Geoff, let's stop you there", said Dawn, "This is beginning to sound creepy; I think you might be Fiona Bruce's stalker, In fact, I have a mental picture of you lurking outside of her house and popping up out of her bush!". The group were silent as Dawn suddenly realised what she had said. From that day on, I cannot watch Fiona Bruce on TV without having a mental picture of myself popping up out of her bush. Three sessions of psychotherapy and hypnosis have failed to help. In case you are remotely interested, Kate Winslett got the nod, but the process was all academic as the drug has never been licensed in the UK, despite moderate success in the US. In fact, the company were deluged with complaints for daring to develop a drug to promote women as "sex objects". The company offices and staff cars were vandalised, and the final nail in the coffin was an editorial in the BMJ which accused the company of inventing a "disease termed female sexual dysfunction".

My media appearances pale into insignificance compared with Dr Bollinger's larger-than-life epic performances. In 2013, at around midnight, I was flicking through the channels on the remote control and had skipped past the X-rated channels when around 582, I came across a familiar face on Fiver 2 plus One. It was Dr B on the couch with 2 stunning interviewers talking with the recently crowned word masturbation champion, Masanobu Sato, from Japan. He had recently regained his world title in San Francisco, breaking his world record with an impressive 9 hours 58 minutes performance as described in chapter one. This was performed, of course, without ejaculation and extended his previous world record by 25 minutes. He was asked whether he thought that the elusive 10-hour barrier might now be within his grasp. He explained that to break this record, he swam twice per week and gained 5kg of muscle to improve his stamina. The camera cut to Dr B for expert comment on Mr Sato's training and dietary schedules. He dealt with searching questions as to whether altitude training might help and whether WADA anti-doping checks should be introduced. For the first time, I saw Dr B completely lost for words, almost as though his agent had given him no prior warning of the subject matter. He pulled it all together by the end with some key tips on techniques to reduce the risk of friction burns. I rang him the next day to congratulate him on his performance, "Oh God", he replied, "I thought I'd got away with that". Luckily, I have the programme recorded as I am sure that it is no longer available.

For those who may be interested, the 10-hour barrier was broken in 2018 by a 40-year-old bisexual American aptly named Drake Hardy (yes, his real name), who had broken the barrier several times in training before eventually officially slashing the record in front of a live audience. For those who thought that the 10-second barrier hundred metres and the 4-minute mile were the ultimate sporting barriers of the 20th century, the new millennium has already seen the obliteration of the 10-hour record, the holy grail of masturbation.

Drake Hardy commented in media interviews that his secret was muscle control through tantric principles. He had previously broken the 10- hour barrier with a partner but commented that she had required a short break every two hours. For those who might have thought that winning the Rugby World Cup in 2019 was the South African sporting highlight in recent years, think again. In December, Zakhele Xulu claimed the 2019 World Masturbation championship in Toronto and, with it, the Jonny Sins Cup. His margin of victory was only 45 seconds, and asked whether he was ever worried that he might not win, he commented, "It was touch and go at one stage". At one stage, it looked as though we might be heading for a photo finish. I always remember Dr B's best tip was to take the back-row seat in the judges' box. COVID-19 pandemic led to the cancellation of the 2020 and 2021 finals, but excitement is building for the 2022 finals in

Tokyo, but the masturbatory world has been thrown into turmoil with talk of a Saudi-based super-league.

In 2015, I was twice approached to appear on Embarrassing Bodies on Channel 4 (as an expert, not an exhibit, to avoid any confusion). Having seen the programme many times, not only did I see this as potentially attracting the wrong sort of publicity, but I felt that I could never face Dawn Harper on camera without thinking about Fiona Bruce's bush. As I stated earlier, I was now even more convinced that I had the ideal face for radio.

In August 2015, I was approached to lead an advertising campaign for a new drug for Premature Ejaculation (PE) called dapoxetine and marketed as Priligy. It was clear that the NHS would be reluctant to fund drugs for this condition, and therefore, a public awareness campaign was required. The theme was "Firing too Quickly". The Media Relations company came up with the idea of using top rugby players. I often wonder how much drug companies pay marketing agencies for these ideas. The TV advert for "Firing too Quickly" involved two matches in bed, supposedly involved in "nooky", and after seconds, one of them strikes, and the flame brings things to an abrupt close. The message is that 20% of men suffer from premature ejaculation, and help is available by going to the "Firing too Quickly" website. The three international rugby players, Danny Care (England), Sean Maitland (Scotland) and Dan Biggar (Wales), must have found this one of their most bizarre promotional experiences and all were very quick to point out that they did not suffer from PE. They were clearly there to get the message across that even the most virile men could suffer from PE. I suspect that they really turned up for the fee, which I hoped was better than mine. They certainly earned it for listening we me witter on about PE for 20 minutes. The following morning, it was up at 7am for a radio phone-in with Dr Hilary Jones, a true gentleman and definitely my favourite TV doctor. We had a great morning dealing with men's sexual issues, an infinitely better experience than earlier sessions with sex therapists.

One of the advantages of looking a bit old and craggy by 2019 was that I was passed over for some projects in favour of younger, more photogenic experts. One such programme was "My sexual fantasy" for Channel 5, which was immediately put onto the series link as compulsory viewing for the Tsar. One of my trendier colleagues from BSSM, Dr Anand Patel, has now emerged as the sexual fantasy specialist. In this programme, several subjects describe their intimate sexual fantasies for the expert, Dr P, to interpret. In a recent episode, one young woman described fantasising about older rich men taking her forcefully and displaying their worldly sexual skills. Dr P was skilfully able to explain everything in terms of her sexual frustrations with past relationships. The second case was a "hunky" man from Barbados who lusted after elderly well-spoken ladies for slow seduction in the women's bathroom. I was less convinced by his explanation that this was a healthy guilty pleasure. Other cases ranged from fantasies over casual lesbian encounters to a man with a long beard seeking mass "dogging" experiences on public heathland. The reassuring message from Dr P and the resident sex therapist was that such fantasies were healthy and should be embraced with no feelings of shame. This was very reassuring for me after weeks of sleepless nights fantasising that I was trapped in Fiona Bruce's bush with no prospect of escape. Dr P has recently popped up on the Riverbank for a chat with Mortimer and Whitehouse, compulsive viewing!

A friendly journalist from the Sun contacts me on a monthly basis for comments on several subjects ranging from Botox injections for PE, vaginal rejuvenation, surgery to restore virginity and the sudden popularity of penile lengthening operations. I have been happy to provide illuminating opinions which usually accurately reflect the conversation. In September 2019, he contacted me about the increase in NHS Penile Implants from 550 per year to over 900 and asked for possible explanations. I explained that this was probably due to several factors. As GPs had been paid to screen for ED, especially in men with diabetes, more men were entering the system, meaning that there would be more who failed, whatever treatment we offered. They, therefore, needed the ultimate "last chance saloon" treatment. In addition, increasing cases undergoing gender transition meant that prosthesis was needed for the female to male patients and therefore increased funding was available for surgeons to conduct more operations. He seemed to take all this on board and thanked me. The following night my younger son arrived back from a stag weekend in Prague. His mates on the plane had all picked up their free copies of the Sun. The front-page headline that greeted them was "BIONIC BONERS ON THE RISE", followed by most of my comments (luckily no photograph), suitably misquoted.

I had now achieved "Legend" status with yet another group of young men.

CHAPTER 12
Secrets of Medical Research

Nowadays, the public expects an immediate answer to all their questions via a search from Dr Google. They do not realise that high-quality medical evidence, as opposed to the "8 out of 10 cats" stuff, takes many years from conception to completion and costs millions of pounds. Usually, the funding comes from commercial sources, such as drug companies, where there has to be a prospect of long-term financial gain rather than addressing the ad hoc search demands of random surfers. These are important principles to remember when reading the following chapter.

I suppose I was always interested in research. Having a physiotherapist as a wife, I first looked at the impact of employing a physiotherapist in primary care and later showed that this could be cost-effective in terms of reduced prescribing of medication and time lost from work. I was awarded two prizes for this work. The first was the Charles Oliver Hawthorn award by the British Medical Association in 1986, and the second was the Duke of Edinburgh prize in Sports Medicine in 1992. The latter was awarded by Prince Philip himself at St James Palace. I remember, having received the prize, accompanied by Sally, we were waiting for Prince Philip to join us for celebratory drinks. His assistant warned Sally that he would go straight for her, clearly based on vast experience. As he entered, it was also as though he was scanning the room... Boring old fart to right, pretty woman left... turn left immediately, and there he was. The rest of us were completely ignored. He had quickly discovered that Sally was a physio and might be interested in his groin strain from an old polo injury. He looked to be guiding her hand in the direction of the royal groin with photographers straining for tomorrow's front page or caption competition for "Have I Got News For You". In the nick of time, his PA directed him down the line, and Sally looked visibly relieved.

My success in Sports Medicine led to a tentative approach from Manchester United to take over from the current GP, who was retiring after 25 years. I was invited to speak at a Sports Injuries day, attended by Alex Ferguson, staff and several players. My 30-minute talk was the last of the day. I soon realised that I had no chance, coming after four orthopaedic surgeons, each armed with 150 slides in 30 minutes. In the end, I had five minutes to do myself justice. The club clearly appreciated brevity. When I saw the job description, I realised that the previous GP had done the job for four directors box tickets and a bottomless bar bill. Later, I was approached by Aston Villa, and Doug Ellis, chairman at the time, held the decision open until my return from holidays. My enquiries confirmed my suspicions that "Deadly Doug "did not get his name by accident and expected 24/7 on-call. I politely withdrew. In 1996, I got to the last three for an interview at Edgbaston for the GP job of the England Cricket Tour to India and Sri Lanka, including the World Cup. I was unsuccessful but subsequently found that this turned out to be the most disastrous tour on record with no wins, and the team doctor and a couple of players returned home after three weeks with severe food poisoning. In 2010, I did accept a job as a medical adviser to the European Golf Tour, which has proved very flexible and highly rewarding.

By 1987, I had started to work on an MD thesis at Keele University, where I had recently been appointed a senior lecturer in general practice. I had begun to cultivate some simple clinical trials on new drugs in the practice. They paid very well in the early years, but with time and increased red tape, they become hard work for seemingly less reward.

It was really with the "discovery" of drug-induced erection in 1988 that my research direction changed. At Keele University, I linked up with Professor Peter Croft and Kate Dunn, a research fellow at the time, to conduct the largest study to that date, looking at the prevalence of sexual problems in men and women and how they are associated with common medical conditions such as diabetes and high blood pressure. From these publications, I was targeted for further studies in drugs to improve sexual function. In an earlier chapter, I described the arrival of Alan Riley and the set-up for the first Viagra studies, and it was clear from very early that this drug would change the world. These studies involved patients with ED being allocated to either Viagra or placebo. They would then keep a diary of all the sexual events, and our role was to collect and collate the results. In 1993, I had a barn converted into a clinic. Luckily, this was before the days of the Care Quality Commission (CQC), as we had the odd field mouse visiting the surgery, no lift, no designated disabled parking and no in-house interpreters. Even worse was my 80-year-old father, who lived upstairs and was prone to wander down unannounced in his loosely fitting pyjamas.

More trials followed, involving similar drugs, vardenafil and tadalafil, and I felt privileged to be part of a golden age for medical research. Each trial involved an investigator's meeting and a great chance to meet colleagues. At one of the earlier ones in London, the first day of the meeting had gone well, and we were sitting down to the conference dinner afterwards. Dr Bollinger was sitting across the table, and I could see signs of the agitated twitch, sweating, and drooping lower lip which could only mean one thing... "corporate chicken with cheap house wine". As usual, his phone was out, and a table already booked in a local restaurant. He looked around the table for possible dining companions, and as usual, I got the nod. Four of us went on for a very expensive French meal, preceded by a libation or three. Then it was on to Dr B's jazz club, where he was warmly embraced by the patron. A magnum of Krug disappeared rather quickly. It must have been 3.30am when we approached the hotel. He paused and exclaimed, "feeling peckish, fancy a little Chinese?". In those days, I felt that I could hold my own, but that night I realised that Dr B was now in a different league. We were back at the hotel just in time for the morning breakfast session of day 2 of the meeting. As always, with Dr B, I never usually contributed to meetings until after the first coffee break.

From 1996 to 2005, there was a steady stream of Erectile Dysfunction trials involving the three oral drugs. These were straightforward, and it was very easy to recruit patients as there was no other acceptable treatment; otherwise, they would have to pay privately. A major eye-opener was the greater frequency of sex in older couples, often multiple times a day. They frequently asked for additional diaries. Despite this high level of use in trials, the NHS decided to restrict tablets to once per week with no evidence to support the decision. I was also able to divert patients from my NHS clinic, ensuring that they had access to the most current therapies and unlimited medication. Involvement in these trials cemented a role as a Key Opinion Leader leading to invitations to international meetings, the subject of another chapter.

Not all drugs were as successful as sildenafil (Viagra) and tadalafil (Cialis). One pharma company developed a drug called Apomorphine (Uprima) which worked differently. Whereas Viagra works by opening the blood vessels leading to the penis, this drug supposedly works by stimulating the nerve pathways from the brain to the penis. Their key message was "Uniting Mind and Body". The studies had been conducted in the US, and they had appointed Dr Bollinger (who else) as their international adviser. Dr B was sceptical of the US data and patient selection, and some of us were not seeing these results in the early patients we treated. Dr B came to me with a protocol for a 2-centre study that we could conduct quickly to address these issues. He drew up a contract with the company, and we signed up for the study. Within weeks, it was becoming clear to the world that this drug was relatively ineffective, and the company decided to withdraw it. Dr B pointed out that he and I had a contract that needed to be honoured. They had to agree and pay up, meaning that effectively we were paid without seeing a patient – top man Dr B.

The next large potential growth area was Premature Ejaculation (PE). Dr Bollinger had been working with Professor Wallace Dinsmore from Belfast and a prominent scientist Mike Wyllie to develop the ejaculometer. This was designed as an experimental model to evaluate oral and topical drugs developed to treat PE. PE was defined as less than 2 minutes after penetration, although this was later revised to 1 minute. The ejaculometer was a primitive electrical device consisting of a timer and a stimulating pad that flicked the penis at a standardised frequency until ejaculation resulted. Our role was to use the device on patients to confirm PE and then later to evaluate the response of active medication and placebo. There were a few logistic issues. The patient had to be connected to the machine, and then, for obvious reasons, the doctor had to start the machine and timer and withdraw from the consulting room. I remember waiting outside the door for one patient, thinking that the machine was rather noisy. I could hear groaning from the room and politely enquired, "Everything OK?" "Nearly there... Ahhhhhh". I guessed from the sounds that he was now actually there. I gave him a suitable time, knocked and entered the room. The timer read 1 minute 40 seconds, so I confirmed his eligibility for the studies. "I'm not sure where it went", he said, "It just shot out; I looked everywhere". This really was a mystery, but I had further patients to see and had to crack on". Twenty minutes later, I was well on with the next consultation and felt a large drip on my head. "What was that?" said the patient. Quickly I thought of a response, "Having a bit of trouble with that roof," hoping the patient would not realise that it hadn't rained in several weeks and we were on the ground floor of a 2-storey building. I wound up the consultation and hastily cleaned up the lampshade. I remember that Sally later asked if I was having a "bad hair day". I often refer to this as my Cameron Diaz moment.

"Another 30 seconds shoiuld do it."

Dr Bollinger, myself and several other investigators were soon at a meeting in 2000 for studies of Dapoxetine, a tablet that works on the brain to delay ejaculation. The protocol was being discussed by a prominent world expert from the Netherlands. He explained that although the timing was crucial and relatively straight forward to measure, it could not be the only standard. Satisfaction with the sexual experience was important, and there were well-validated questionnaires to access this. The final and crucial issue was the concept of Control. He deliberated, "Now, that's when things start to get really sticky". He was clearly totally unaware of the significant of the statement. These trials were truly fascinating. It was more reliable when the partner used the stopwatch as it reduced the pressure on the man. The downside was that she was now a subject in the study, causing logistic issues.

There were several spin-off trials in the PE programme. There was considerable concern that the partner issues in PE were not being addressed as they were unlikely to complain for fear of upsetting her subject. This study involved advertising for couples on local radio to attend the centre. This was going to capture couples with and without PE. Subjects and their partners would be paid to complete confidential questionnaires to detect whether partners of men with PE were suffering themselves and experiencing distress. As we were essentially paying couples to have sex whilst using a stopwatch, we had hundreds of responders. Among them was an undercover journalist who rather embellished the standard information that my nurse was reading from the script. The "expose" in the Birmingham Post described us as an "exclusive private clinic", paying couples to have as much sex as possible and in *as many positions as possible*. Although this was described as an "Observational Study", this did not mean that anybody would be watching. This was full-page coverage with a picture of a scantily clad couple in a lusty pose underneath the huge headline, BONKERS!

Subsequently, we conducted further PE studies involving a local anaesthetic spray that often made both couples numb such that neither knew if anybody had come. We drew the line on one involving injections of Botox into the penis.

As we were now the first port of call for companies with sexual medications, many other companies came to us. One company had a needle-free injection of an ED drug that essentially "blasted" the drug through the skin but left the skin raw and bleeding. One involved an inhaled drug, which was curtailed as some patients dropped blood pressure and fainted. We made the right decision not to be involved in these.

We were approached by one company with a hard sell for an ED drug that involved rubbing a nitrate cream on the penis prior to sex. The principal was that nitrates are used to treat angina, open blood vessels and increase flow. If applied as a cream, this might promote erection. We first learned of the study when the CEO took Dr Bollinger and me to dinner at a Michelin-star restaurant near Vilamoura in Portugal. He made the major mistake of handing the wine list to Dr B. For some, this had been the final blunder of their careers. When the bill arrived, I saw the chap's knees buckle under the shock.

At the investigator meeting in London three months later, Dr B had been unable to make it due to a Masonic Lodge meeting but joined the group at our London hotel for a nightcap at around 10.30 pm. I went to bed at around 11, but on checking out the following morning, I discovered two bottles of Bollinger Reserve added to my room bill, amounting to £350. I was fairly certain that I had only had beers. I paid up and emailed Dr B. The reply came back, "Oops, Champagne Charley strikes again!"

Despite our concerns, we decided to take part in the Nitrate cream study. Our third patient, Mr Richard Head, was attending for his first visit on a day when the CEO of the company was onsite, dealing with some administrative issues. Richard, or Dick as he preferred, was very chatty as I applied the first dose of the messy cream to his penis. We were just getting ready for the blood test and ECG when he sat up, slumped forward, and crashed to the floor. It was time to implement all my CPR training. His airway was clear. I put him in the recovery position and ascertained that he was still breathing and had a weak pulse. I suddenly thought that he would still be absorbing the drug, so I pulled down his trousers and his pants and wiped all the surplus drug from his penis. It did cross my mind how the CCTV footage of the incident might look to the General Medical Council (GMC) in the event of a formal investigation. Over the next 10 minutes, he recovered. We decided, of course, that he should withdraw from the study and that we now needed to complete a serious adverse event form. I informed him that the CEO of the company was in the office and asked whether he would like to give him some feedback. "I certainly would", replied Dick, "Where is he?" I went into the office, only to learn that the CEO, having been told what was going on, had decided that he had a pressing appointment, compelling him to leave at short notice via the back door. Other investigators had similar experiences, and multiple sites withdrew. Rather than accepting that this drug has no future for ED, the company continues to conduct trials of this product.

Around 2002 there was, at last, interest in treating postmenopausal women with low sexual desire. The difficulty in female trials was the lack of objective measurement, as erections and ejaculation are relatively simple to assess. Female symptoms could be more readily linked with depression, relationship problems, body image issues, menopausal symptoms, or indeed ED or PE in the partner. It was essential to screen women carefully, to exclude these other issues as much as possible. Investigators all required special training in the use of newly developed questionnaires, especially for these studies. The first trial involved a low-dose testosterone or placebo patch for post-menopausal women. The results were promising, and the patches were licensed in 2006, but for a narrow indication of women with surgically induced premature menopause. By 2010, it was evident that this indication was too narrow for commercial success, and the patches were withdrawn.

The next important study was Flibanserin, a centrally acting drug developed to treat women before menopause with acquired low sexual desire, meaning that the problem had not always been present. The media hailed this as "Pink Viagra", but, of course, it was nothing remotely like a pink version of the blue pill. We were one of only three UK centres to conduct this trial, meaning that, essentially, I am one of three UK doctors to have clinical experience with this drug. From our point of view, the results seemed encouraging. We remember one woman who had never had a significant relationship but was able to meet a partner and get married as a result of the drug. They were absolutely delighted and thanked us profusely at the end of the trial, even inviting us to the wedding. Sadly, the trial ended, and the company were unable to provide further drug on "compassionate" grounds. We later heard that her problems had returned, and she had split with her partner. This centrally acting drug to increase a woman's desire for sex encountered strong resistance from the feminist lobby in the US but was controversially licensed there in 2015. The drug has been moderately successful, as it seems to be effective in a selected group of women. There are no signs of a UK licence.

I was at Waterford airport on May bank holiday Saturday, returning from an exhausting golf tournament in Ireland, when my phone went. Dr Bollinger's blood pressure was causing problems, and he was advised to pull out of two presentations on Flibanserin at the American College of Obstetricians and Gynaecologists (ACOG) in New Orleans, commencing the following day. Dr B felt that I was the only person who could possibly stand at a day's notice. I had to say yes or no immediately as I would only have a few hours between flights. Realising that I still owed Dr B big time for presenting him as the media anal sex expert – the answer was yes. On arrival home, Sally was not amused that I was straight back to the airport again, but a glimpse at the contract and fee was greeted with the words, "You must go". It was a great trip, and most agreed that I was an adequate stand-in for the great man.

In 2002, clinical trials for testosterone therapy in men were taking place as new products were now available. The men most affected by low testosterone, termed hypogonadism, were men with T2DM, obesity, or those taking regular painkillers. The first study involved either active or placebo gel and yielded positive results. Based on this clear benefit, in 2006, I set up my own study of long-acting testosterone injection or placebo in 200 men with T2DM. This study was a career-defining moment for me, and there is much more about this in the chapter intitled "serious stuff". Through my excellent links with local general practices, we screened over 1000 patients to identify men for the study and have now continued to follow up with these men for 10 years. I negotiated the budget, devised the protocol, co-ordinated the centres and worked with a specialist statistician who managed the data and all statistical aspects of the study. We gave the study the acronym BLAST (Birmingham, Lichfield, Atherstone, Sutton Coldfield and Tamworth). After five years, we found that 13.3% of those with normal testosterone had died, 20% of those with low testosterone UNTREATED but only 3.6% of those on treatment. Best results were seen in men over 70, perhaps the least likely men to receive a prescription from their GP. We also found that taking a tablet for ED also significantly lowered the risk of dying. There are two large studies expected in the next three years that will address these issues, but remember, you heard it here first.

To date, the BLAST project has yielded 14 papers and counting. It remains today the largest and longest placebo-controlled study of testosterone injection therapy in men with diabetes. Without a doubt, treating men with low testosterone has been the most rewarding aspect of my medical practice, but more about that in the final chapter.

Over the last 25 years in sexual medicine, I have made many friends and contacts all over the world. There are many places around the world where I know that I could turn up and be treated like a long-lost friend, and they all know that the reverse is true. The unifying link is a sense of humour. If you can't laugh about sex, then you can't laugh about anything. This is reflected in much of the published research.

The most famous publication was the "Sex in the MRI scanner - 1991" from Sabellis *et al* in the Netherlands. This remains the most downloaded BMJ paper of all time. The author was also one of the 12 subjects who had sex within the scanner in the rear entry position. I had seen further papers presented by a French team at a later ESSM who decided to repeat the work, and why wouldn't one? My take-home message had been the intense self-control required to keep absolutely still for 10 minutes after full penetration. Although dismissed by the editor as "hardly as important as the moon landing", we learned that the penis developed a boomerang shape, with a third of the erect length being in the penile root. The vagina lengthened during sex, and the uterus enlarged and rode up minimally. Other female subjects allowed images to be taken at various stages of masturbation, adding much to what we previously knew about female orgasm.

Many studies have looked at the important issue of sex and athletic performance. An Italian study in 2008 suggested that football strikers were more likely to score after sex the night before. This reminded me of one of my boyhood heroes who was the hugely talented 70s Leicester and Liverpool striker Frank Worthington. In his autobiography "One hump or two", he reported regularly having sex at half-time during first-division matches. In contrast, world cup managers traditional banned sex before matches. Sven Goran Eriksen, famous for his own sexual exploits, encouraged WAGs at the 2006 World Cup and England flopped. In 2010, Fabio Capello banned sex during the tournament, and England flopped again. The reality is that sex consumes around 50 calories, the equivalent of climbing two flights of stairs, which is totally insignificant for a trained athlete. Boxing and Rugby coaches were worried that ejaculation might deplete testosterone and reduce aggression, whereas the evidence is that prolonged abstinence, certainly of longer than three months, significantly reduces testosterone and hence aggression.

In 2014, I set out to see whether the Italian footballer study would be valid for older men playing golf. As mentioned earlier, a good acronym is important for any study, so I came up with the Sexual Habits of Ageing Golfers or SHAG study. The beauty of this study was that, whereas there are relatively few goals in Italian football, ageing golfers frequently take over 100 strokes per round. Conveniently, all shots are recorded on the golf club website as a statistical record of performance. I was advised by my statistician to start with a small pilot study to test the methodology. I gave 20 randomly selected golfers a record card to complete, recording the timing of sexual activity over a 3-month period and then downloaded their scores from that period. We found that there was a weak positive correlation between sex the night before a round with a mean 0.2 stroke improvement. Unfortunately, the frequency of sex in the ageing golfers was only 1-2 times per month. This allowed me to make 3 important conclusions:

1. Ageing UK golfers have significantly less sex than Italian footballers

2. Ageing UK golfers should probably have more sex

3. More studies were required.

I decided to apply for a 5S research grant (The Scandinavian Society for the Study of Sexual Statistics), and my pilot SHAG study was accepted for a poster presentation at the 5S conference in Sweden in 2015. On the plane to Stockholm, I found myself sitting next to a blonde Swedish Researcher who spoke with great enthusiasm about her oral presentation on "Penile length and Girth – the 20-nation study". She had received an earlier society grant and had spent three years visiting 20 countries and measuring the penile dimensions of

100 random males of matched age from each country. With great excitement, she told me that the results were to be revealed for the first time at the meeting, but if I swore to keep her secret, she would reveal all. As we were getting on so well, I promised. She revealed that the longest penis at mean length of 5.5 inches was the American Red Indian, but the greatest girth at 4.02 inches were Italians, who, according to secondary endpoint, were also the best lovers. This should come as a surprise to nobody. Anxious to impress, I responded, "Absolutely fascinating; I can hardly wait for the presentation; by the way, I haven't introduced myself; the name is Tonto Corleone". On this occasion, my grant application was unsuccessful.

Research from North Carolina State University hit the CNN headlines a few years ago with the finding that women who practised regular fellatio with swallowing significantly reduced their chances of breast cancer. I presented the findings at a couple of meetings over the next month. The research, conducted by Prof Kramer and his team, followed two groups, 6,246 women ages 25 to 45 who had performed fellatio and swallowed on a regular basis over the past five to ten years, and 9,728 women who had not or did not swallow. The group of women who had performed and swallowed had a breast cancer rate of 1.9 percent, and the group who had not had a breast cancer rate of 10.4 percent. The CNN website had a million hits in two days. It seemed that we had a definitive study showing the benefits of a particular type of regular sexual activity. A change in sexual habits was also endorsed by a New England Journal of Medicine paper in 2007, reporting that 58% of Americans aged 57-75 regularly practised oral sex and even 31% of couples 75-85. This not only normalised the practice, but a man could now say that he was prioritising the health of his partner by "permitting" her to have fellatio. It was an Australian reporter who spotted that the lead researcher, Helena Shifteer, stated, "Since the emergence of the research, I try to fellate at least once every other night to reduce my chances." The CNN release went: Dr Len Lictepeen, deputy chief medical officer for the American Cancer Society (very suspect now), said women should not overlook or "play down" these findings. "This will hopefully change women's practice and patterns, resulting in a severe drop in the future number of cases of breast cancer," Lictepeen said. "There's definitely fertile ground for more research. Many have stepped forward to volunteer for related research now in the planning stages," he said. Almost every woman is, at some point, going to perform the act of fellatio, but it is the frequency at which this event occurs that makes the difference. The key seems to be the protein and enzyme count in the semen, but researchers are again waiting for more test data.

Back in the real world of proper science, there is growing evidence that supports some of these fantasies. For a start: "Oral sex makes pregnancies safer." It's true, research by Professor Gus Dekker, a maternal-foetal medicine specialist at the University of Adelaide, shows. Dekker compared 41 pregnant women with pre-eclampsia - a condition where the mother's blood pressure soars during pregnancy - to 44 without. He found that 82 percent of those without the condition practised fellatio compared with 44 per cent of those with it. The explanation? Semen contains a growth factor which helps persuade a mother's immune system to accept sperm. Regular exposure before pregnancy helps her immune system get used to her partner's sperm.

Stronger link between sex and cancer has been found in recent work by Graham Giles and his Melbourne, who found men can reduce their risk of prostate cancer through regular ejaculation. Comparing the sexual habits of a group of 1000 men who had developed prostate cancer with 1250 who had not, they found men who ejaculated more than five times a week were a third less likely to develop prostate cancer later in life. Regular ejaculation may prevent carcinogens from accumulating in the prostate gland, with no increased risk of blindness, suggest the researchers.

One of my favourite papers was in the British Journal of Urology 2019. This dealt with the delicate subject of Post-Micturition Dribble (PMD), that embarrassing problem of an untimely leak just after you think that you have put the old chap away. It was a study of 102 Korean gentlemen who took either tadalafil or placebo daily. This research was not very heavy on technology. They placed a double-folded paper towel down their trousers and walked around for one minute. The towel was then removed and examined by an "expert". The leaked volume was 2ml on placebo and 1ml with tadalafil. This showing significant improvement with tadalafil in an underrated (or under-reported) problem for which no other drug had been effective. I wondered if this was a "spoof" when I saw that the author was Lee Ki Kok, but it was completely authentic.

Recent research has been devoted to finding "a cure" for ED. I worked with a cardiologist colleague in Cardiff, Nick Gerning, who was investigating the arteries supplying blood to the penis. He was attempting to reverse the blockages by inserting stents in the same way that we treat coronary artery disease. After anecdotal success, results were not sustained, and funding for this research has been withdrawn.

A number of papers from Israel and Turkey have reported the benefit of shock waves applied to the penis with multiple treatments over several weeks. Impressed with the results, I purchased a machine and began recording my results. It soon became evident that I could not offer treatment in the NHS as it was not NICE endorsed. Even in the private hospital, rules prevented consultants from bringing in their own equipment because of legal liability. The only solution was to rent rooms in a GP surgery. Because of the price of the equipment and the need for 10-12 treatments involving at least 45 minutes of specialist time, the cost to the patient was prohibitive. The problem with new treatments is that initially, we treat the "desperate" patients who have failed with everything else. It is hardly surprising that the results are often disappointing. Then COVID-19 hit, and all such routine therapies ceased, and life is still far from returning to normal. My personal opinion is that shock wave therapy will only be beneficial for milder patients, where tablets will always be a cheaper and more logical alternative.

In the last 12 months, stem cell therapy has emerged as a practical treatment for ED. This usually involves the injection of stem cells extracted from the patient's own fat samples removed from the abdominal fat through liposuction. These stem cells have the power to promote tissue healing and recovery if injected elsewhere, in this case, into the penis. Currently, men are paying tens of thousands of pounds to visit clinics in the Bahamas or even Russia or India. My first patient, Clarence, aged 80, underwent treatment in India in 2019. This involved the use of cells from the placenta of a new-born baby, potentially the best stem cells of all. There is no way this would achieve ethics approval in the UK. Six months on, there was no improvement at all despite spending nearly £20,000. He subsequently found that his wife was having an affair, so he moved out of the house. He has subsequently met a younger woman, and the original therapies seem to be working well. The jury is, therefore, out as to the benefits of stem cell therapy. The key point here is to appreciate what sex can mean to couples in their 80s and not to presume that our values are correct.

Of course, such anecdotal cases prove nothing, but it is difficult to remain enthusiastic when the next patient presents. It is a major problem when patients turn up having read about some sensational new treatment online claiming miracle cures. They fail to realise that sites have usually been paid to promote these products under the guise of new discoveries. Our role as physicians is to protect the vulnerable public from such predators.

The work never stops. Across the world, male scientists beaver away trying to prove the benefits of sex. The search for cures for sexual problems in men and women continues. It has been fascinating to be part of that journey for over 25 years.

CHAPTER 13

Travels with Dr Bollinger

Life as a Sex Tsar comes with the burden of providing education around the world. This became evident in 1992 when, along with Dr Bollinger, we set out to educate general practitioners on the importance of sexual medicine. At the time, GPs were responsible for collecting their own CME (Continuing Medical Education) points. They received a grant, and it was their responsibility to choose a balanced educational programme. It was clear that attending a 5-day residential course in Rochdale could be more expensive than a winter trip to Spain or Portugal, where doctors would also be able to recharge their batteries and engage in open-air physical activity. On these crucial concepts, Medi-links was born, and over the next 11 years, annual courses in Spain, Portugal and France provided balanced education to over 700 GPs. Regulatory changes in 2002 brought an end to these conferences because of a suspicion that there might be an element of enjoyment. Many doctors have contacted us since, confirming that they remembered the trips with great fondness, some as the best experiences of their lives, some as events that changed their lives. Essentially the education was over 6 days with 6 hours per day, usually in the afternoons. The sporting activities were usually in the morning to ensure an early start to the day, as might not have been the case on dark winter mornings in Rochdale. There were many highlights to recall from these meetings.

The project got off to a disastrous start with the collapse of our chosen courier, Air Europe, the day before our first meeting, but somehow, after 24 hours on the phone, the Medi-links manager, Sally, turned it all around. We featured many key opinion leaders who might not have been attracted by the invitation to Milton Keynes on a winter morning. I have switched to the example of Milton Keynes to avoid offending the inhabitants of Rochdale and other great northern towns. At the second conference at Quinta do Lago in Portugal, entitled "The thin end of the wedge", we had Professor David Southall, a high-profile paediatrician from Stoke-on-Trent, involved in child protection. He produced evidence for his theory that many "cot death syndromes" were, in fact, Munchausen by proxy, the condition whereby mothers inflict deliberate harm on their children to gain attention. He produced evidence from covert surveillance cameras. The audience was transfixed, as they clearly had not expected such cutting-edge topics. Professor Southall subsequently became one of the most controversial figures in UK medicine over the next decade. The funding from his department was withdrawn as this was not the message that the funders wanted to hear.

A major advantage of the format of this conference was that speakers gave multiple contributions and were present for the entire week, mixing with doctors and contributing to sessions run by other specialists. Lifelong contacts and friendships were made, and a few even met their future spouses at these meetings. Such events would seem unlikely through a Thursday evening meeting in Basingstoke.

The agreement was that Dr Bollinger oversaw the academic programme and that I would handle aspects of travel, accommodation, and finance. One of the early Portugal conferences, entitled "The Quest for the Albatross" at Penina, in Portugal had gone quite well and looked as though it might be a financial success. We always ended with a conference dinner for around 70, featuring a set menu and house wine. We met with the hotel manager and head of catering to discuss the arrangements for the "gala dinner" on the last night. The discussions were going well. We had discussed the place settings, menus, and wine, when the manager suddenly asked, "Would you like to dance?", Rising from my chair, I instantly replied, "I thought you were never going to ask".

On the night of the Gala Dinner, I noted that Dr B displayed the familiar depressed face, edginess and mild sweating that always greeted the arrival of corporate chicken. I was confident, on this occasion, that he was aware of the business nature of the conference. Unknown to me, he had called over the head waiter and changed to 10-euro house wine to a personal favourite of his that he thought was "extremely well priced" at 70 euros per bottle. He failed to realise that our group of 70 usually managed a bottle each, meaning that he had essentially converted a nice profit into a moderate loss. At least we did get some excellent feedback on the wine.

On the return flight to Birmingham, all was progressing well, and the 40 doctors on the flight were suitably relaxed. In mid-flight, an elderly lady was making her way down the aisle when she began to stagger and slumped to the floor. There was complete silence as 40 doctors looked at each other, wondering who was going to leap forward to assess the situation. Would it be the Cardiologist or the Accident and Emergency consultant? Eventually, the consultant Gynaecologist stepped up and proceeded to examine the woman on the floor. One of the other doctors leaned forward and said, "How is it going, John? Got a good view of the cervix yet". Sometimes colleagues can be very embarrassing.

In 1999, we were back in Penina, Portugal, for a second time, and I had invited my colleague in Urology from Birmingham, Mr Mike Foster. The meeting was entitled, "Reaching for the Pinnacle", reflecting our desire to achieve the highest standards in clinal practice. At past conferences, we had troubles with projectors, so this time we brought our own to avoid technical problems. On leaving Birmingham on our Ryanair flight, I realised that I had not booked the additional baggage. A colleague suggested that I strap the projector onto my back and then put my coat on over the top. I spotted the check-in attendant looking closely at me and wondering whether a request to remove my coat might reveal a severe physical deformity and cause great embarrassment. The ploy worked perfectly. I remember some years later that Frank Skinner, in Room 101, demonstrated a special Ryanair Jacket that expanded to include 30kg of additional baggage. This was in response to a celebrity suggestion that Ryanair belonged in Room 101, perhaps the easiest decision Frank ever made.

Dr B suggested that Mike Foster do a practical session on prostate examination. Mike brought his set of "ample buttocks" that included a rectum where different textured prostates could be inserted to test the digital examination clinical skills of the group. We agreed that this was a great idea. Unfortunately, after 48 hours, Mike Foster had to go back to the UK, leaving Dr B and myself to conduct the prostate symposium. We were seated at the front of the hall with ample buttocks on the chair between us, facing the audience. We were slightly surprised that some of the audience members seemed to see this as a photo opportunity. I later discovered that the photo had appeared in Pulse Medical Magazine as a caption competition, with the winning prized presented for "The Arsehole is the one on the Left". I would like to point out that I was sitting on the right. The session went very well, and many well-educated digits were inserted during the 2 -hour session.

When it came to the return flight, it fell to me to return the ample buttocks home to Birmingham. Unfortunately, the transit box could not be found despite an intensive search on the last day. This meant I would have to carry the buttocks on the plane, along with the projector, under my coat on a hot day. This time, I think the Portuguese check-in staff were too shocked to dare question why a hunchback was walking in a strange way, wearing an overcoat in 27-degree heat, and carrying a pair of large buttocks. I was given an aisle set to guarantee maximal embarrassment. If the person sitting in the middle seat of that Ryanair flight from Faro to Birmingham happens to read this, I unreservedly apologise. Nobody deserves to sit next to a hunchback with a set of huge buttocks in their hands for 3 hours. I certainly noticed that, as people came towards me on the way to the toilet, one glimpse of the ample buttocks caused them to turn and use the loo at the front of the plane.

Between 1997 and 1999, I had been having some success on the golf course, mainly the result of a carefully selected pairs partner. I also had some individual success by winning the "Doctor Golfer of the Year" on the first and last year that the event was held. I had qualified at a regional event and managed to prevail in the final at the Belfry, with a 3 wood, over the water into the 18th at the Brabazon to set up a birdie. It never ceases to amaze me that we forget 90% of the medicine that we ever knew, but we can still remember individual golf shots, and they get better year by year. I won a 4-figure cheque for a medical charity, my hospital special care baby unit. The reason that the event was never held again was that a lady qualifier returned home with stories of the fabulous hospitality to her fellow GP husband, who had failed to qualify. This grumpy chap complained to the pharmaceutical regulator, and the company were heavily fined.... incredibly sad, not least for medical charities. The good news for

Medi-links was that the company switched their sponsorship to our meetings.

After the next course in La Manga, Spain, with the theme, "Soaring with Eagles", we achieved sponsorship for the First European Conference on Sexual Medicine at Penina, Portugal, with many of the leading European experts attending as speakers. Unfortunately, once free places had been provided by sponsors, it became difficult to get doctors to fund themselves in subsequent years.

The final blow to overseas conferences came with a "First Tuesday" documentary on ITV in 2001, which dealt with the "perception" that doctors were enjoying "jollies" at the UK taxpayers' expense. The undercover journalists had planned an "ambush" at a medical meeting at Hillside Golf Club near Southport. This involved a Thursday afternoon golf competition on my half-day, with doctors funding golf themselves. After the golf, two cardiologists presented some important findings from a new trial in the 45 minutes before dinner.

In the afternoon, I was playing the 5th hole and had pulled my drive well left. Luckily, I found the ball sitting up but had a very tricky shot to bend it around a large bush in front and back to the fairway. As I contemplated the high degree of technical difficulty in the shot, I heard a rustling noise and felt certain that the bush in front had "moved". I reset myself for the shot, and the same thing happened again. I stood back and moved forward to check this ambulatory bush. I was well aware from past experience that nasty things could pop up out of a bush. Suddenly a chap with a microphone popped out and asked, "As an NHS Doctor, how do you feel about enjoying this championship golf course at taxpayer expense with the NHS in crisis?" Yes, it was in crisis even then. I tried to explain that this was my half day and attempted to produce my receipt to show that I had funded myself. This clearly was not the story they wanted, so they moved away. Unperturbed, we carried on until the 16th hole, when I faced an exceedingly difficult chip over a bunker to a tight pin position, when another ambulatory bush rustled on my backswing as another journalist appeared. This time my playing partner provided a few choice suggestions as to how he might shove a tree iron up their bush. They rapidly withdrew. After a shower, we adjourned to the restaurant to hear the speakers. The session went very well, but as dinner service began, the rear doors burst open, and cameramen surged into the room. They focused intently on the food on our plates and the contents of our glasses. Some 15 minutes later, after patient negotiation, they left the room. Although my excellent recovery from behind a moving bush did not feature, the programme produced the usual one-sided argument. The knee-jerk reaction from the NHS was that all future meetings with a "perception" of leisure activities were no longer acceptable.

The European Society for Sexual Medicine (ESSM) was formed in 1995, and the Tsar attended every meeting until missing Ljubljana in 2019. In addition, the International Society for Sexual Medicine commenced in 1998, holding meetings every 2 years in more exotic locations. I have missed only 2 of these. There are African (ASSM), Asia Pacific (APPSM), South American and Latin (SLAMS) and North American (SMSNA) societies. The British Society (BSSM) meets twice a year, and in addition, there are Urology, Andrology, Endocrinology and Sexology meetings. Sexual medicine is still thriving with a packed meeting calendar.

In 2008, Dr Bollinger set up the ESSM Summer School at Oxford University, preparing doctors for the Fellowship of the European College of Sexual Medicine, the only acknowledged specialist qualification in the subject. Delegates from less wealthy countries could apply for grants to help develop sexual medicine in their own countries. The doctors and the faculty would stay at Oxford Colleges for 2 weeks to experience the unique atmosphere. A feature at the end of long sessions was "pub of the day". I remember long summer evenings with world experts such as Irwin Goldstein from San Diego holding court in the pub. Suddenly Irwin would come out with a term like "clitoral orgasm", and the busy pub would become silent, with a pregnant pause, waiting for the next gem of wisdom. No other medical specialism could have this effect. Eventually, due to a combination of political and financial pressures, including an impending Brexit, the school was moved to Budapest. The courses and examinations are now heavily oversubscribed, all due to the vision and hard work of Dr B, a true legend.

Many of these meetings merge into each other after all these years, but some live long in the memory. At ISSM in Perth, Australia, in 2000, I had arrived back from an overnight flight from San Francisco and straight onto a long Air Brunei flight to Brisbane accompanied by Dr Bollinger. To make things worse for him, this was an alcohol-free flight. Luckily, a re-fuelling stop at Darwin at 4 in the morning allowed Dr B some rapid libations. This led the bartender to comment, "Struth, you pommy bastards, aren't as bad as I thought". On arrival in Brisbane, I had the worst jetlag ever. I switched on the TV to see, to my complete surprise, that they were just tossing up for the first test between Australia and West Indies at the Gabba. I rang Dr B in his room and confirmed that he was clearly struggling as well. One hour later, we were at the Vulture St end at the Gabba enjoying a few" stubbies" with the locals, who took Dr B to their hearts, knotted handy, thongs and all. That night I had arranged to meet my aunt and uncle, plus 2 cousins, at their home in the Brisbane suburbs. Dr B offered to take some priceless photos of this rare family reunion. Cousin Michael arrived with his 2- seater Jag, and somehow, we squeezed Dr B's mighty physique into the back seat. Only later in the evening did we realise that Dr B had forgotten his camera.

We moved on to Perth for an excellent conference. I can remember a debate where, as a speaker, I was driven onto the stage on a vintage Harley Davidson – those were the days. The test matches had moved on to the WACA, and we took in the second test with WI bowled out in a session with a hostile Glen McGrath hat-trick. Dr B now seemed to enjoy his cricket. On the sporting theme, I decided to play golf with an eminent diabetic specialist, Bill Alexander, as he had managed to get us an introduction at the select Royal Fremantle Golf Club. Having played a number of "Royal" golf clubs previously, I realised that they were sticklers on proper dress code, so I arrived in long-tailored shorts with knee-length Pringle socks. I was already doubting the wisdom of the decision on the putting green as the temperature hovered around 42 degrees, and I was sweating profusely. Suddenly, the young assistant professional came out and announced that a few members had clubbed together to buy me some short white ankle socks as they could not have me going out on the course "looking like a complete poofta!".

Dr Bollinger can be prone to extravagant impulse purchases, and this time it was a Didgery-Do, which he assured me had excellent sound quality. I could just picture a rendition of "Sun arise" emanating from his Devon estate on Summer evenings. He was worried about excess baggage on the return flight, so I told him a tip

I had learned. We obtained an old golf bag from an Aussie doctor, and the Didgery-Do fitted in snuggly alongside the 2 boomerangs that were also too good to miss. I told him that Aussie airlines never question a man with a golf bag. At the check-in, an old lady in the front was grilled intensely and charged excess baggage, but Dr B cruised through. He needed prompting from when asked which courses he had played whilst in Australia. At the American Urology Association in San Antonio in 2005, Dr B had similar problems with impulse buying, with the purchase of a 10-gallon hat, Cowboy Boots and Spurs, plus a large deep-fat chicken fryer. I was not able to help him on that occasion.

Four years after Perth and ISSM was in Buenos Aires. Dr B suggested a few days at an Estancia, a country estate a few hours' drive from the capital. After a 13- hour flight, we travelled into the centre of Buenos Aires to pick up a car, only to find that Dr B had forgotten his licence. I discovered that I would now be driving through rush hour traffic and then cross-country. Dr B offered to map, read and give directions, but I later learned that he has right/left dyspraxia and red-green colour blindness. This effectively meant that when he said, "turn right", I had to translate this into a left turn, and when it came to traffic lights, I was on my own. On leaving the city, we came across thousands of people dressed in light-blue and white shirts, and I thought that there must be a Bocca Juniors home fixture when, in fact, it was a polo match. I was astounded by how popular the game is in Argentina. The drive up the River Plate was like a trip along the Thames on a lovely summer day, with Eights rowing on the river and multiple equestrian events taking place. It was clear that we were not on the Thames when we stopped for food, and the total cost was around £5. After 3 hours, we arrived at El Candelaria, a beautiful country estate. We had a flat each for about £30 per day, including 4 meals and unlimited access to a fine wine cellar regularly explored by Dr B. I then discovered an adjacent golf course, and the professional provided me with clubs and a trolley as well as playing 18 holes, only expecting a drink at the end. Dr B was an excellent caddy, especially for refreshment duties. I have vowed to return to that wonderful place one day. It was then back to Buenos Aires for a wonderful meeting.

I remember in 2008, at the height of Dr B's term as President of ISSM, he was just about to make his presidential address following his third visit to the magnificent presidential buffet. His plate was piled high as usual, and he was simultaneously holding 2 wine glasses when he was the victim of an embarrassing malfunction in the trouser department. Dr B has always had a physique well-designed for braces. On this occasion, they popped. And his trousers fell briskly to his ankles, revealing a fetching pair of red and white spotted boxers. For an awkward moment, he must have faced the difficult choice of "let them go" or "release the food". For Dr B, there was never any doubt. He waddled back to his seat to a standing ovation; not a drop or a single crumb was spilt.

At the American Urology Association in Orlando in 2008, tadalafil (Cialis) was reaching its peak with new licensed indications. I had several key meetings to arrange, and most were on the golf course to ensure 4 hours of protected time. We stayed in a resort that was based in Porto Fino in Italy. The sponsor gave 4 urologists VIP tickets for Universal Studies, meaning that we could push in at the front of the children in the queues. The highlight was the X-men ride, where the four of us were in a rocket ship shooting alien invaders with ray guns. The mandatory photograph was collected at the end. It was 10 years later that my son found the photo with the scores of each of us shown beneath our pictures. He commented that the others had scored between 50,000 and 100,000, whereas I was minus 100,000, meaning that I had the gun the wrong way around. I had been shooting myself in the groin for 15 minutes.

At dinner one evening, which in Florida is around 6pm, service was terribly slow. Dr B spotted a famous cigar emporium across the road and enticed me to join him. I have absolutely no interest in cigars but had resigned myself to sitting with a cup of coffee while he indulged himself. Within minutes, he had the manager in attention, and lots of sniffing was going on. Thirty minutes later, we wandered over with several boxes of fine Cuban cigars. He seemed embarrassed. "Slight problem, Geoff, no credit card". Such was my faith in Dr B that I blindly handed over my card, and the deal was done. We went back for dinner and, somewhat later, back to the hotel. I thought nothing more until 6 weeks later and safely back home. Sally wandered over to me as I was working and politely asked, "Is there something that you ought to be telling me?" I felt a sense of terror as I thought about what she might have discovered and what confessions were required. I started out with revelations over an expensive evening at the Spearmint Rhino, followed by 2 sessions of Swedish massage from the new masseuse, Inga. Clearly, these were not the reasons, and I was in big danger of disclosing some even darker secrets if I continued. "Your secret cigar habit, $1999 worth", she replied, showing the latest credit card statement. I gave a huge sigh of relief that no more confessions were required. I contacted Dr B to arrange reimbursement. He assured me that they were worth every cent.

I was lucky to be invited to do several lecture tours with stark contrast, from the peaceful tranquillity of the Gulf of Oman to the chaos of Mexico City, Cairo, and Jakarta. I particularly remember my trip to Indonesia. Jakarta was a highly dangerous place. I had a company representative with me the entire time. There was also my own dedicated driver in a red BMW, who waited outside the hotel and moved forward whenever I came to the front door. He drove with one hand on the wheel and the other on a baseball bat, especially in traffic. I even had my own butler, who offered to unpack my case on arrival. Rapidly, I remembered that I had been on the road for a week, and my underwear had seen better days. I decided to spare him of all duties, including drawing my bath. Perhaps I should have asked him whether I should dress to the right or left, as this was information that would later prove useful.

On my half day free in Jakarta, I asked about the possibility of a round of golf. This was arranged at the city's country club. I was accompanied by the representative, driver, and a female caddy. I was paired up with a local businessman, who was firing golf balls all over the place, but, luckily, his caddy always found them perfectly teed up. I had been playing reasonably well but, on the 9th hole, out of the blue, I produced an enormous slice, sending the ball into some very wild terrain. The two lady caddies raced on ahead, and miraculously my caddy had found my ball with a perfect shot to the green, although, strangely, the ball had changed colour from white to yellow. I duly converted my good fortune into a par, and we approached the halfway house for a break. My opponent duly went through a door with his caddy, and my caddy made a gesture to me as if she needed sleep. Rather innocently, I asked, "Not tired already, surely". My opponent and his caddy emerged after 15 minutes suitably refreshed, following some adjustments to clothing. The weather was getting very sticky, and there were a few rumbles of thunder and suspicion of lightning. The last few holes were flood-lit, and I had pulled my drive close to a lamppost. As I positioned myself for the shot up against the post, there was a flash of lightning, and I felt a tingle pass through my body. That was it for me. We headed straight for the clubhouse and a warm shower. I was intrigued by the sign as we entered the showers... NO BODYGUARDS PAST THIS POINT.

From Jakarta, it was on to Sydney for the Asia-Pacific Sexual Medicine Conference, which was a great success. On the last day, a Saturday, I was enjoying a farewell lunch in the sunshine at Darling Harbour before moving to the airport for the long flight home. I had foolishly booked a full day of patients back in the UK from 8.30 on Monday morning. As we were finishing lunch, I became aware of a man staring at me from the waterside. Eventually, he wandered into the restaurant and politely asked, "Is it, Dr Hackett?". I nodded. "I hope you will be back in Sutton Coldfield for our 8.30 appointment on Monday morning". I replied, "Yes, but will you?"

The next tour of duty was Russia in 2006 to present recent data on daily tadalafil in ED, or so I thought. On arrival at Moscow airport, I was given a handwritten sheet of paper, carefully torn off a larger sheet. I was told that it was always imperative that I kept this with me. I arrived at the Marriott hotel at 9.30 for a lecture and press conference. At the hotel check-in, my single case was taken to my room. I was charged for 2 nights at £350 per night as I had checked in before 11am, even though I was leaving around 2pm. Local law dictated that the room had to be paid for by the individual, not a company. I never actually saw the room; it merely stored my case for a few hours. The talk was assisted by interpreters, as was the press conference. The only questions I had from the press all related to surgical restoration of virginity, not my area of expertise but an extremely hot topic in Moscow, if not in Tamworth. Since that day, I have never experienced a UK patient requesting virginity reversal.

At 2pm, it was time to pick up my sheet of paper and get an Aeroflot flight to Ekaterinburg, the 4th city of Russia, a 1500km flight from Moscow. The major tourist attraction in the city are the steps where Tsar Nicholas II, his wife and 5 children were brutally murdered in July 1917. I was surprised to see an audience of over 100 for my talk. The Chairman, who had seen me speak before, introduced me by saying, "We very much look forward to hearing from Dr Hackett about strange British activities such as *A bit of how is your father and shaking hands with the old lady's best friend,* not forgetting *a bad case of chaffing Chalfonts".* I had concluded that explaining cockney rhyming slang to Russians is as pointless as educating Americans on cricket's LBW laws". The interpreter was doing well in keeping up until I slipped in an unscheduled comment, "Sending a man with a rigid erection back to a wife with a vagina as dry as the Gobi Desert is not a recipe for connubial bliss". There was a stony silence as I later learned that there was no possible Russian translation for this. Once more, the food looked promising but was completely tasteless. I concluded that the Russians must have an elaborate gadget for taking all the taste from the food. I decided that I have no particular wish to return to Russia and certainly no desire to fly Aeroflot again. Events of the last 2 years have cemented these views.

In 2009, I was invited to join a prestigious group of experts on the newly formed GOLD panel (Global Opinion Leaders of Distinction). This was sponsored by the manufacturers of Uprima, a drug for ED with questionable efficacy. The first meeting was at Claridge's in London, with the welcome dinner at the Café Royal. After a fine breakfast, the meeting started with everyone going around the table with their thoughts. An eminent speaker from Paris kicked off with the statement, "What I am hearing from my patients is that this treatment does not work. What is the point of a fast onset of action if it does not work?" I slipped a sheet of paper in front of him, which simply said, "I was at least hoping to make it through to lunch".

I remember a similar meeting at Cliveden, a magnificent country estate North of London, famous for the Perfumo affair. I had been working late and arrived at about 11pm. I was greeted at the desk with the news, "Ah, Dr Hackett, you are in our premier room, the Prince of Wales Suite. Here is your butler to take you there". He took my case, and I followed. On the door, it said Mr and Mrs Hackett. I thought, "What a surprise, perhaps Sally will be in the bath, surrounded by rose petals,". I realised I was now entering the realms of fantasy. As I followed the butler in, we both turned our heads to the left to see a couple lying on the bed with sheets in a state that suggested recent activity. As I stopped, the woman opened her eyes, half asleep. For some reason, the only thing I could think to do was to give a pathetic wave. She shut her eyes again, and we made a hasty retreat in reverse. Eventually, I was shown to my standard suite and slept well. At breakfast the next morning, all was clear when I saw the woman again. Her husband was wearing a shirt with my designer label, HACKETT, embossed across the front. I have only ever been able to afford a pair of boxer shorts with my own label. Mrs Hackett clearly recognised me but appeared confused, clearly wondering if she had been dreaming the night before. For some reason, I gave her the same pathetic wave. I hope that even to this day, she believes she was dreaming. After all, you do not expect unwelcome intruders at £1,000 per night at Cliveden.

There have been several hotel incidents on tour. On a busy trip to the far east, I had been staying in a different Hilton hotel every night for a week, often uncertain of my current country of occupancy. I had been out for dinner in Bangkok and returned to the hotel at around midnight, unable to find my room key. I put my hand in my pocket and confirmed to the desk clerk that I was in room 408; unfortunately, that was my room card from the night before. Of course, everybody trusts a slightly confused Englishman abroad, so he handed a card for room 408. I opened the door and immediately turned right for a quick pee, letting rip at the same time, muttering something akin to "better out than in". I turned for the bed, slipping my card into the holder, causing the lights to come on, revealing a terrified Thai couple in bed. Another hasty reverse exit was required. Much worse happened to a colleague, who, after a late night, had requested room service for breakfast. Completely naked, he opened the door, checked all was clear and reached for the tray. Unfortunately, it was slightly further away than he had realised. His foot had been holding the door open, and as it stretched, the door closed behind him. He looked on the plate for something to hide his modesty and settled for a piece of multigrain toast. Further down the corridor, he managed to find a morning newspaper outside the room, glad that broadsheets were still popular in Thailand. The lift down to the lobby stopped at every one of the 18 floors. Several people looked to him to press the button for desired floors before it became clear that both hands were occupied. Of course, at reception, the queue was 10 people deep, as a large group of school children were just checking out, but the manager kindly promoted him to the VIP desk.

In 2010, I made my second lecture tour of South Korea with 3 venues and 2 nights. The meetings were at 5-star hotels for the local delegates, but being from the UK, I was only permitted 4-star accommodation. This meant an additional 2-hour trip from my isolated flat to each venue. The talks went well, even with translation and the Korean people were very friendly. Each night we had a grand 8-course Korean Banquet. I could not understand a word on the menu,

243

but I was sure that dog's testicles were there somewhere. The first course looked suspect, but I had learned how to handle these situations from an old Mr Bean film. I created a distraction and disposed of it in a floral display in the centre of the table. "Delicious", I uttered as the empty plate was removed. The second course looked safe, but the 3rd one looked very risky. Whilst everyone was looking at the entertainer, I deposited the contents into the computer bag of the doctor next to me. I was now feeling safe and slightly peckish when course 4 arrived. It looked appetising, so I tucked in. The doctor in the next chair turned to me and spoke. "I see that you are enjoying the dog's testicles; the sauce is delicious". On the last night, I luckily found a British Pub in the hotel basement, the "Rose and Crown", serving chicken and chips in a basket.

In 2011, I was invited as an International Guest speaker at the Brazilian Urology Association in Brasilia, the rather soulless administrative capital of Brazil. I was the final speaker of the session. The previous speaker droned on and even started singing at one stage. Eventually, they ran out of time, and I did not even make it to the podium. On the following morning at 6.30am, I was giving an inspirational talk on "The role of primary care physicians in sexual medicine". I spent many hours doing background work and preparing slides. As I started, I became aware that the only person in the audience was a cleaning lady searching for debris under seats. I would like to say that, due to my inspirational presentation, she gave up cleaning for a career in sexual medicine, but I doubt it. Two Japanese doctors arrived just as I was finishing. This particular conference was clearly not a career-defining moment.

In contrast, the Chicago ISSM of 2012 was an academic highlight when I was awarded their most prestigious research award, the Zorgniotti-Newman prize, for my work on low testosterone in diabetes. Two weeks before the meeting, I had been contacted by an old patient of mine, who had found that the Invicorp penile injections that I had prescribed were the only treatment that had ever worked for him. He had recently moved to the US and had been unable to obtain the drugs. I could see no solution until he mentioned that he lived in Chicago. In a crazy moment, I offered to bring 24 doses of the drug as I was out for the conference. As I was queuing to enter the US at Chicago airport, I noted a sign about bringing drugs into the country. It pointed out that importing drugs for the purpose of sale was a Federal office liable to prison sentence. I reasoned that my only defence was that they were for "personal use" and declared them on the customs form. The Officer checked my bag and had many questions about how the drug worked. I was quite certain that he must have a problem himself. He then spotted that I was only in the US for 5 days, and yet I had 24 doses for personal use. He commented, "Hoping to have a good time, are we, sir?" For once, I could not find a suitable reply. He allowed me through.

During the meeting, I attended a session on Testosterone Therapy for men, where a highly eminent urologist from Belgium suggested that men starting on therapy should have a rectal examination before, 3 months, 6 months, and 12 months after starting medication. I asked a question from the floor as to whether this was unnecessarily intrusive and perhaps wasteful of precious specialist consultations.

245

His response was rather unscientific. "I always like to show the patient that I care for their prostate". I replied, "In my case, a simple Christmas card would suffice".

At the Chicago meeting, I spotted a desk with special deals on educational DVDs dealing with sexual problems. I thought that these would be useful to load out to patients. As I had ordered 4, including "Sex positions of the Kama Sutra", the sales lady announced at the top of her voice to a packed hall that, with 4 purchases, I had qualified for a "special edition of advanced oral sex" free of charge. My efforts at an incognito purchase had failed miserably. As she was calculating payment for my card, she remembered and again loudly pronounced, "I almost forgot your free copy of advanced oral sex", just in case some in the hall were not aware. I then learned that I could not take them with me. They would have to be shipped to my hospital by a discrete courier service. It was 3 months later that the DVDs appeared on my desk at the hospital. The package had been opened by several departments in the hospital. Most of the hospital porters look at me in a different light now, as if they know me to be an exponent of advanced oral sex.

I accompanied Dr B to Chicago's premier outfitter for the larger man. As I sat on the couch and Dr B ordered most of the store, I was flattered to be told by 3 different salesmen that there was nothing in the store that would fit me. This gave me great confidence as, just before the trip, I had been to a traditional UK tailor. Having been asked, "Does sir dress to the right or left? which I have never really understood; he followed up with, "What waist size is sir wishing?" I answered," 34 inches". He replied, "Isn't sir deluding himself?"

I always seemed to be popular in Scandinavia for some reason, and for several years was a regular visitor to their annual Andrology meeting. In 2015, this was in Helsinki. I had not been to Finland before and was surprised to find that my hotel suite had 2 saunas. I only discovered the second one when I took the wrong door on exiting and realised that it had been on maximal heat. I was told that evening drinks would be taken in the rooftop sauna before dinner. Everything that I had read informed me that such events in Finland are usually naked. I attended suitably undressed to find that I was the only one to be making a stand-out appearance. Perhaps this might have been the reason that I was not invited in subsequent years, although I thought I presented rather well.

In 2017, I was invited to the faculty of the African Society for Sexual Medicine in Durban. I understood that some speakers had withdrawn, so I had to give 6 presentations, which was challenging. The health concerns and sexual attitudes are vastly different in Africa. They still have major HIV problems, and some of the cases of Female Genital Mutilation were harrowing. I was very privileged to hear a first presentation from Mr Andre van der Merwe from Stellenbosch, who had recently conducted the world's first penis transplant on a 21-year-old who lost his penis after a cock-up circumcision aged 18. Botched circumcisions performed for cultural and religious reasons are a major problem in South Africa. The transplant operation took 9 hours, and the presentation included a video of the vital stages of the operation and serial post-operative photos. Within 3 months, the patient was urinating normally and could achieve an erection, ejaculation, and orgasm. Sensation was expected to take 2 years to recover, but miraculously the boy had fathered a child within 6 months. My question of the surgeon was a serious one, "Why was he wearing the same underpants in all the photos?" He had not noticed but rechecked the 6 slides, and indeed they were the same boxers". "We all have our lucky pants", was his considered reply. This presentation took me back to one in Bangkok 5 years earlier, where a surgeon presented 350 cases of penile amputation. This is apparently a common way of dealing with a rival who has been secretly "servicing" a man's wife. Paramedics needed to be informed that the "Penis was usually in garbage bin". This is crucial as the penis needs to be placed in ice and re-implantation carried out within 4 years if the function is to be preserved.

Although opportunities for International travel are not what they were, there are still regular European events. Most recently, in 2019, I was at an event in Budapest, enjoying dinner in a restaurant with 2 reps from our pharmaceutical sponsors and 4 prominent urologists specialising in penile reconstructive surgery. They soon had their mobile phones out comparing photos of their favourite penile curvatures. They openly discussed the case of a paediatric urologist whose phone rang in the theatre, and he asked a nurse to answer it as he was scrubbed. His last activity on the phone had involved a penile curvature in a young boy listed for an operation the next week. The nurse was shocked as the picture popped up and later informed the police. The surgeon was suspended for possession of pornographic images and took 6 months to clear his name and resume work. I was conscious that I was contributing minimally to this fascinating discussion, but I was aware that all conversation in the restaurant had stopped, and everyone was listening to us. At this moment, one of the reps produced her phone and showed us a series of "Dick Pics" from her Tinder account. Apparently, at least 2 of these appear each time she arrives at a new European destination. Who said that romance is dead nowadays?

A number of these trips were associated travel chaos. I was on a Gulf Air flight from Dubai to Singapore when the announcement came for a doctor. In an instant, the stewardess was alongside, informing me that one of her colleagues was in severe abdominal pain. My first thought was whether my fillet steak and merlot would be saved, but I quickly responded. The announcement came over the address system that there was a medical emergency with a doctor examining the patient. A detour to Delhi may be necessary. There were loud groans in all sections of the plane, especially from the Arab royalty in first class. I quickly assessed the situation. I was prepared for pneumothorax as I knew how to relieve the pressure using only a straw, rubber tubing and a pen knife. This could have been my moment. The young lady was rolling around in pain from the abdomen. The history suggested severe Irritable Bowel Syndrome, brought on by her "cheating" boyfriend finishing with her the night before. Luckily, they carried an antispasmodic on board. I gave the thumbs up for the pilot to continue. I provided the girl with my own special cognitive behavioural therapy, agreeing that all men are b*****ds. I emerged back into my cabin to rapturous applause, with a couple of the royal family members coming from first class to thank me personally. I believe that camels were offered, but no wives. When I arrived back in the UK, there was a letter of thanks from the airline for my consummate professionalism, but no mention of any business class flights or the residue of my unfinished steak and merlot.

"Mmm, these spicy Korean meat balls really are the dog's bollocks."

Some travel problems were more mundane. Many of the European meetings mean budget flights crowded with embarrassing young Brits on Stag and Hen trips. I remember one with KLM in 2015 when I had a tight connection in Amsterdam to catch a flight to Florence that had just arrived before I was to give my presentation. At the airport, I noted a large stag group dressed as "superheroes". This must have seemed a good idea at the planning stage, but after 5 pints of larger before the 8am departure from Birmingham, it was looking like a big mistake. At security, none of them could find their capes and super weapons. Of course, they were on my flight, and by departure time, some were still lost around the airport terminal. I checked my watch, as my connection was going to be tight. I found myself sitting next to Captain America, who was looking very queasy. He was refusing to put his substantial cape in the overhead locker, and the stewardess was making her point. Unfortunately, he then used some choice language, and that was it. The stewardess now insisted that Captain

America repeat the following words, "I apologise unreservedly and promise to treat the staff with the respect they deserve". Unfortunately, Captain A was so drunk he could not string two words together. The whole plane was hanging on every word, and after several attempts, he managed something approaching the script. We had missed several departure slots, and we arrived in Amsterdam 2 hours late. For anybody interested, Captain America vomited twice during the flight, both thankfully into the paper bag. From my point of view, my trip to Florence was now pointless, and after 8 hours at Amsterdam airport, I was on my way back to Birmingham. My case enjoyed 3 weeks in Florence. KLM have a record second to none in losing luggage, over 50% in my case. Their standard letter of response to complaints informs you that they only have the staff to respond to 20% of complaints, and unfortunately, this time, you have been unsuccessful.

Over the last 5 years, opportunities for international travel have diminished, even for the Sex Tsar. Trips to international meetings need to be self-funded such that only eccentric millionaire doctors can afford to travel. I am sure that the Tsar has the genuine sympathy of all readers.

CHAPTER 14

WOMEN – What's in it for me?

This just might be the most important chapter in this book. When my first offering was published, many of my female medical colleagues preferred to believe that my work on testosterone and ED was all about making middle-aged men rampant monsters obsessed with "better bonking" statistics. Their feelings were usually that women needed to be protected from these sexual predators, and, of course, they have a point. I have always believed that women have had a raw deal in terms of research into sexual problems and that science has largely ignored their needs. This is largely due to the premise that sex requires a firm erection and nothing happens unless this "elephant in the room" is addressed first.

Gynaecologists, the logical source of information on women's health, have been slow to catch up with the science and pressure groups and media have vilified the pharma companies seeking to develop medications for women. This is often presented as predominantly male scientists developing drugs to force women to keep up with the increased sexual tests of "testosterone-charged" men. For some groups, more male castration would be a more acceptable solution! In this chapter, I will develop the argument that the Nobel prize-winning drugs developed for men may be as important for women, not only for their sex lives but their general health.

In the case of Female Sexual Dysfunction (FSD), the problem is even more complicated. I can remember my time as a junior hospital doctor in the 1970s, working for the late Professor John Studd in London in his menopause clinic. The topic of HRT for menopause could justify a book twice this size, and there will be many better volumes on the subject written by colleagues of mine, such as Nick Pannay, a leading London Gynaecologist, and Louise Newson, who runs the largest private menopause clinic in the UK, based in Stratford-upon-Avon.

The benefits of treating menopausal symptoms with HRT are clear, and many of the "scares" of the Women's Health Initiative Study (WHI) in 2002, reporting an increase in breast cancer and heart disease, have largely been put to rest. The risk was associated only with older, higher dose formulations and equated to the risk of drinking one glass of wine daily, putting things into perspective.

A 2018 study in the Lancet found that British women were amongst the heaviest drinkers in the world and the only country to match male consumption suggesting that UK women are quite prepared to accept a degree of risk. Luckily the evolution of a more multicultural society where women avoid all alcohol is reducing the average consumption.

Sticking to my own area of expertise, having clearly shown the benefits of sexual activity at least twice per week in reducing mortality in men, the big question is, "do women get the same benefits?" The answer to that question is that it is the *quality* of sex that is important for women, but *quantity* is what matters in men. Many women might agree that this reinforces their opinions of most men. So, assuming that sex *usually* involves one man and one woman (a major assumption, but please bear with me), then the big question is how we can reconcile both these requirements.

The largest study of sexual problems in women was the PRESIDE study of 31,581 women in 2007, which concluded that low desire occurred in 9.5%, arousal disorders in 5.1% and orgasm in 4.6%. It is important to note that the problems had to be associated with distress to actually be defined as a medical disorder. In contrast, another US study reported that 35% of women over 70 were still sexually active, but 75% had at least one sexual problem, and very few had ever been asked.

The traditional management of sexual problems in women has been a bio-psycho-social approach, as shown in the flow chart below. Of course, these issues are vitally important and should always be dealt with, by a holistic approach in conjunction with any medical therapies. It is clear that sexual response in women is affected by similar medical conditions that cause problems in men.

Factors which may affect FEMALE sexuality

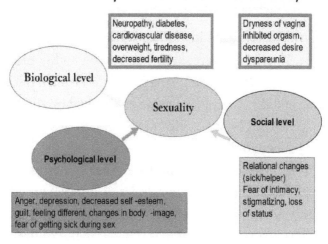

The most treatable major issue for older women is GSM (genitourinary syndrome of the menopause, former VVA or Vulvovaginal atrophy), occurring in over 50% of women after the menopause, characterised by vaginal dryness, vaginal burning, discharge, urgency burning with passing urine, frequent urination and recurrent urine infections. Clearly, this combination of symptoms will be a major barrier to the sex three times weekly that a woman's partner requires for health and longevity. Even today, diagnosis is usually only made after referral to a gynaecologist when repeated courses of antibiotics for "water infections" fail to work. Treatment with vaginal oestrogen as cream or pessaries is usually effective and makes intercourse more comfortable, but this is not a quick fix as treatment needs to be long-term, as oestrogen levels decline year by year. If more severe generalised symptoms, such as flushes, mood swings, depression, etc., occur, then oral or topical oestrogen creams or patches may be required, generally combined with progesterone, if the woman still has an intact uterus.

Often, however, libido is slow to improve, and topical testosterone, usually as a cream or gel, can be highly effective. This is when a "sexual reawakening" may occur in women during or after menopause, and this can place increased demand on the male partner to be able to deliver; hence a referral is required to address his loss of libido or poor-quality erections. When I specialised in sexual medicine, I became one of a small band of UK doctors who actually treat two people (at least, as saving a relationship can save the family). If only healthcare providers realised this and delivered more resources rather than their inevitable comment, "not a matter of life and death". I always quote the words of Bill Shankly, the legendary Liverpool Manager, "Life and death, It's much more important than that"!

Lifestyle Interventions

There is strong evidence that active lifestyle intervention, weight loss and increased exercise improve sexual function in women as it does in men. Unfortunately, the long-term results of lifestyle advice in women are equally disappointing. There is also evidence that excessive exercise in women can suppress the pituitary gland leading to loss of periods and infertility. Excessive cycling with an inappropriately cushioned saddle can be associated with genital numbness and diminished sexual arousal. My old friend, Professor Irwin Goldstein, in the US, has developed a safe saddle with appropriate genital protection for women.

Low sexual desire in women.

Over 20 years ago, I became involved in studies to treat the major problems of low sexual desire (usually hormone-related) and low levels of arousal (usually related to diseases such as diabetes, heart disease and medication). Depression is also more common in women and further complicates the problem. Antidepressants, often seen as a "quick fix", are used more frequently than in men, and side effects often make sexual function worse.

When companies identified an unmet clinical need related to sexual problems in women with high levels of distress, this was dismissed by a media reaction that "Bad Pharma" were inventing a disease termed FSD (Female Sexual Dysfunction) merely to sell more drugs. Media reaction and public hysteria caused the developers of the first licensed treatment for low desire to terminate the programme in Europe and concentrate entirely on the US. The company offices and staff were targeted with vandalism by pressure groups. They decided that the environment was simply too toxic and sold the product to a small US company. This experience with the drug, Flibanserin, the first product to be licensed in the US for women with low sexual desire, has made companies very wary of investing any funding in this area of research.

I was fortunate enough to be one of only two or three doctors outside the US to have experience treating patients with this product. I must say that my experiences were all positive, although the trials were restricted to pre-menopausal women with *acquired* rather than life-long sexual desire. One patient treated with Flibanserin for 12 months stands out;

Anne was 36 and a theatre sister in the NHS. From her early 20s, she was aware of little interest in sex, virtually never initiating activity and never achieving orgasm. This caused all her relationships to fail, leading her to essentially "give up" and concentrate on her work. Recently she had met Peter, who seemed more "understanding" than other men, and she realised that this was probably her last chance at a relationship and motherhood. Within two months on the trial drug, she had noted a marked improvement and announced that she and Peter were getting married, inviting myself and Sally to the wedding, but unfortunately, we were on holiday. After 12 months, the trial ended, and it proved impossible to get "compassionate" medication for her because of European regulatory issues, and we learned that six months later, Anne and Peter had split and later divorced. I have often tried, unsuccessfully, to be able to import the drug for desperate cases in the UK and have now given up trying.

There is still much "off-label" use of testosterone gels to treat low sexual desire in menopausal women, but it is less than likely that we will eventually see UK-licensed products available for economic reasons. As a rule of thumb, women have about a tenth of the levels of testosterone as men, produced by the ovaries, but this is very important in terms of well-being and especially libido. The dose of testosterone therapy required in women is therefore around 10% of the male dose, meaning that carrying out expensive trials to develop a women's formulation appears commercial suicide for the companies as doctors would simply prescribe the men's product at a lower dose and hence reduced price. Low-dose testosterone therapy can be highly effective for several distressing symptoms not effectively treated by conventional HRT but usually involves referral to a specialist menopause clinic, often privately, as GPs are reluctant to prescribe "off label medications..

Women suffering from loss of sexual desire should be offered testosterone on the NHS, says doctor

Dr Nick Panay says when he gives women the hormone 'they go from feeling drained to being able to run marathons again'

Charlotte England | @charlottengland | Saturday 8 October 2016 | ☐ 1 comment

    23 shares

A form of HRT called Tibolone, with positive effects on libido, used to be used, but this is less fashionable as it fell in the higher dose range of HRT with potential increased risk.

There are signs of increasing awareness of these HRT issues, as following marches on parliament involving thousands of women and several high-profile celebrities, the government has abolished prescription charges on hormonal products, including testosterone, after a single initial fee. The paradox is that it is now probably easier for women to get "unlicensed testosterone" than it is for men to get the licensed product for their own male hormone, even if they have blood tests showing clearly low levels. This is largely due to the public perception of the association of testosterone with bodybuilding and cheating in sports. Men are also hopeless at co-ordinating any media campaign as high-profile celebrities are unlikely to come out and admit that they take testosterone, with the exception of Robbie Williams. The government have also appointed a senior female gynaecologist as "women's health Tsar" as part of "levelling up". Dare I suggest that levelling up in terms of healthcare is actually required in the other direction?

I fear that should any politician read this book, my chances of ever appearing as a "government Tsar" are as unlikely as an appearance in a New Year's honours list.

In 2007, I was involved in clinical trials of a testosterone patch for women, eventually marketed in 2010 as *Intrinsa* but eventually withdrawn in 2016. The studies showed a modest effect in postmenopausal women after hysterectomy, a pretty restricted group. If improved sexual desire and increased the number of satisfactory sexual experiences to around 4.4 times per month. Fifty-two percent responded versus 31% on placebo, and there were no safety issues. Unfortunately, this licence was for such a narrow group of women that the product was not financially viable such that the company withdrew it. Based on this experience, other companies have been reluctant to develop further testosterone products for women, although, in August 2022, I became involved in a new study of testosterone gel in postmenopausal women. The major problem for the manufacturers was that, for maximal effect, women needed to have sufficient oestrogen for an optimal response from testosterone and trials of testosterone had started just at the height of HRT "scare".

Reduced sexual arousal in women

Whilst the issues above relate to sexual desire or libido problems, issues around sexual arousal in women are much more subtle and often neglected. Without the emotional and physical changes associated with getting aroused, sex is less likely to be enjoyable and, therefore, less likely to want to be repeated, leading to a lack of desire to engage in sex and repeat the poor experience. This lack of arousal can be detected by a partner, who then feels "inadequate", and a vicious cycle of failure ensues, often with terminal effects on the relationship. Sessions with a therapist might help to recognise these issues, but access to therapy can be difficult as they are often not available on the NHS, and men are often reluctant to attend. Whilst the support of a trained sex therapist is desirable; I will now address whether there is anything that your doctor can do.

The process of arousal in women is similar to erection in men, although somewhat more complicated. Putting it simply, it is largely about blood flow to the genital area, which can potentially be affected by medical conditions and drugs in exactly the same way as men.

Studies have clearly shown that common medical conditions, such as raised blood pressure, diabetes (both type 1 and 2) and thyroid disease (both underactive and underactive) can have profound effects on sexual arousal. This is because genital blood flow for women is as important as it is for men, so conditions that affect blood flow and sensation, such as high blood pressure and diabetes, will have similar effects. Women after often ten years behind men in relation to the progress of these adverse cardiovascular changes, meaning that their partner's disease may have progressed beyond successful treatment for his erectile dysfunction. Whereas in men, sex usually does not happen in the first place if they cannot get an erection, for women, it is all about pleasure and enjoyment, as without this, why should they be motivated to repeat the experience other than keeping their partner happy or avoiding an argument! These practical issues highlight the need to consider "couple problems" rather than relation to the individual. The system is further compounded by where men get referred to a urologist and women to a gynaecologist, who probably hasn't examined a man in 25 years.

Women, therefore, need to be aware of these issues and be prepared to discuss the problem with their GP, who has the benefit of seeing men and women on a daily basis. Whereas younger women might be prepared to discuss such issues with the doctor providing contraceptive or postnatal care because they can see a possible link, they do not do so for these other "medical" conditions. Likewise, a doctor will ask about lots of symptoms commonly associated with these conditions but rarely mention sex, as "best not to go there" or "best not to open Pandora's box". I remember a partner coming to me complaining that I had asked a couple of ladies in the diabetic clinic about their sex lives and actually used the term "orgasm". The paradox was that at the time, GPs were paid bonuses for asking men with diabetes about their erections on an annual basis. Incidentally, this was only for one year. When the payment was withdrawn, the GPs promptly gave up asking the question. I sometimes think that we have lost the plot.

If blood flow to the genital area is also important for women, then might not the medications that assist men also be helpful for women? After all, our blood vessels are essentially the same. The answer to this question is undoubtedly "yes", but this has been difficult to prove scientifically, and therefore drug companies have been reluctant to go there, especially as they would probably face even more media criticism, not to mention endless cheap "pink Viagra type jokes". Once again, by the time that the companies began looking at this, we were well down the 15 years to patent expiry such that they would never have got a penny back on their clinical trial investment. Clearly, no government would ever see such projects as a priority for taxpayers' money.

There is clear evidence that the PDE5 inhibitors such as sildenafil (Viagra) and tadalafil (Cialis) increase blood flow to the clitoris and vagina, increasing engorgement and lubrication, but measuring this scientifically proved challenging. It is important to realise that these medications will only improve AROUSAL and NOT DESIRE, so the best results in trials were shown in younger women, especially those with type 1 (usually insulin-dependent) diabetes and those on LONG-TERM ANTIDEPRESSANTS. The benefits are improved feeling of engorgement, sensation (69%) and lubrication (50%), with 20-30% showing response to placebo. Less impressive results are seen in post-menopausal women, probably because many would need to be on HRT and/or testosterone, and the trials were conducted in the US at the height of the anti-HRT lobby.

Another major problem was that men more frequently initiate sex, so therefore taking a drug an hour before would involve all sexual activity being pre-planned, which might be a major relationship change for couples where the male has nearly always initiated sex, especially if he has to take a tablet before sex as well. Therefore, the use of daily tadalafil might have some major advantages for women to enable them to be spontaneously responsive, but this might be impractical for older couples where sex might only take place once or twice per month. This regime might also upset feminists who might feel that women were being treated with "daily drugs" to facilitate them as "sex objects" for male gratification. Once again, what should be seen as a logical treatment for the medical complication of chronic disease, in much the same way as diabetes causes cold, numb feet gets complicated by ethical, gender and religious issues purely because sex is involved. I always saw this issue as just as important for women with diabetes and high blood pressure as it was for men, but this got me into trouble.

Many drugs adversely affect sexual function in women, antidepressants, drugs for epilepsy, tranquilisers, blood pressure medications, even statins, and of course, oral contraceptives. Both overactive and underactive thyroid problems are associated with sexual problems. The issue is that women are seldom if ever, asked! This is because the loss of erection is pretty obvious in men, but lack of arousal in women is much more subtle, and questions about "engorgement of the clitoris" or "increased lubrication" do not flow too readily into the conversation during routine consultations, especially with barriers of age, gender, and ethnicity.

With regard to medications, there are a few clear issues; most antidepressants and tranquilisers are bad for sexual function, as are most older drugs for epilepsy. Beta-blockers are bad because they restrict blood flow to the extremities. Drugs ending in -SARTAN (called ARBs) are better for sexual symptoms than those ending in -PRIL (called ACE inhibitors), so a simple switch might help sexual function, especially as the latter group can also cause a tickly cough often not easily relate to the drug by the patient.

Do drugs like daily tadalafil have the same benefits for women?

The next issue is whether daily tadalafil 5mg might have the same benefits in patients with chronic conditions as we have seen in the early chapters in men, and the simple answer seems to be "yes". The way in which these drugs act to improve blood flow and improve the function of arteries is no different in men and women, and development was advanced in treating both men and women before the interesting side effect of improved erections changed the direction of research for economic reasons. There is also considerable experience of use in women as it is licensed to treat pulmonary hypertension, a very serious condition affecting the major arteries in the lung and the efficacy and safety show no difference between genders. In fact, the largest trial was made up of 80% of women, who took doses up to 40mg daily, *eight times* the standard UK daily dose, with only mild side effects.

Trials in diabetes have, in fact, suggested possibly *greater* effect in women because they generally have the less severe disease than men. This means that women are likely to be less insulin resistant and require less medication, potentially slowing the progression of the disease. Of course, the underlying issue in all these cases is that tadalafil is only licensed for pulmonary hypertension in women and is now cheap, so no drug company will be motivated to spend millions on long-term trials with no change in financial returns. Furthermore, as tadalafil daily has been licensed to treat enlarged prostate in men, small trials have shown benefits in "overactive bladder" in women. This is a distressing condition associated with an uncontrollable urge to pass urine frequently, often uncomfortable, and occasionally resulting in leakage. Another study from Turkey showed significant benefits in bladder pain syndrome and interstitial cystitis that had failed to respond to other conventional treatments. There are likely to be fewer side effects than other medications used for these problems. Unfortunately, UK women are unlikely to receive treatment because of the fear of using "off-label" medication. By the time a fully funded clinical trial programme has been developed leading to any licenced product, it will be too late for any women reading this book.

These conditions affect sleep, day-to-day living, and *sex life*. Lifestyle changes can be helpful, losing weight and controlling tea, coffee and alcohol but are rarely a solution. Drugs currently used to treat it predominantly alter the nerve supply to the bladder. These can cause dry mouth, dry eyes, blurred vision and constipation and also sexual problems associated with dryness and altered sensation. Botox injections into the bladder or nerve reconstruction are used in severe cases. A 2017 study in 96 women showed that daily tadalafil for three months was effective in symptom control in bladder symptoms and well tolerated. Once again, it is unlikely that any company will apply for a product licence for this indication as tadalafil is generic and cheap, but women are more likely to prefer a drug that has minimal side effects, possible cardiac benefits and improves sexual function rather than one that has adverse side effects.

Two cases come to mind that demonstrates these points, and particularly the importance of treating couples, not just the individual:

Case 1

Paul, a doctor aged 62, suffered from T2DM and raised blood pressure for years. I had treated him with daily tadalafil, and his symptoms had improved. This had unmasked problems in his wife, Jean (63), who also suffered from diabetes and felt that her sex life

266

was over because of Paul's problems. They attended for Paul's follow-up and asked if I could help Jean. I prescribed a low dose of testosterone gel and then added daily tadalafil 5mg daily. Within weeks there was a dramatic improvement, not only in her enjoyment of sex but more so in the improvement in sensation in her legs. Paul commented that she was happier, more alert and had much more energy. She had now overtaken him in the bedroom, and he asked if I could step up his treatment. Jean subsequently attended a diabetes clinic follow-up and was advised by the consultant to stop the tadalafil as it was "not licensed in women". After six weeks, all her symptoms returned, and she went back onto tadalafil, and they all remitted. Four years she remains in fine form, and her diabetes control, circulation in the legs and mental function is better than several years ago.

Case 2

George was 62 with T2DM. He had ED for 10 years and was using Caverject injections into his penis before sex as tablets had stopped working. He was feeling tired and thought that the days of sex had passed. I checked his testosterone level and found that it was very low at 5.2 nmol/l (normal levels are above 12nmol/l). He responded very well to testosterone gel and started responding to Caverject injections again. His wife, Doris, was 56 and had bilateral breast cancer 10 years ago, and her ovaries and uterus were removed for ovarian cancer five years ago. She was unable to take HRT but used a vaginal oestrogen pessary twice a week but still found sex was not enjoyable. I added a pump of testosterone gel on Saturday morning, and they were both able to have sex regularly on Saturday night.

267

These cases show that there is much more that can be done to help women by thinking outside the box and being prepared to use established safe drugs outside their product licence, having discussed the issues with the patient. One might have expected that the couples above would have given up, but these cases show just how resilient patients can be and demonstrate that although sex is "not a matter of life and death, to many, it is actually more important than that!

What about the other benefits of daily tadalafil for women?

In the earlier chapters, I explained that tadalafil and sildenafil (Viagra) were both developed to treat *heart disease in men and women* until a chance side effect led to the men in the trials being reluctant to return the unused tablets!

It should therefore come as no surprise that these drugs are actually very good for a large range of heart-related conditions in both sexes. I have described that various studies have shown reductions in heart attacks and death from a range of conditions. Tadalafil will be more useful as a single tablet remains active for at least 36 hours, whereas sildenafil is effective for 4-6 hours and would therefore need to be taken three times per day. This also means that women are likely to see the same benefits in terms of improved blood flow to the lower limbs and improvements in diabetes and kidney function. There are, however, a few medical conditions that are far more important for women.

The most important of these is dementia, and 65% of sufferers are women and results from brain scans show us that brain cells deteriorate at a faster rate in ageing women and women live on average 3-4 years longer. This means that they are likely to live longer with all the associated stress of this terrible disability. Heart health is also important in dementia, suggesting that blood flow and oxygenation are important, and therefore, a drug such as tadalafil, shown to increase blood flow and, therefore, oxygenation, would be likely to reduce dementia risk. Brain scans on patients on tadalafil show increased blood supply to important centres associated with memory and cognitive function within weeks. Hormones also play a part, and oestrogen is beneficial, yet doctors are reluctant to prescribe HRT in older age due to perceived cardiac risk.

Women also suffer circulatory problems with cold hands and feet, and women, especially migraine sufferers, are twice as likely to suffer Raynaud's syndrome, a condition where the fingers and toes become acutely cold and painful frequent changing colour. Obviously, a drug taken regularly to improve blood blow will reduce the severity of Raynaud's, and this has been shown in several trials.

Migraine, more common in women, is also related to sudden changes in the blood vessels in the brain, which cause pain by stretching nerve endings in the blood vessels and muscles. A drug such as daily tadalafil can prevent these sudden changes through a gradual background relaxation, but large trials have been restricted by the lack of a licence for women and the low likelihood of trials being sponsored with a generic drug.

Osteoporosis is also more common in women due to the loss of oestrogen after menopause. Daily Tadalafil increases bone mass by stimulating the action of cells that produce new bone cells.

Although bowel cancer is more common in men, especially Afro-Americans, it remains a significant cause of cancer death in women. Reduction in cancer rates and mortality in men has been shown with tadalafil and sildenafil with regular dosing, and this effect is likely to be the same for women.

Tadalafil – the Heptathlon drug for women?

I often refer to tadalafil as a "heptathlon" drug in women and a "decathlon" drug for men. A heptathlete would be unlikely to make the Olympic team for any of the seven individual events, just as tadalafil might not be first or second in class for the above conditions, but just as we judge the Olympic Heptathlon Champion, such as Jessica Ennis in 2012 (see below), as the greatest all-round athlete, then perhaps tadalafil is the best overall health drug, the heptathlon champion, certainly better than taking seven different supplements. Your doctor is unlikely to appreciate these arguments and would usually be thinking only about the NICE recommended licence drug for each individual condition, not the global health picture. That selected drug may even have adverse side effects on the other "decathlon events". The problem is that patients never realise the benefits of a preventive drug as they never expect to get any medical conditions and treat good health as "standard".

CHAPTER 15

Your doctor won't see you now!

"In my opinion, people who continually make sweeping stereotypical generalisations are all the same" - Geoff Hackett 2021.

In many ways, men are their own worst enemies. They take more risks. They drink too much, smoke too much, experiment with drugs, drive too fast, fight too much and engage in dangerous activities. In addition, they rarely see doctors between the ages of 12 and 40, except for accidents and injuries, usually associated with risk-taking and alcohol. Women consult health care professionals three times more often than men up to the age of 60, after which events catch up with men, and they consult just as often.

Men die on average four years earlier than women, and this "gender gap" is greater in certain parts of the country, such as the North East. In fact, life expectancy for men can be 6-7 years less in men in the most deprived versus the most affluent areas. Men have higher rates of death from cardiovascular diseases such as heart attack and stroke. Men also have higher rates of T2DM and increased associated mortality. They also have higher mortality from all types of cancer, excluding the "sex-specific" ones such as breast, uterus and ovary. This increased mortality is largely related to late diagnosis. An excellent example is malignant melanoma of the skin. Women get more melanoma, but men die much more frequently because they present later.

The real question is, "What can we, as men, do about this?" The first answer to that question is that we cannot rely on the healthcare system to sort this out for us. Certainly, the events of the last five years have caused us to rethink the whole concept of "NHS care for all, free at the point of delivery.

The "decline" of general practice

As GPs are essentially "self-employed contractors", they have responded to the demands of their clients. If three times as many women come to see the doctor, then the service they provide has developed to address those needs. This is essentially the same response that any business would take to assess its client base in order to retain and attract new clients. If the general practice demand is for consultations related to contraception, maternity, mother and baby, breast screening, HRT, and well women, then the healthcare appointments and personnel have been tailored to meet these demands. If the service is not considered satisfactory, patients will go elsewhere. Very commonly, a woman will be greeted at reception with the words, "Well, Mrs Brown, you'll be wanting an appointment for one of our lady doctors". Often the patient is not asked; it is the assumption of the virtually 100% female reception staff that this will be the case. The result of the increase in demand for female consultations led some years ago to positive discrimination towards medical school places. A General Medical Council report in 2015 showed that 59% of GPs under 50 were female versus 37% over 50. The corresponding figures for hospital specialists were 38% and 25%.

The primary care gender issue is worsened by the way GPs are remunerated. Whereas a percentage of GP incomes is from "capitation fees", essentially the numbers on their list, a substantial element of income is from "item for service payments". In the case of female patients, income will clock up with contraception, maternity, breast and cervical screening, and well-woman and menopause visits in some cases. There are no male-specific payments. Although prostate screening has been introduced in many countries, the UK stance has always been that such a programme would not be cost-effective. We, therefore, have a situation whereby any female registering with a GP is a much better financial deal for the practice. Likewise, a female GP might also represent better value. It would, of course, be illegal for any practice to accept female patients in preference or for any practice to advertise for a specific gender of a doctor. The reality was that if I was to hold a clinic in one room, seeing men with erection problems, whereas a lady partner in the next room running a contraceptive clinic, I would bring zero income to the practice, whereas she would bring in several hundred pounds. I would also receive a visit from the community pharmacist for being a prescribing "outlier" in terms of ED medication, which would come with financial penalties. If I were to attempt to justify my prescribing because I was offering a better service, this would be perceived as arrogant and critical of other practitioners.

In 2013, it appeared that NICE had finally got the message when they introduced a payment policy for GPs in return for asking men with diabetes about their erections once a year. As evidence, they cut and pasted the evidence that we had provided seven years earlier. At that time, NICE invited the Tsar, Professor Mike Kirby and Dr David Edwards, a GP from Chipping Norton, to a meeting in Birmingham to discuss this subject. We invited Dr Graham Jackson to join us. We then received a message from NICE to say that he must not attend because "he knows too much"! From that day on, Graham Jackson lived with that title. In fact, at ISSM in Beijing in 2016, after his death, I was invited to do a memorial lecture in his honour entitled, "Dr Graham Jackson, the man who knew too much". He left us with memorable quotes:

"The way to a man's heart is through the penis", not a suggested route for a coronary angiogram!

"ED = ED = ED", meaning erectile dysfunction = endothelial dysfunction = early death.

"Viagra is a serious heart drug, highjacked by urologists". The readers of this book will soon realise the truth of this statement. I fondly remember that Graham used to do his presentation at meetings immediately before mine. Once, he once announced, *" After 30 years as a consultant cardiologist, I am reduced to a career as Geoff Hackett's warm-up act!"*

It seemed no accident that these payments to GPs for one year coincided with the availability of cheap generic Sildenafil. Immediately GPs hit the 80% target and collected the cash. Twelve months later, the payments were withdrawn on the basis of "simplification". A year on, we were back to square one, with only 10% of men being asked. If ever there was an example of what was needed to improve outcomes in men's health, this was it.

In 2015, I conducted an audit of GP practice websites involving 262 GPs (142 female and 120 male). Whereas 68% of female doctors expressed an interest in women's health, only 1% of male doctors expressed an interest in men's health, and he was working for me as a clinical assistant at the time and has since retired! In 2018, the chance of a patient finding a GP who has declared interest in men's health would be negligible. Having been involved in the training and motivation of GPs for over 25 years, we still have only a handful of GPs with interest in men's health scattered around to country. Most of these are getting older, with little sign of younger ones coming through to fill the gap. In contrast, there are a significant number of private menopause clinics employing GPs with a passionate interest in women's health.

As mentioned in an earlier chapter, there are 14 Women's hospitals in the UK and no Men's hospitals. When I am at a loose end, I often drive to the reception of Birmingham Women's hospital and ask for the Men's hospital just to see the reaction. In other European Countries and the US, Men's hospitals do exist, often termed Andrology Departments, but few men or women in the UK would know what this term means. As mentioned in earlier chapters, medical students receive extensive training in women's health and virtually nothing that addresses the needs of men. The Royal College of GPs has a spokesperson on women's health but not one for men. I ring the RCGP from time to time asking for this non-existent person and often encounter the response, "Why would we possibly need a men's health spokesman?". The answer is, of course, that men have the greatest need. If research had identified an ethnic or religious group who were suffering from health inequalities, there would be an immediate government initiative to address this. Finally, there is even a government minister for women and not one for men. All these issues led me to give talks and write articles entitled "Short Brutal and Nasty – it's a Man's life.

Men are not going to change their behaviour overnight, and women quite rightly expect the highest standards of healthcare to address their needs. Their preference to have this delivered by physicians of their choice must be appreciated. The physicians providing these important services also deserve to be paid appropriately for their work. Women might also argue that we should not be funding drugs for men's sexual satisfaction from precious NHS resources when no such therapies exist for women. It is, therefore, totally understandable that the NHS pharmacists have targeted these drugs for potential cost savings. The reality is that, in 2020, an entire year's treatment with Sildenafil costs the same as *a single tablet of Viagra in 1998,* and a prescription charge costs roughly ten times more than the real cost of a month's supply of the drug. Four years after the licence of Viagra, two further drugs, Tadalafil (Cialis) and Vardenafil (Levitra) were approved, and these are now also available in cheaper generic form. The recent crisis in the NHS due to COVID-19, with the cancellation of routine services, is likely to lead to an appraisal as to what the public can expect from the NHS in future. It is unlikely that such discussions will target morning erections and "mojo preservations" as top priorities for the future.

A particularly vulnerable group are young men between 15 and 25, who rarely access GP services, mostly relying on the internet for medical advice and turning up in casualty as medical emergencies. Such a case was Zack, who obviously had major issues with his penis size, especially in relation to the models in various medical magazines. He had read that a third of the true length of his penis was actually "inside", meaning that it was below the skin. As he was obsessed with measuring his penis regularly, he decided to measure it from the "inside" using the nearest thing at hand, which was a USB cable. Unfortunately, his interpretation of "inside" was to insert the USB cable down his penis, with the unfortunate result shown in the x-ray below, requiring two hours of surgery to repair the damage. Perhaps a timely visit to his GP and referral to the "small penis clinic" might have prevented this disaster.

A teenage boy required surgery after getting a USB cable stuck inside his penis. The 15-year-old boy from the UK was attempting to measure the inside of his penis with the cable as a form of "sexual experimentation" when it knotted and he became unable to remove it.

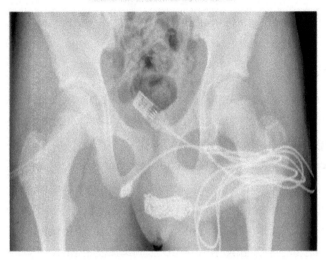

If we accept that there are inequalities in health care that the NHS are failing to address, we need to be practical as to what can be done to address these issues. The only solution for men is to take control of their own health, and this concept will form the basis of the rest of the chapter.

The exercise and lifestyle message

Hardly a day goes by without an article pointing out that we are facing an epidemic of obesity and T2DM, and the UK is second only to the US and Mexico. Mediterranean countries figure much better in this respect. In the UK, the population of men from southeast Asia, and particularly the Indian sub-continent, are at especially increased risk. The fundamental process at play is "Insulin resistance", meaning that these tissues are less sensitive to the effects of insulin, and the body produces more insulin to try to counter this resistance. The higher levels of insulin are associated with increased "Inflammation" and the production of "Inflammatory proteins" that damage our arteries through a process called "oxidative stress". Whenever you read about vitamins and supplements, you will see that the main claim for benefit will usually be that as "anti-oxidants", they reduce this oxidative stress.

The clear advice would be to switch to a Mediterranean-type diet rather than a US high carbohydrate type. The Mediterranean diet is essentially based on whole grains, fish, olive oil and nuts, fresh vegetables and fruit, with red meat confined to once per week. There is considerable evidence to support the long-term health benefits, including weight reduction and reduced insulin resistance. Rather depressingly, a 2020 study in the British Medical Journal reviewed 15 types of diet across a host of clinical trials and confirmed that they are all equally successful over a 6-month period but lose their effect by 12 months. These findings suggest that fundamental changes to the dietary patterns of a lifetime are very difficult to maintain. The counter-argument, of course, is that unless you do lose weight in the first place, you are unlikely to be in the 10% who do maintain that weight loss. In recent years, the basis of the NHS approach has been to turn the responsibility back onto the patient to modify their own health and reduce the burden on the NHS.

The benefits of exercise on insulin resistance are clear. A 45-minute episode of moderate aerobic exercise will improve insulin resistance for 16 hours. The important point is that the move from no exercise to a moderate level shows the greatest benefit. Walking, jogging and cycling are sufficient forms of exercise, and there is a little additional benefit in pushing exercise levels to excess.

We should, of course, look to reduce unnecessary stress in our lives and focus on our most important relationships, especially with our partner. We should discuss openly what is important to us in the relationship and listen to their wishes. We should try to negotiate common ground and don't let old feuds continue. We should concentrate on what brought us together. It might have been a sexual attraction, so we need to work on returning to sex and intimacy the way it was as much as possible. Forgive, forget and move on. Whilst on clichés, Life isn't a rehearsal, so don't put these things off. Get them sorted now and start enjoying life again.

Morning erections, the holy grail of men's health!

I now move on to some more specific advice. A man's erection, especially the spontaneous ones in the morning, are the best predictor of a man's heart health. This has been shown many times, and every study has come to the same conclusion. Men should rejoice over every firm morning erection. If you can hang a towel over it, then sing hallelujah! As a leading American Cardiologist said in the 80s, "If you can't get an erection, your heart is heading in the wrong direction". A question about your erection should be part of every health check at your GP surgery. It is more important than asking about smoking. If the doctor or nurse forgets, remind them. The 5-question Sexual Health Inventory for Men (SHIM) is in the appendix of this book, and I suggest that you fill it out and take it to your doctor or nurse at every health check. They are being negligent if they do not ask, so don't let them get away with it. Only by constantly reminding them will they get the message. Likewise, anyone paying a fortune for a private health medical should point out that failure to ask about erections means that the medical is not fit for purpose. Studies show that the average interval between losing erections and a cardiac event is 3-5 years, so a man cannot wait for a doctor to get around to asking. As recently as April 2022, a fifteen-year follow-up of men in the European Male Aging Study (EMAS) confirmed that *morning erections* were the single best predictor of whether a man would have a heart attack or die prematurely within the next 15 years.

Asking the right questions

The aspiration of every doctor is to have a disease, clinical sign, or test named after them. I would like to present my major contribution to medical science, *"Hackett's two cough test"*. Men with high blood pressure in the UK are usually treated with a drug called Ramipril, which belongs to a class called ACE inhibitors. These have a slightly adverse effect on erections and a bothersome side effect of an irritating cough in 15-20% of patients. An alternative and slightly superior drug would be Valsartan or Losartan, a group called ARBs, which improve erections. Whenever I asked GPs to switch the medication to improve a man's erection, they completely ignored my suggestion. I then decided to tell the patient to give a little cough at the start of the consultation. The GP would usually stop for a few seconds, but with a second cough, they would ask the patient when this cough started. An answer of "Shortly after starting those blood pressure tablets" would result in an immediate switch from ACE to ARB, with improved erections. Hackett's two cough test works every time. In mild cases of ED, this medication switch may be all that is required. I would invite readers to try this "two cough test" on their GP; it works nearly every time.

Forty per cent of men aged 40 and 50 per cent aged 50 suffer from erectile dysfunction (ED), and these men are at 46% increased risk of a heart attack and need investigation. Do not let a doctor tell you that this is "normal" (so is death) or "just due to stress". Do not accept advice to "chill out" or "man up". In some cases, if a man has excellent morning erections but loses them during sex, then "performance anxiety" may be an issue, but cases should never be dismissed as this without investigation. Excellent performance with one partner but not with another would so-called situational ED would also suggest performance anxiety. All men with ED need their blood pressure and heart checked, plus blood tests for diabetes, cholesterol, and a morning testosterone level, ideally with a test called SHBG (sex hormone binding globulin). SHBG is a compound produced by the liver. It tightly binds to testosterone rendering it inactive and, therefore, reducing the amount of free "active" testosterone in the circulation. SHBG rises with age and is the main cause of the fall in free testosterone as we get older. Even more important is to "know the level of SHBG before deciding on therapy.

The Health Benefits of Sex

In earlier chapters, I described the benefits of sexual activity in reducing the risk of cardiac death by 50% in men having sex more than twice per week. This has been confirmed in at least three studies. A study from Sweden also showed the benefits of regular sex, but the quality was more than quantity when it came to women. The Tampere study from Scandinavia showed that regular sex reduced the chances of developing ED, and another study showed that men who were not having morning erections developed structural changes in the penis, which could become irreversible with time. These studies effectively demonstrate that the adage "Use it or lose it" is 100% true. It is, therefore, important that we do not simply treat this evidence with a smutty giggle but embrace it proactively.

Loss of Erections are an important warning sign of heart disease.

The importance of ED as an early warning sign of heart disease cannot be overstated. The mechanism for this is explained by the "Arterial Size Hypothesis". The process by which the arteries function poorly is termed "Endothelial Dysfunction. Our arteries are lined with a thin layer of cells called the endothelium. If this thin layer, like clingfilm, covering all our arteries were to be peeled off, it would cover a tennis court. If this layer is damaged, then cholesterol is deposited on the damaged areas, leading to "plaque" which will narrow the arteries. "The arteries to the penis are 60% of the diameter of the coronary arteries, and ED appears when there is around 50% narrowing. In contrast, men can have 70% narrowing of a coronary artery without any symptoms. We regularly put our penis through this "stress test" every time we have sex, whereas we might rarely put our heart to such stress testing. If the appearance of ED comes 3-5 years before a heart attack, then the clock is running. Action needs to be taken promptly to diagnose and address all the factors that are narrowing the arteries. These include diabetes, high blood pressure and raised cholesterol. The important message is that if you have ED, these problems should be addressed much more proactively rather than just token efforts to "exercise more and eat less fat". Many cardiologists believe that "a man with ED has heart disease until proven otherwise". Others would prescribe a statin to lower cholesterol in all men with persistent ED. We are clearly dealing with a chronic disease process here, and it is vital to treat the disease process and not just a symptom.

The Importance of Prostate Disease

As men age, they develop more symptoms related to their prostate, that small gland, normally the size of a walnut (25ml), situated just below the bladder. Traditionally we thought that this was a simple matter of the prostate growing with age, but we now know that prostate symptoms, such as going to pee more often, poor stream, delay in peeing, dribbling and getting up more at night, are closely related to ED, diabetes, high blood pressure and raised cholesterol. Essentially the prostate is also a victim of insulin resistance, oxidative stress and poor blood supply. If left untreated, men will often need surgery to address these symptoms in later life. I need to emphasise that this is Benign Prostate Enlargement and not Prostate cancer, although regular sex and more frequent ejaculation have also been shown to reduce the risk of prostate cancer. Daily tadalafil has been licensed to treat enlarged prostate for several years and has been advocated as a first-line treatment across Europe for men with both ED and enlarged prostate. Unfortunately, NICE, in the UK, has never produced guidelines on ED and declined to look consider tadalafil when they produced prostate guidelines. Tadalafil 5mg daily, apart from improving symptoms, increases blood supply to the prostate and reduces inflammation. This mechanism is highly likely to significantly improve the overall health of the prostate, but the long-term clinical trials that we need will take several years. Men in their 50s and 60s now do not have the time to wait for these perfect studies. Most urologists realised these benefits of daily tadalafil and have been taking it for years, in my case, 12. The benefits were brought home to me when I popped into the loo just off the patient waiting room one day. As I emerged, two ladies were sitting just outside, and one said: "Oh, it's you, doctor; we thought a horse was loose in the building".

As physicians, we need to give the best advice based on our current knowledge and experience.

The role of ED drugs

In 1998, Viagra, the first of a group of drugs called Phosphodiesterase Type 5 Inhibitors (PDE5-Is) were licensed. We all got used to the concept of taking a "blue pill" an hour before sex and being told they "Might be dangerous". PDE5-Is work by increasing the level of a chemical called Nitric Oxide (NO) in the blood vessels and other tissues. NO opens the blood vessels and increases blood flow. The discovery that this increase in blood flow in the penis could produce an erection was a chance finding in trials where the drug was being used to treat heart disease. The decision of the manufacturers to focus on ED was a commercial one, but it should come as no surprise that these drugs are also very good at what they were developed for – heart disease. This raises two important issues. Firstly, an effective drug for ED should not be restricted to once per week, as the function of the penis needs to be improved every day of the week, not just for 1-hour on a Saturday night. Numerous studies have shown that partners dislike this weekly "sex on demand" and would prefer to initiate sex on occasions when *they* are in the mood. If this has been a pattern throughout their relationship, then this is what we should aim to restore. Secondly, if men with ED frequently have undiagnosed heart disease, then surely taking a drug that is good for the heart would be sensible.

Let us deal with the idea that these drugs might be dangerous. In the early stages, men with advanced heart disease, unable to walk more than a few yards without chest pain, decided to "roll back the years" with long nights of passion. As sex involves physical effort, equivalent to walking a mile in 20 minutes or climbing two flights of stairs, clearly, the hearts of these men were not capable of this level of effort. They were also unlikely to heed the warning signs, especially after a large meal and bottle of wine. The problem with Viagra (sildenafil) is that it is short-acting and would need to be given 2-3 times per day, whereas the second drug in this group, tadalafil, lasts more than four times longer, so it is suitable for daily dosing. ED, as explained earlier, is part of a chronic disease process, namely endothelial dysfunction (remember ED=ED=ED). Taking a tablet before sex treats a *symptom*, whereas taking a daily medication treats the disease process (endothelial dysfunction). When a man goes online or to the pharmacy for Viagra Connect, he is not treating the disease process, which will continue to develop. In 2-3 years, the narrowing will have progressed, and the Viagra will stop working. By this stage, other arteries will also have narrowed, and the heart attack may be quick to follow. Daily medication treats the disease process, as well as the symptoms. Recent studies show that daily therapy with PDE5-Is, such as tadalafil, significantly reduces the risks of a heart attack.

The problem was that having been licensed nearly 4 years later than Viagra; there was a long period where tadalafil (as Cialis) was much more expensive, such that the NHS would have been in considerable financial difficulties had these theories been allowed to develop. For example, between 2014 and 2018, generic sildenafil was 17p per tablet and branded Cialis daily was £55 per month. The NHS response was to only endorse sildenafil and ban the use of Cialis, creating the impression that there might be some "concerns" about the drug. In late 2017, tadalafil became generic, and the NHS price for the daily dose fell to £4-5 per month or around £5-6 on private prescriptions. The NHS continues to endorse only sildenafil at four tablets per month for 80p rather than 28 tablets of tadalafil at £4-5.

This has created a very difficult problem for specialists. Patients referred to hospitals will have tried and failed on the regime of four sildenafil per month, the only one provided at NHS cost. Daily tadalafil works in half of these patients where on-demand sildenafil failed, but men cannot understand why they must pay privately, even if they are over 65 and on benefits. Why should men have to go through the indignity of having to fail on many occasions before they receive a prescription that was known to be more effective in the first place, especially when the normal sexual function can be restored for the cost of a pint of lager for a month's treatment?

I now dread the questions, "what would be the best treatment for me to take, doctor?" or even "what would you take if it were you? " Should I give the honest answer based on the latest information from international conferences and publications, or should I state the official NHS policy, even if I know it to be financially based and at least five years out of date. Most doctors working in the NHS will, without hesitation, recite verbatim the official NHS position with no mention of any alternative approach. The General Medical Council, however, informs us that we must be open and honest with patients at all times. The mission statement of my hospital trust was CARING, ACCOUNTABLE, SUPPORTIVE and HONEST. Many of you will notice that this acronym actually spells CASH.

Beyond a shadow of a doubt, that treatment is tadalafil 5mg daily, but I will now be contradicting their GP and his NHS advisers, who continue to be unaware of the progressive research on this subject as, after all, "It isn't a matter of life and death, is it?". I would suggest that a heart attack in 3-5 years is actually a matter of life and death.

Are "specialists" a danger to your health?

At first sight, this might seem a ridiculous suggestion, but let me explain. In the "old days", a GP would make a decision to refer to a "specialist", and the patient would then return to discuss his opinion. The lack of GPs has led to patients circumventing this process and self-referring to experts, often located through an internet search. The drawback here's that consultants or "specialists" might know a lot about their narrow subject but very little about other specialities. The problem is that patients present with "symptoms" that cross many specialities. Consultants are now slaves to so-called "evidence-based medicine" and need to follow NICE guidance, specifically related to their own speciality, but frequently ignoring the impact on other body systems. The following example will demonstrate this:

Lee Ki Kok, aged 52, was the manager of a local Chinese restaurant. He noted that he was getting up several times per night to pass urine and had noted that this was taking a long time, followed by a lengthy dribble afterwards. This is causing him (and his wife) severe distress. Mr Lee was also being treated for early diabetes and blood pressure with medication. His GP has referred him to Mr Richard Cummings, a consultant urologist. Within 10 minutes, and after a thorough rectal examination, he advised a medication called tamsulosin to treat the symptoms, recommending a follow-up in 3 months. Mr Lee was not asked about morning erections or anything about his sex life and relationship. In fact, he is suffering from erectile dysfunction and premature ejaculation (PE), and the prescribed medication causes a retrograde ejaculation (RE) back into the bladder, makes his erections worse and causes him to be light-headed on standing up as it interacts with his blood pressure medication. Mr Cummings could have been prescribed tadalafil 5mg daily, which is almost as good as tamsulosin, the NICE endorsed treatment. Tadalafil would also have improved his ED and PE, avoided RE and reduced his risk of heart attack by 40%. In reality, Mr Cummings was following NICE guidelines drawn up by other expert urologists. These guidelines, however, do not consider any of the other aspects of his health that fall outside urology, nor the impact on his sex life and relationship as Mr Cummings remit was to address Mr Lees' urinary problems. An experienced GP would have been very useful in this case.

The problem here is that the medical profession demands long-term clinical trials providing Evidence-Based Medicine (EBM) to establish these licensed indications. This process costs millions of pounds and takes several years. This process simply does not make economic sense, and in this case, the evidence was developed when tadalafil was £1 per month, and tadalafil was £55 per month, not now that tadalafil is generic, costing less than four pounds per month. The other multiple preventive benefits for the prostate, kidneys, nervous system, diabetes, cancer reduction, mood and mental function are discussed in another chapter, but because these are not "licensed" indications, doctors must refrain from discussing them. Under severe time pressure, they default to only dealing with the one problem defined in the referral, as in the case of Mr Lee, to the detriment of his general health.

The importance of Counselling

Essentially what we are talking about here is proper patient-centred counselling. Let us now consider the practical issues of all this, and here I will use the example of an Irish patient of mine, Paddy McGinty, aged 56.

Paddy developed ED, loss of interest in sex, low motivation and felt "washed out". He arranges to see his GP, Dr Seamus O'Toole. Paddy has read some articles and wonders if he might have low testosterone, so Dr O'Toole takes some blood and finds that his levels are around 7 nmol/l and offers him an antidepressant as a "pick-me-up". He informs Paddy that his blood tests are in the" normal range", but Paddy asks for a referral to a urologist, so he is referred to Professor Phil McCrackin. He advises him that he needs "thorough counselling" before testosterone therapy is prescribed. Paddy has done some research and came across this paper from 2021, from the US, written by experts who conducted the largest trial on testosterone therapy.

Benefits and Risks of Testosterone Treatment in Men with Age-Related Decline in Testosterone.
Dos Santos, MR & Bhasin, S. Annu. Rev. Med. 2021.72:75-91

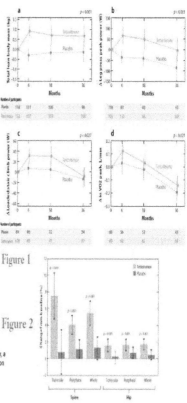

Figure 1

Figure 2

Abstract

The substantial increase in life expectancy of men has focused growing attention on quality-of-life issues associated with reproductive aging. Serum total and free testosterone levels in men, after reaching a peak in the second and third decade of life, decline gradually with advancing age. The trajectory of age-related decline is affected by comorbid conditions, adiposity, medications, and genetic factors. Testosterone treatment of older men with low testosterone levels improves overall sexual activity, sexual desire, and erectile function; improves areal and volumetric bone density, as well as estimated bone strength in the spine and the hip; corrects unexplained anemia of aging; increases skeletal muscle mass, strength and power, self-reported mobility, and some measures of physical function; and modestly improves depressive symptoms. The long-term effects of testosterone on major cardiovascular events and prostate cancer risk remain unclear. The Endocrine Society recommends against testosterone therapy of all older men with low testosterone levels but suggests consideration of treatment on an individualized basis in men who have consistently low testosterone levels and symptoms or conditions suggestive of testosterone deficiency.

Figure 1 - The effects of testosterone treatment for 3 years on lean body mass (a), peak leg power (b), loaded stair climbing power (a measure of physical function) (c), and VO2 peak (maximal oxygen uptake at peak exercise intensity, a measure of aerobic capacity) (d) in older men with low or low normal testosterone levels in the Testosterone Effects on Atherosclerosis Progression in Aging Men (TEAAM) Trial.

Figure 2 - The effects of testosterone treatment relative to placebo on volumetric bone mineral density in older hypogonadal men. The data are derived from the Bone Trial of the Testosterone Trials (See slide 23 also)

Imagine what happens when Paddy goes to see the expert after he has been feeling dreadful for the past five years and has waited twelve months for an appointment. The specialist, Professor McCrackin, tells him that his testosterone is low and discusses possible testosterone therapy. Clearly, the Prof expects the consultation to go something like this:

He tells him that testosterone therapy improves overall sexual activity, sexual desire, and erectile function. Paddy answers, "no, the wife is not interested in any of that any more".

He tells him that it improves bone strength, muscle mass, strength and power whilst also correcting anaemia. Paddy answers, "no, not interested in any of that, quite happy being weak and flabby. We just stay in watching daytime TV". Next, he is told that it improves mobility and physical function, and Paddy answers, "no, we don't do much nowadays, so mobility is not required". As for depression, Paddy states that he and his wife are quite happy being miserable. . Professor McCrackin goes on to say that the long-term effects on the heart and prostate are "unclear".

Paddy leaves, completely reassured, thoroughly counselled and quite prepared to wait another 20 years until Professor Phil McCrackin contacts him to confirm that the treatment is completely safe, as he wouldn't want to risk any side effects.

What patient would decline treatment if informed of all these potential benefits listed by these authors? Despite this, their society, the US Endocrine Society, does not recommend Testosterone Therapy but feels that guidelines need to be "patient centred!!" Paddy feels that he suffers from virtually all of these symptoms and that his work and relationship with his wife, Mary, is suffering.

Professor McCrackin merely councils him that he would not recommend testosterone therapy because the "long-term safety for the heart and prostate is unclear". Paddy leaves the clinic and returns home.

The Professor would argue that the first duty of a diligent doctor is "to do no harm" and that "lack of any evidence of harm" is not "proof of safety". Yet the trial to prove absolute safety is unlikely to be done because it will need thousands of men over many years and potentially will cost several million pounds. Professor McCrackin's *main interest is prostate cancer, and he knows that 1 in 8 men will get prostate cancer in their lifetime, so 1 in 8 men started on testosterone therapy will get prostate cancer, even if the treatment has absolutely no adverse effect. The problem is that the patient would immediately look to blame the therapy, rather than many years of poor lifestyle, and potentially seek legal claim against the specialist. The Professor knows that it only takes one or two of these cases to make his life a misery, so he defaults to the "first do no harm theory". Additionally, both he and the GP will be taking on additional long-term follow-up without payment and recognition, so taking the conservative approach of an anti-depressant is the "safer option".*

It is no wonder that patients are seeking help from outside the NHS by gaining specialist physician access from Men's Health Websites such as www.tedshealth.com or seeking inexpensive private blood from thriva.com or medichecks.com.

Various issues that I have raised in this chapter might clarify why so many doctors are leaving the NHS. Personally, I felt that I have received little support from the NHS in my efforts to improve the health of men. When all my partners referred all the men with erectile dysfunction to me, instead of gratitude, I was identified as being a "prescribing outlier", potentially "poorly performing", and advised to reduce by prescribing closer to the national average. How was I expected to be able to treat all the patients referred to me and still remain an "average" prescriber? What other career would expect highly trained professionals to find job satisfaction in aspiring to mediocrity? I believe that these two cases show that, in some cases, specialists can endanger health, especially if confined to work under time restraints and restrictive guidelines

What is wrong with general practice?

Once more, this is a question that could fill an entire book. I would gladly write this if any publisher was remotely interested in approaching me. I will keep my answer short as this is the final chapter.

It is pretty clear that there is a crisis in general practice, and I am regularly engaged in discussions with a group of former PWC accountant partners (who retired at 50-55 on full-salary pensions) as to how pathetic such "highly paid" so-called medical professionals are letting the population down! As someone who spent nearly 30 years as a GP, I feel inclined to fight back. In the previous chapters, I have clearly been positive about the "golden years" of general practice when this was a very rewarding career. Unfortunately, there has been too much "tinkering and regulation" often in the name of "quality". This has generated thousands of additional jobs, all designed to reassure the public that their doctor is not only safe but can be compared with others by arbitrary "quality parameters" often related to "cost-effectiveness". The final nail in the coffin for flagging doctors has been the juggernaut of annual appraisal and revalidation, which consumes hundreds of hours of meaningless navel-gazing and "reflection", another term which should be condemned to the dictionary of shame.

The appraisal and revalidation process has not only been a massive drain on the taxpayer but, more importantly, has taken potentially important healthcare professionals out of patient care. I actually trained as an appraiser for five years for the "easy money" but eventually found it monotonous and soul-destroying. In my case, every five-year revalidation cycle made me question as to whether to go on. In contrast, the rewards of working as the "Sex Tsar" have been a complete career rejuvenation.

Having just recovered from a COVID-19 infection and 18 months off work, the medical advice was to take things very gently on my return. I subsequently learned that before resuming work, I had to pass my delayed appraisal. I calculated that I spent over 64 hours in preparation for this most recent appraisal involving fifteen online modules, including an eight-hour one on safeguarding children, which was totally irrelevant to my work as I do not see children. Each time I had to pay £1500 for this process. After each module, doctors have to achieve 100% on a multiple choice examination, but I found that post-COVID, I had nodded off for five minutes around four hours into the session, so I got a couple of questions wrong. This meant that I had to do the whole MCQ test again. The next time I got a different question wrong. This was far more intense than the real job, but there was no softly-softly approach from the appraisal team. The revalidation process is even more demanding and often irrelevant for a doctor nearing the end of his career and not seeking long-term professional development.

A colleague told me that his solution was to take a picture of each of the slides on the phone so that he could get the questions right! This sounds rather like passing your medical finals by seeing a "leaked version" of the exam paper beforehand or winning a golf tournament by not including the shots taken when nobody was looking.

I am certain that, across the whole country, annual appraisal plus five-yearly revalidation causes doctors to give up a year or two early because they cannot face the tedious process again. Coming on top of three years of turmoil from COVID-19, revalidation will be the final straw for many, resulting in early retirement and the loss of many centuries of medical expertise. Unfortunately, these meaningless concepts are too firmly ingrained in the medical psyche, and too many professionals have opted out of direct patient care and are in gainful employment on the appraisal/revalidation juggernaut for significant changes to be contemplated. Essentially, for many, general practice has ceased to be rewarding, and this problem will not be solved by even more regulation. I would suggest that readers might ask their GP, if they can find one, for their opinion of appraisal and revalidation just to check out the response. We need to reduce the regulation on GPs, stop the "league table mentality" and encourage and reward innovation and sub-specialism. Too often, GPs have to apologise for being "just a GP". In the "good old days" we used to meet consultant colleagues "as equals" at regular meetings, but nowadays, GPs dictate letters to "dear Cardiologists", and education takes place at home in the evenings in front of a laptop watching zoom meetings.

In this short chapter, I have tried to bring together some serious issues from my work over the last thirty years and offer some positive advice to readers as to what they can do to improve their health and their personal happiness. For any physicians reading this book, I can totally recommend a career in sexual medicine.

Hopefully, the next Sex Tsar is out there somewhere.

CHAPTER 16

– LIFESTYLE – WHAT DOES AND DOES NOT WORK?

Whereas others are much better placed to write book chapters on lifestyle, a book such as this would be severely lacking if such a topic was not discussed. This is, therefore, my take on what is important and what works and what does not. Of course, lifestyle advice is important, but often this can be overstated and is often seen by patients as the doctor seeking to blame the patient and transferring the burden back onto the victim. Luckily, I have recently been involved in writing chapters for the 4th edition of Men's Health 2021, which covered this topic in detail. I will attempt to cover the issues concisely.

In all countries of the world, men have shorter lives, but the perception has been that women have longer but experience greater misery. The gender gap in mortality in the UK had been falling steadily from 5 years at the turn of the 20th century to 3.7 years in 2019 but widened to 4.0 years by 2021 as a result of increased covid deaths in the first year of the pandemic, which saw the greatest increase in mortality since world war II. By 2020, the average life expectancy was 79.9 years for men and 83.6 years for women. Social deprivation is an important factor, with male life expectancy ranging from 83.5 to 74.1 and women 86.4 to 78.7 between the 10% least-deprived and 10% most deprived areas. Clearly, recent events in

Ukraine will be associated with the gender mortality shifts unlikely to be seen with disease.

Whereas most minority ethnic groups had <u>lower overall mortality</u> than the white UK population, this effect was lost due to increased covid-related mortality in Pakistan, Bangladeshi and Black Caribbean men.

There are multiple reasons for the gender mortality disparity:

Globally there are an estimated 929 million men and 175 million women smokers, but in the UK, the ratio is much closer, with 15.3% of men and 13.7% of women smokers. This is interesting as the UK has been among the highest in the world in terms of anti-smoking campaigns and regulations, suggesting that the messages are less effective for women, although there are possible ethnic and cultural influences.

Globally there are estimated to be 237 million men and 46 million women with alcohol use disorders. In the UK, 26% of men and 12% of women are drinking at dangerous levels, with the greatest risk in the 45-64 age group, although those under 25s are more likely to binge drink. Levels of drinking increased during Covid isolation. This again suggests that health promotional activities might have limited effect.

Men have a less healthy lifestyle with fewer health-promoting activities. Worse outcomes are compounded by the fact that the NHS offers more health screening to women than men, for example, breast and cervical screening, where there is no prostate screening programme. GPs actually get paid more for caring for women patients than men, especially if we include contraceptive and maternity payments.

Men eat more red meat and less fibre, fruit and vegetables. Their dietary habits are likely to deteriorate with the loss of a regular partner.

Key Determinants in the Health of Men

Men are less likely to conduct self-examination (e.g., melanoma and testicular cancer)

Men use less sun protection and are less likely to seek help when skin damage occurs.

They are less responsive to health information and promotion. The expectation is that the healthcare system will chase them, whereas women chase the system to make sure that they achieve their goals.

They have fewer social networks and fewer, less intimate relationships and friendships. Those men who live without a partner are the least healthy and die earlier. Hence it is important to maintain healthy sexual relationships, as sexual issues are a frequent cause of relationship failure. Men have less social support, and even healthcare centres have become more feminine environments.

Men consume more alcohol, drugs and tobacco products. Consumption increases in response to relationship failure.

They are more likely to drink-drive and not use seatbelts.

They engage in higher-risk jobs and pastimes. They even introduce increase risk to supporting their favourite football team.

They have more sexual partners. Once again, risks are greater with the breakup of long-term

Men respond less well to stress and have worse coping strategies (e.g., more alcohol and increased smoking)

Men underreport symptoms and delay seeking help. This has become more obvious since the covid outbreak, and the decline in available appointments is likely to have a greater impact on men. The internet has become a major source of information, often inaccurate, leaving them vulnerable to commercial exploitation.

Men are less likely to take medication for depression or seek counselling. They are more likely to resort to alcohol or drug as a solution.

Men are 3 times more likely to commit suicide, yet women make 3 times the number of attempts. As one psychiatrist once said to me, if you want a job done properly, get a man to do it! I explained that I could not possibly comment. Despite these figures, women are more likely to be referred for counselling and support services.

What should we do about exercise?

Several studies have confirmed the importance of regular exercise. Standard advice is for men aged 19-64 to accumulate 150 minutes of moderate-intensity exercise per week, ideally spread across the week in bouts of 10 minutes or more (30 minutes on 5 days a week would be ideal). Seventy-five minutes of High Intensive Training (HIT) might be easier to achieve for some. Those who are least active and who achieve even moderate targets get the greatest benefit in reducing risk.

Muscle strengthening exercises involving the major muscle groups should be performed for at least 15 minutes twice per week.

Overweight men will achieve health benefits even if they do not lose weight.

Targets are the same for men of 65 and over may need to start at 5 minutes and gradually build up to 10-minute sessions. Regimes should include balance training at least twice per week. Older men should start at 50% of these targets and gradually increase over time. Older men should focus on resistance training to prevent age-related loss of muscle mass. Recommendations should be tailored according to the individual's needs and disabilities. Generally, the risks of ill health arising from physical inactivity outweigh the risks of injury, although injured patients often do not see it that way. Healthcare professionals can help individuals to achieve their aims by setting achievable goals to enable patients to reach their full potential.

Older obese men with type 2 diabetes or chronic kidney disease may have low testosterone levels in around 40% of cases, and this may need to be addressed to achieve maximal benefit from exercise (see earlier chapters). As a rough guide, a waist circumference of over 40cm or BMI of over 40 kg/m² is associated with reduced survival of 8-10' an equivalent risk to smoking 20 cigarettes per day.

Diets

It would be possible to write an entire book on specific diets, but the important lesson is that CALORIE control is important. Many patients become obsessed with reducing fat content, only to increase carbohydrate consumption due to hunger. Balanced diets include the Mediterranean diet (see below), the Zone Diet and Weight watchers (www.weightwatchers.com). Some patients find the Atkins diet (high fat, low carbohydrate) effective for rapid weight loss. The premise is that carbohydrates increase insulin secretion, which induces metabolic changes that lead to weight gain. Some experts advise this as a jumpstart to weight loss, but the headache, bad breath, flatulence and constipation can be bothersome.

The Fast Diet (also known as 5:2 diet) was developed by Dr Michael Mosley and Mimi Spencer and is based on intermittent fasting 2 days per week. On the other 5 days, men require 2400 calories per day and women 2000 calories.

Low-fat diets are falling out of favour as recent thinking recognises the benefits of mono-and polyunsaturated fats and the detriments of saturated and trans fats.

Mediterranean Diet

Phytonutrients

Phytonutrients such as polyphenols, flavonoids, polyphenols and polyunsaturated fatty acids (PUFAs) can reduce the risk of several chronic diseases by switching on genes that promote health and reverse disease. Foods rich in phytonutrients include red, yellow and orange fruits and vegetables, dark green leafy vegetables, dark blue purple and red fruits, cruciferous vegetables, citrus fruits, flaxseed, legumes, soybeans, tea, sea vegetables and spices, especially turmeric, rosemary and purple sage.

As a general rule, the more colour in the food, the more likely the benefit. Remember that these metabolites will have low benefits compared to licensed pharmaceuticals with proven efficacy. They may prove relatively expensive and require high levels of motivation and persistence to see long-term benefits. Alas, they qualities are often deficient in many high-risk patients.

Questionnaires to assess men's health

Below are 2 simple questionnaires to quickly assess your own health. The AMS (Ageing Male Symptom) assess the likelihood that a man might have low testosterone levels. It contains helpful information that might help your doctor with the diagnosis. The SHIM (Sexual Health Inventory for Men) is helpful to diagnose erectile dysfunction, and the score defines severity and helps you to evaluate response to any therapy. You will remember the ED is a strong predictor of cardiac risk within the next 3-5 years, as is loss of morning erections. It would be wise to print off your scores and take them with you to the doctor. There will then be no excuse that these issues were overlooked because he was too busy. I am sure that he will thank you for being helpful!

AMS Questionnaire

Which of the following symptoms apply to you at this time? Please, mark the appropriate box for each symptom. For symptoms that do not apply, please mark "none".

Symptoms:	none	mild	moderate	severe	extremely severe
Score =	1	2	3	4	5
1. Decline in your feeling of general well-being (general state of health, subjective feeling)	☐	☐	☐	☐	☐
2. Joint pain and muscular ache (lower back pain, joint pain, pain in a limb, general back ache)	☐	☐	☐	☐	☐
3. Excessive sweating (unexpected/sudden episodes of sweating, hot flushes independent of strain)	☐	☐	☐	☐	☐
4. Sleep problems (difficulty in falling asleep, difficulty in sleeping through, waking up early and feeling tired, poor sleep, sleeplessness)	☐	☐	☐	☐	☐
5. Increased need for sleep, often feeling tired	☐	☐	☐	☐	☐
6. Irritability (feeling aggressive, easily upset about little things, moody)	☐	☐	☐	☐	☐
7. Nervousness (inner tension, restlessness, feeling fidgety)	☐	☐	☐	☐	☐
8. Anxiety (feeling panicky)	☐	☐	☐	☐	☐
9. Physical exhaustion / lacking vitality (general decrease in performance, reduced activity, lacking interest in leisure activities, feeling of getting less done, of achieving less, of having to force oneself to undertake activities)	☐	☐	☐	☐	☐
10. Decrease in muscular strength (feeling of weakness)	☐	☐	☐	☐	☐
11. Depressive mood (feeling down, sad, on the verge of tears, lack of drive, mood swings, feeling nothing is of any use)	☐	☐	☐	☐	☐
12. Feeling that you have passed your peak	☐	☐	☐	☐	☐
13. Feeling burnt out, having hit rock-bottom	☐	☐	☐	☐	☐
14. Decrease in beard growth	☐	☐	☐	☐	☐
15. Decrease in ability/frequency to perform sexually	☐	☐	☐	☐	☐
16. Decrease in the number of morning erections	☐	☐	☐	☐	☐
17. Decrease in sexual desire/libido (lacking pleasure in sex, lacking desire for sexual intercourse)	☐	☐	☐	☐	☐

Have you got any other major symptoms? Yes ☐ No ☐

If Yes, please describe: _____

Total Score	
<26	no/little complaints
27-36	mild
37-49	moderate
50+	severe

304

Name:_____Date: _____

Sexual Health Inventory for Men
Patient Instructions

This questionnaire is designed to help us quantify and treat your erectile dysfunction. You will be asked to complete this questionnaire in the future to measure the success of the treatment.

Over the past six months:
0 Meaning no sex drive – 5 normal sex drive

1. How do you rate your **confidence** that you can get and keep an erection?
      0   1   2   3   4   5

2. When you had erections with sexual stimulation, **how often** were your erections hard enough for penetration (entering your partner)?
      0   1   2   3   4   5

3. During sexual intercourse, **how often** were you able to maintain your erection after you had entered your partner?
      0   1   2   3   4   5

4. During sexual intercourse, **rate your ability** to maintain your erection to completion of intercourse.
      0   1   2   3   4   5

5. When you attempted sexual intercourse, **how often** was it satisfactory for you?
      0   1   2   3   4   5

Add the numbers corresponding to the questions 1- 5.
Your score: _____

If you scored between **1-7**, you may have severe erectile dysfunction.
If you scored between **8-11**, you may have moderate erectile dysfunction.
If you scored between **12-16**, you may have mild to moderate erectile dysfunction.
If you scored between **17-21**, you may have mild erectile dysfunction.
If you scored between **22-25**, you have normal erectile function.

Lightning Source UK Ltd.
Milton Keynes UK
UKHW020750290123
416118UK00012B/1577